The
Canadian
Postmodern

The Canadian Postmodern

A Study of Contemporary
English~Canadian Fiction

LINDA HUTCHEON

Toronto   New York   Oxford
OXFORD UNIVERSITY PRESS

Oxford University Press, 70 Wynford Drive, Don Mills, Ontario, M3C 1J9

Toronto   Oxford   New York   Delhi   Bombay   Calcutta   Madras   Karachi
Petaling Jaya   Singapore   Hong Kong   Tokyo   Nairobi   Dar es Salaam
Cape Town   Melbourne   Auckland

and associated companies in
Berlin   Ibadan

CANADIAN CATALOGUING IN PUBLICATION DATA

Hutcheon, Linda, 1947-
The Canadian postmodern

Bibliography: p.
Includes index.
ISBN 0-19-540668-0

1. Canadian fiction (English) — 20th century —
History and criticism.*   2. Postmodernism.
I. Title.

PS8199.H87 1988   C813'.54'09   C88-094599-0
PR9192.5.H87 1988

Cover photograph: Nigel Scott, *Maillot Noir et Blanc*,
June 1986 (Julie diving). Used by courtesy of the
Jane Corkin Gallery, Toronto.

OXFORD is a trademark of Oxford University Press

2   3   4   -   1   0

Printed in Canada

91-3244

Contents

Preface

Robert Kroetsch once said that literary history is 'very radically storymaking'.[1] If that is so, then this book consists of a set of stories made from literary historical storymaking. For a period of about four years I did little else but read Canadian fiction. In this I was driven by both pleasure and guilt, for I had agreed to write the chapter on 'The Novel 1972-84' for Volume 4 of the *Literary History of Canada* (University of Toronto Press) before realizing just what that would entail. In order to try to understand some of the things I saw happening in Canadian fiction during those years, I found I had to work them out in detail, mostly for my own benefit. Some of these self-help efforts eventually became articles or talks. Many of the essays in this book are constructed out of those attempts to understand, but they have all been extensively rewritten to fit the present context: an investigation not into the general phenomenon of postmodernism, but into the particular forms in which it appears in contemporary Canadian fiction.

Another point of literary—or critical—history should be mentioned here as well. Coinciding with my reading of this fiction was the first major change in general orientation in many years within the field of literary studies. This change, associated with the advent of what is called 'literary theory', has been seen either as tolling the death knell of the humanities or as offering the hope of intellectual salvation for English departments, depending on one's literary politics. As a comparativist whose own theoretical orientation had shifted from resolute formalism through (and because of) reader-response considerations to some mix of feminism and (what was labelled) poststructuralism, I too had come to question the way I had been taught to read—and, in turn, teach—literature by my 'liberal humanist' education.[2] My increasing self-consciousness about my own class, gender, and ethnic background had for some years been suggesting to me that perhaps what had been taught to me as universal and eternal was, in fact, the creation of a particular historical time and place, as well as race, sex, and class. Laurie Ricou once signalled, with considerable self-conscious humour, his awareness of the critic's need to situate him/herself: he subtitled one of his essays 'Journal Entries from a Capitalist Bourgeois Patriarchal Anglo-saxon Mainstream Critic'.[3] Despite the irony, the impulse to situate is important . . . and postmodern. This book is directly a product of my own positioning as a Canadian woman of Italian immigrant origins, an English-speaking (though trilingual) product of the sixties (in political terms), who is now a mainstream academic, though with fairly fresh scars from the 'sessional appointment' wars that are still raging in the universities.

Although I am a Canadian (and, more specifically, a Toron-tonian, I fear), this book is for me not a 'painful patriotic duty', but rather a means of getting my 'bearings', to use Northrop Frye's terms.[4] It is also my way, however inadequate, of respond-ing to the recent challenge thrown down by Ted Blodgett:

> . . . one of the reasons the Canadian literatures are looked upon with a kind of benign diffidence by those unacquainted with them derives from our failure of imagination as critics. We have not been bold enough in spirit to find ways of establishing, so to speak, the context that would make them significant to imaginations formed on European cultures.[5]

Since that diffidence often extends to those who *are* acquainted with Canadian literature (or who think they are, or who should be), this is an important challenge, and postmodernism seems a likely context in which to address it. Formed out of North and South American as well as European cultures, postmodernism both confronts and goes beyond the problematics of colonial dependency, offering a new context in which to view the specificities of Canadian writing.

As a cultural practice that has actually been defined, in part, by the impact of feminism, postmodernism is of particular interest to me as a woman too. As both reader and teacher I have been influenced by what feminist theorists have argued about the particularities of en-gendering in education. Certainly I no longer read books the way I once did: that eternal universal Truth I was taught to find has turned out to be constructed, not found—and anything but eternal and universal. Truth has been replaced by truths, uncapitalized and in the plural. And Canadian novels by women have become important in my own understanding of how cultural notions of the feminine are inevitably inscribed by and in language. The challenges this fiction offers to fixed genre boundaries (the novel vs. the poem, the short-story collection, the essay)[6] and its willingness to confront both political and social issues have pushed postmodernism in directions it might not have taken otherwise: to contest Man (in all 'his' universality) is not necessarily to discover Woman—or women.

The postmodern 'different', then, is starting to replace the humanist 'universal' as a prime cultural value. This is good news for Canadians who are not of Anglo or French origin—that is, for a good proportion of the country's population today. As the daughter of an Italian construction worker I always knew I was not the usual stuff of which academic literary critics are made. But times change. And postmodernism offers a context in which to understand the valuing of difference in a way that makes particular sense in Canada. As expatriate Canadian filmmaker and critic Laura Mulvey has put it: 'Canadian culture is not yet a closed book. The historical anomalies that Canada has grown from make contradictions visible. Uniform national identity is challenged by a pride in heterogeneity and difference.'[7]

Nevertheless, I am also part of the Anglo-Canadian context, by virtue of name and language, if nothing else. This book reflects that fact in its focus on only English-Canadian fiction, though the Québécois context is invoked at various points. This deliberate limitation reflects an unwillingness on my part to obscure what I see as the important differences between French- and English-Canadian culture and literary history. That is another book, still to be written. In English Canada George Bowering can rightly claim that 'as soon as an author begins to fool seriously with the trappings of the conventional novel, he is relegated to either neglect or notoreity, both places outside the mainstream',[8] but in Québec a different literary tradition makes radical experimentation almost a kind of norm: the French *New Novel* and even the *New New Novel* offered francophone writers and readers an infamous alternative to realism. The issue is, of course, much more complex than that because of politics, and this is so even today, when feminism has essentially replaced Québécois nationalism as the political basis of writing, at least for many women writers in Québec. (The particularities of postmodernism in this context have been dealt with already in the fine book by Janet Paterson, *Moments postmodernes dans le roman québécois*.) But the work of Hubert Aquin and the theorizing of *Parti pris* have had their impact on English-Canadian fiction, as has the work of Nicole Brossard and Madeleine Gagnon. The political is an important part of the Canadian postmodern. In poet/critic Douglas Barbour's terms, 'language . . . always / political because man / is'.[9] So too is woman.

The postmodernists writing today are, like myself, products of the sixties, those paradoxical years of political engagement and self-indulgence. Their work, like this book, may question authority—in all its guises—but often it offers no final answers; indeed, it is suspicious of the very notion of final answers. The interrogative is the mode of the postmodern, and this book wants both to enact and to describe that mode. There is clearly a danger inherent in this questioning stance, though: the danger of bad faith. To question must be to self-question, as well. I have tried to be aware of the pitfalls of writing within the academic mainstream, pitfalls that Louky Bersianik has articulated in her characteristically pointed fashion:

> Since it is not unusual for teachers and critics to be to a greater or lesser degree members of literary chapels, they all share with the priest the power of *consecration*: they 'officiate' before a congregation of the faithful (i.e., of those who have faith in literature), deciding that certain works will be handed down to posterity and that others will remain unknown. They are decision makers.[10]

In this book, as in the classroom, I have always tried not to 'officiate' in evaluative or consecrating terms, but I also see that even the choice of which books to mention is both an evaluative and a consecrating act, whether I like it or not. And I openly admit that I do enjoy and consider successful the fiction I am writing about here.

In their self-reflexivity, Canadian postmodern novels offer yet another example of the self-conscious or 'meta-' sensibility of our times, that is, of the awareness that all our systems of understanding are deliberate and historically specific human constructs (not natural and eternal givens), with all the limitations and strengths which that definition entails. These are novels that admit openly they are fiction, but suggest that fiction is just another means by which we make sense of our world (past and present) and that, as such, it is comparable to historiography, philosophy, physics, sociology, and so on.

It would seem that it is the particular relation to the historical past that is crucial to postmodernism in the visual arts as well as in literature. As Chantal Pontbriand has argued, Canadian art (painting, sculpture, installations, video, performance, photography) has flourished in the postmodern context, partly because of the historical field of reference it invokes. For the Canadian postmodern, history is 'a vast theatre in which a drama is unfolding, that of representation, or of art itself'.[11] Unlike the art or literature of modernism, the postmodern uses its tendency towards self-reference as a way both of engaging with its own past, usually through irony and parody, and also of engaging with its audience. In Canada there is almost an *embarras de richesses*, so many works that rethink history and its relations to both the aesthetic and the political: even a partial list would have to include the work of the Public Access Collective in Canadian public spaces, Murray Schafer's rock/opera/performance piece *Patria I*, the films of Michael Snow, the 1986 symposium on 'Artists. Television' (which aimed at opening up constricted notions of broadcasting), not to mention more plays than I could ever list or the documentary long poems of Stephen Scobie, Daphne Marlatt, Robert Kroetsch, and so many others.

My focus in this book, however, is on the contemporary Canadian novel. What I have tried to offer is what Steve McCaffery (via Georges Bataille) once called a 'general economy', a perspective that is 'concerned with the distribution and circulation of the numerous forces and intensities that saturate a text'.[12] Because both that text and its critic are specifically Canadian here, this economy of the postmodern will have to be limited to that context.[13] But that is not really a problem, I think. Margaret Atwood once said that there is no such thing as 'truly universal literature', partly because there are no 'truly universal readers'.[14] And this book reflects the Canadian 'storymaking' attempts of one particular Canadian reader, writing for Canadians.

Notes

1 Robert Kroetsch in Shirley Neuman and Robert Wilson, *Labyrinths of Voice: Conversations with Robert Kroetsch* (Edmonton: NeWest Press, 1982), p. 196.

2 Dennis Lee has succinctly defined liberalism as teaching that 'men inhabit an objective and value-free universe, which we know and re-fashion through calculating reason. The cosmos consists of objective phenomena, together with the perceiving subjects who discover the laws of their regularities' (*Savage Fields: An Essay in Literature and Cosmology* [Toronto: Anansi, 1977], p. 50).

3 Laurie Ricou, 'Phyllis Webb, Daphne Marlatt and Simultitude: Journal Entries from a Capitalist Bourgeois Patriarchal Anglo-saxon Main-stream Critic', in *A Mazing Space: Writing Canadian/Women Writing*, ed. Shirley Neuman and Smaro Kamboureli (Edmonton: Longspoon/ NeWest Press, 1986), pp. 205-15.

4 Northrop Frye, *Divisions on a Ground: Essays on Canadian Culture*, ed. James Polk (Toronto: Anansi, 1982), p. 120.

5 E. D. Blodgett, 'After Pierre Berton What? In Search of a Canadian Literature', *Essays on Canadian Writing* 30 (1984-5), p. 63.

6 See Louise Dupré, 'From Experimentation to Experience: Québécois Modernity in the Feminine', in *A Mazing Space*, p. 358 especially.

7 Laura Mulvey, 'Magnificent Obsession', *Parachute* 42 (1986), p. 11.

8 George Bowering, *The Mask in Place: Essays on Fiction in North America* (Winnipeg: Turnstone Press, 1982), p. 31.

9 Douglas Barbour, 'Poetics 19: home/space', in *Boundary* 2 3, 1 (1974), p. 180.

10 Louky Bersianik, 'Aristotle's Lantern: An Essay on Criticism', in *A Mazing Space*, p. 40.

11 Chantal Pontbriand, 'The Historical Factor: A Fundamental Theme in Canadian Contemporary Art', *Parachute* 47 (1987), p. 51.

12 Steve McCaffery, *North of Intention: Critical Writings 1973-1986* (Toronto: Nightwood Editions; New York: Roof Books, 1986), p. 201.

13 For a more general account of postmodernism, see Linda Hutcheon, *A Poetics of Postmodernism: Theory, History, Fiction* (London and New York: Routledge and Kegan Paul, 1988).

14 Margaret Atwood, *Second Words: Selected Critical Prose* (Toronto: Anansi, 1982), p. 345.

Acknowledgements

I

As I mentioned in the Preface, this book grew out of attempts to work out for myself various issues arising from the writing of the chapter on the novel for the fourth volume of the *Literary History of Canada*. For this reason I have appended that chapter to the essays here, as a way of offering the general context in which this study came about. Some of these chapters began as occasional pieces—for a particular conference, issue of a journal, collection of essays. In rewriting and refocusing this material, I have tried to erase the traces of occasional-ity and concentrate on the investigation of the postmodern that, in fact, I discovered to underlie all my work over this period of time. The essays are primarily organized by issue, though the work of certain writers gets separate treatment, in part because of its important role in the public debates that surround the notion of a Canadian postmodernism.

In detail, then: the introductory Chapter 1 here is a longer and differently focused version of an article written for a Modern Language Association of America volume edited by Arnold E. Davidson, *Studies on Canadian Literature: Introductory Critical Essays*.

Chapter 2, 'Caveat Lector: The Early Postmodernism of Leonard Cohen', reworks part of a 1974 article in *Canadian Literature* and a monograph on Cohen written in 1982 for ECW's *Canadian Writers and their Works* series. That study is more general and, to my embarrassment, resolutely declines to come to terms with the notion of the postmodern; this one is more specifically focused on *Beautiful Losers* and tries to deal with this novel's early manifestations of what has come to be seen as postmodernism.

Most of the third chapter, 'The Postmodernist Scribe: The Dynamic Stasis of Contemporary Canadian Writing', appeared in 1984 in the *University of Toronto Quarterly*, after being presented in 1982 at the McMaster University English Association Symposium on Canadian Fiction and Film. The version here has been altered to avoid redundancy in the context of the book and to bring the terminology in line with that used throughout this study; this includes gender pronouns—again, much to my embarrassment.

The same is true of Chapter 4, 'Historiographic Metafiction', which was first read to the Association of Canadian and Québec Literatures and then published in *Essays on Canadian Literature* in 1984, but there have been considerable additions to this version.

Chapter 5, 'The Postmodern Challenge to Boundaries', is an odd amalgam of bits of material from two 1984 reviews written for *Canadian Literature* (of Clark Blaise's *Lusts* and Michael Ondaatje's *In the Skin of a Lion*) and a piece that appeared in 1985 in Sam Solecki's collection of essays on Ondaatje called *Spider Blues*.

The most re-written of the essays that have already been published elsewhere is Chapter 6, '"Shape-Shifters": Canadian Women Writers and the Tradition'. I found that it had to be reformulated, largely because of the rest of the book in which it first appeared, Shirley Neuman's and Smaro Kamboureli's *A Mazing Space* (1986), but also because of the many new essays and books on feminism in general and Canadian women writers in particular that have come out since its writing. Part of the extended analysis of Aritha Van Herk's *No Fixed Address* is a reworked longer version of my review of the novel in *Dandelion*.

The last two chapters have never been published elsewhere. Since 1978 I have written a number of pieces on Margaret Atwood, none of which has satisfied me. The doubled context of post-modernism and feminism has finally given me a framework that seems right, and Chapter 7, 'Process, Product, and Politics: The Postmodernism of Margaret Atwood', is the result. The final chapter is by no means final, in that it offers no answers to the questions posed by postmodernism addressed in the book. In writing about 'Mr Canadian Postmodern'—Robert Kroetsch—I realized that I had, in fact, written a summary of all the concerns raised by the postmodern interrogations of literary and historical assumptions. There seemed little else to add in conclusion, and so the study ends with 'Seeing Double: Concluding with Kroetsch'. The Appendix, from the *Literary History of Canada*, is the cause of it all and has a lot to answer for.

II

In the writing of any book there are always numerous personal and intellectual debts incurred—for everything from general encouragement to specific ideas. This book was over ten years in the making, and so the list is particularly long here, including friends, colleagues, and, especially, students—since Canadian literature is, for myself and most of my generation, an area of study learned through trying to teach others.

Two friends and colleagues in particular must be mentioned at the start, however, since their work accounts for two of the obvious gaps in this study. Janet Paterson's incisive readings of Québécois postmodern fiction in *Moments postmodernes dans le roman québécois* (which was being written at the same time as this study) helped me to define for myself the differences between the literatures of our two founding cultures that made me limit my own investigation to English-Canadian fiction. In addition, her acute and thoughtful comments on many of the chapters here have been invaluable to me, as has her constant willingness to thrash out problems involving general and specific aspects of postmodernism.

My second particular debt of gratitude is to Magdalene Redekop, who was writing *Alice Munro and Our Mock Mothers: Reading the Signs of Invasion* as I was working on this book. Her bringing together of feminism and (what I, if not she, would call postmodern) theoretical challenges to realism and to narrative strategies in general have influenced me greatly—and, in fact, have prevented me from daring to write here about Alice Munro. The chapter, or rather, the book, on her work has already been written. My thanks too for Maggie's patient and provocative readings of certain chapters of this book and for the many pleasurable hours of discussion our common interests have provided.

Since I began working in Canadian studies as a teacher, as a reader reading with others, there are literally hundreds of students who probably ought to be listed by name here. However, let me mention in particular those, working at various universities in the past, who allowed me some entry into their thinking-processes at some point in their graduate dissertation work: Lee Easton, Sylvia Söderlind, Lorraine York, Glen Deer, Christine Niero, and Rosmarin Heidenreich. A special debt must be acknowledged to those Comparative Literature students at the University of Toronto who, since 1984, have formed a (self-motivated) study group of which I have been fortunate to be a part and whose own work in postmodern Canadian literature has influenced mine in countless ways: Wendy Waring, Marie Vautier, Carla Visser, Lorna Hassell, and Winfried Siemerling.

Many other people have read parts of this book in its various forms and offered criticism and comments to which I hope I have done some justice in rewriting: Bill Keith, Ted Chamberlin, Ted Davidson, Joan Coldwell, Sam Solecki, Shirley Neuman, Smaro Kamboureli, Laurie Ricou, Robert Lecker, Bill New, Gay Allison, Aritha van Herk, Robert Kroetsch, Timothy Findley, and Rudy Wiebe. I would also like to thank the audiences whose critical responses to oral versions of some of the ideas here helped me refine them and make them more precise and understandable: those at Trent University, the University of Calgary, the University of Saskatoon, McMaster University, the University of Toronto, McGill University, the University of New Brunswick, and the University of Ottawa. With all this help, this should probably have been a much better book; its limitations and errors are mine and mine alone.

Gratitude—or blame—is also due to Richard Teleky of Oxford University Press (Canada), whose idea this book was. For its generosity and faith, the Killam Program of the Canada Council must be thanked most sincerely; without the support of its Killam Research Fellowship, I would probably have taken another ten years to finish this book.

A final thanks to my spouse, Michael, as always, for everything.

Chapter 1

Introduction

The 1960s are generally accepted as the years that saw the flowering of Canadian fiction. The provocations were diverse: nationalist sentiment, government support for publishers and artists, and the general feeling that in cultural terms Canada had finally ceased to be what Earle Birney once called a 'highschool land / deadset in adolescence'. Despite the continued strong presence of traditional realist fiction by Morley Callaghan, Robertson Davies, Hugh MacLennan, W.O. Mitchell, and others, something new began to appear in the seventies and eighties. What the rest of the world was starting to call 'postmodernism' had arrived in Canada—but the form it took was a distinctly Canadian one. In order to make clear its distinctiveness, I should first explain what I mean by this cultural form to which we have given such a seemingly provocative label. Despite the frequency of the term 'postmodern' in the criticism of literature, the visual arts, and architecture, its definition remains decidedly vague. From what I can glean from the *usage* of the term, 'postmodernism' would seem to designate art forms that are fundamentally self-reflexive—in other words, art that is self-consciously art (or artifice), literature that is openly aware of the fact that it is written and read as part of a particular culture, having as much to do with the literary past as with the social present. Its use of parody to echo past works signals its awareness that literature is made, first and foremost, out of other literature. But there is a problem with this definition: it could also be a description of the earlier modernist art of the beginning of the century, with its belief in the autonomy and self-sufficiency of the art object. The continuity between the modernist and the postmodernist is a very real one, but what distinguishes them, I would argue, is that in the postmodern this self-consciousness of art *as art* is paradoxically made the means to a new engagement with the social and the historical world, and that this is done in such a way as to challenge (though not destroy) our traditional humanist beliefs about the function of art in society.

Let me clarify this modernist/postmodernist distinction with an example: both Sheila Watson's *The Double Hook* and Margaret Laurence's *The Diviners* are 'metafictions' (fictions about fiction). They are both very aware of the process of creating order through myth and art. Despite what some critics would call postmodern techniques (fragmentation, parody), both novels reveal more a *modernist* search for order in the face of moral and social chaos than a *postmodern* urge to trouble, to question, to make both problematic and provisional any such desire for order or truth through the powers of the human imagination. What many American critics have called postmodernism—the extreme non-representational textual play and self-reference of 'surfiction'[1]— is, in this context, yet another form of (late) modernism, the logical extreme of its aesthetic (and aestheticist) tenets and its romantic faith in the imagination. Postmodernism, as I see it, is more paradoxical and problematic, as witnessed perhaps by the continuing debates on its definition. It both sets up and subverts the powers and conventions of art. It uses and abuses them in order to suggest that we question both that modernist autonomy and any realist notion of transparent reference. In other words, the postmodern novel is neither self-sufficiently art nor a simple mirror to or window onto the world outside. Yet in another sense, as we shall see, it exploits the power of both concepts of the function of art.

Walter Pache has argued that in Canada postmodern writers have clearly responded to American forms of metafiction.[2] No doubt this is true, but in Canada there is very little of the extreme formalism of 'surfiction'. This has led Stanley Fogel to claim that metafiction is 'almost completely absent' from Canadian literature.[3] While this statement is partly the consequence of his particular and polemical focus on the core of books always taught and read, that is, on the received 'canon' of 'Can. Lit.', it is typical of a common view of Canada as a kind of cultural backwater, always copying what the Americans do, twenty years too late. For Fogel the Canadian lack of formal experimentation and ideological engagement that he associates with metafiction (pp. 15, 18) is the result of the fact that Canadian writers are unencumbered by the 'ideological baggage' of American novelists. But surely it is more a matter of Canadian writers' just having *different* ideological baggage, baggage that includes not a revolution and a civil war, but a more conservative cultural history as a colony. This is indeed a history that may make for more deference to authority (pp. 22-5) and a greater need to sustain a distinct cultural identity than can be found in the United States—or in Britain. In other words, Canada has never really been in synch with the US in terms of cultural history, so it is perhaps unwise to look for parallels today, even if we do stick with the generic label of 'postmodernism'.

However, Canada's own particular moment of cultural history does seem to make it ripe for the paradoxes of postmodernism, by which I mean those contradictory acts of establishing and then undercutting prevailing values and conventions in order to provoke a questioning, a challenging of 'what goes without saying' in our culture. Whether postmodern writers be Canadian or Latin American, British, American, Italian, or German, they are always in a sense 'agents provocateurs'—taking pot-shots at the culture of which they know they are unavoidably a part but that they still wish to criticize. This almost inevitably puts the postmodern writer into a marginal or 'ex-centric' position with regard to the central or dominant culture, because the paradox of underlining and undermining cultural 'universals' (of revealing their grounding in the 'particular') implicitly challenges any notions of centrality in (and centralization of) culture. Since the periphery or the margin might also describe Canada's perceived position in international terms, perhaps the postmodern ex-centric is very much a part of the identity of the nation. In postmodernism, though, the centre and the periphery do not simply change places. Nor is the margin conceived of only as a place of transgression. The periphery is also the frontier, the place of possibility: Kroetsch's border town of Big Indian in *What the Crow Said* is deliberately on the border of Alberta and Saskatchewan; Hodgins' Vancouver Island is self-consciously on the edge of the continent.

Margins also challenge borders as limits. Marshall McLuhan[4] once called Canada a 'border line case', and certainly it is a vast nation with little sense of firm geographical centre or ethnic unity: the multicultural mosaic is no melting pot. In fact, we might be said to have quite a firm suspicion of centralizing tendencies, be they national, political, or cultural. In literature there is a parallel suspicion of genre borders. In Kroetsch's terms:

'modern literature closed the boundaries; what is needed is a breaking across these boundaries, a post-modern literature.'[5] The margin or the border is the postmodern space *par excellence*, the place where new possibilities exist. Or, as McLuhan put it: 'The hidden borders in men's minds are the great vortices of energy and power that can erupt and spiral anywhere' (p. 241). It is also, however, the place where the centre is paradoxically both acknowledged and challenged. This is the case whether that centre is seen as elsewhere (Britain, the United States) or as localized in, say, Ontario. Canada can in some ways be defined as a country whose articulation of its *national* identity has sprung from *regionalist* impulses: the ex-centric forces of Québec, the Maritimes, the west. Its history is one of defining itself against centres. Eli Mandel has called this a perennial tension in Canadian life 'between English and American influences on our life and culture, tensions manifested in familiar and different views of our history: between those who believe the lines of power run North and South and those who believe they run East and West, between those who hold the Laurentian thesis of Innis and Creighton or those who, like Underhill, are continentalists, between those who say Canada exists *because* of its geography and those who say it exists *despite* its geography'.[6]

Canadian writers, then, may be primed for the paradoxes of the postmodern by their history, as Leonard Cohen saw in *Beautiful Losers*, and also by their split sense of identity, both regional and national. Canada's major historical figures look like almost deliberately postmodern creations: Louis Riel may be an archetypal marginal ex-centric, both inside a dominant culture (French-speaking and church-educated) and outside it (Métis and a renegade rebel). Perhaps the ironies and contradictions of postmodernism are the most apt mode of expression for what Kroetsch has called the 'total ambiguity that is so essentially Canadian: be it in terms of two solitudes, the bush garden, Jungian opposites'.[7] The postmodern irony that refuses resolution of contraries—except in the most provisional of terms— would appear to be a useful framework in which to discuss, for example, the obsessive dualities in the work of Margaret Atwood (body/mind; female/male; nature/culture; instinct/reason; time/ space; lyric poetry/prose narrative) or the echoing doubling of (and within) characters and plots in the novels of Kroetsch. Perhaps 'postmodern' is the best way to describe the genre paradoxes in the works of Michael Ondaatje (are they biography? fiction? poetry?) or Alice Munro (are they short-story collections? novels?). Certainly contemporary Canadian fiction is full of examples of a postmodern challenge to the boundaries of specifically 'high art' genres: comic books and movies (*Beautiful Losers*), detective stories (*The Telling of Lies*), and sports tales (*Shoeless Joe, Home Game*) are among the 'contaminating' popular cultural forms infiltrating postmodern Canadian fiction today.

In 'Progressions Toward Sainthood: There is Nothing to Do but Die'[8] Aritha Van Herk offers a fictional dialogue between Jeanne d'Arc and Louis Riel on the subjects of religion, politics, martyrdom, and, especially, the cultural representations of the ex-centric by both the 'date-compilers' and the creative writers (George Bernard Shaw and Rudy Wiebe). Though four and a half centuries apart in time and of different genders, the woman and the Canadian find that they have much in common. (This will not surprise those historians of Canadian literature who have long noticed the strong female presence within the Can. Lit. canon: from Moodie and Traill through Ostenso, Wilson, and Montgomery, to Laurence, Gallant, Atwood, Thomas, Munro, and the list gets longer each day.) I know I am not alone in suggesting a parallel analogy here between the position of woman writers (anywhere) and Canadian writers working in English. In both cases there is a necessary self-defining challenging of the dominant traditions (male; British/American). What Stan Fogel calls Atwood's obsession with 'character formation and the difficulty of maintaining ontological security' (p. 116) is also true of much fiction written by women today, and the reason is an obvious one—and it is *not* that women writers are by nature more conservative and traditionally realist. The reason is that you can assume selfhood ('character formation') or 'subjectivity' only when you have attained it. Subjectivity in the Western liberal humanist tradition has been defined in terms of rationality, individuality, and power; in other words, it is defined in terms of those domains traditionally denied women, who are relegated instead to the realms of intuition, familial collectivity, and submission. I exaggerate only slightly in my rhetoric here, for the last ten years of feminist research have argued most convincingly for the historical existence of these two differently en-gendered modes of subjectivity.

If women have not yet been allowed access to (male) subjectivity, then it is very difficult for them to contest it, as the (male) poststructuralist philosophers have been doing lately. This may make women's writing *appear* more conservative, but in fact it is just *different*. Women must define their subjectivity before they can question it; they must first assert the selfhood they have been denied by the dominant culture. Their doubled act of (literally) 'inscribing' and challenging subjectivity has been one of the major forces in making postmodernism such a resolutely paradoxical enterprise. I think there is an analogy to be made here with the situation of the Canadian writer, female or male. Why do Canadians still produce books in 1987 called *A Passion for Identity: An Introduction to Canadian Studies*?[9] What Fogel sees as important to postmodernism in America—its deconstructing of national myths and identity—is possible within Canada only when those myths and identity have first been defined. Like women writers in general, Canadian novelists must return to their history (as do Wiebe, Swan, Bowering, Kogawa, and so many others) in order to discover (before they can contest) their historical myths. American ex-centric writers have done the same, of course (Afro-Americans and women of colour, especially). However, Canadian writers have first had to deconstruct *British* social and literary myths in order to redefine their colonial history: myths such as those of glorious war (in Findley's *The Wars*) or imperialistic exploration (in Bowering's *Burning Water*). Through the use of parody they have also contested the canonical myths and forms of European and American literatures, such as the picaresque (in Van Herk's *No Fixed Address*), the *Künstlerroman* (in Munro's *Lives of Girls and Women*), the Grail legend (in Thomas's *Mrs Blood*), and the western (in Kroetsch's novels).

A number of critics lately[10] have noted the relationship between the national search for a cultural identity and the feminist seeking for a distinctive gender identity in terms of the paradoxical (and I would say, postmodern) recognition and combatting of 'colonial' positions toward the power of dominating cultures. They have pointed to shared themes of powerlessness, victimization, and alienation, as well as to a certain ambivalence or ambiguity that makes both Canadians and women open, tolerant, accepting, yet also at times angry and resentful. Lorna Irvine believes that the female voice 'politically and culturally personifies Canada'.[11] On a national level, male aggression is usually associated, by analogy, with the United States, while Britain represents the stifling force of colonial tradition. As Mavis Gallant ironically put it, 'The father in Canada seemed no more than an apostle transmitting a paternal message from the Father in England—the Father of us all.'[12] Unlike Quebec women writers, who practise a more overtly radical subversion, those writing in English (like their male counterparts, in many cases) use a more disguised form of subversion, which only implicitly questions the prevailing authority. In so doing they also challenge related liberal-humanist notions of art as original and unique, notions that are tied up with (male) notions of individual subjectivity. And they often do so by means of parody: by first recalling the (male; British/American) canonical texts of our culture, both 'high' and popular, and then challenging them by undoing their status and power. The frequent use of verbal irony and word play in the work of Kroetsch, Atwood, and Thomas, for example, is another way in which the ex-centrics, be they Canadians, women, or both, can subvert the authority of language, language seen as having a single and final meaning. Not surprisingly, language has been called the major issue in the general history of decolonialization,[13] whether in terms of gender or of nationality.

Parody and irony, then, become major forms of both formal and ideological critique in feminist and Canadian fiction alike. The reason is, I think, that they allow writers to speak to their culture, from within, but without being totally co-opted by that culture. The irony and distance implied by parody allow for *separation* at the same time that the doubled structure of both (the superimposition of two meanings or texts) demands recognition of *complicity*. Parody both asserts and undercuts that which it contests. For example, many critics—from Northrop Frye to D.G. Jones—have argued for the importance of the Bible and biblical structures in Canadian literature, but novels such as Cohen's *Beautiful Losers* or Findley's *Not Wanted on the Voyage* parody those structures and narratives in a typically postmodern way, both exploiting and subverting their undeniable cultural authority. Kroetsch's novels assert the male myths of the quest journey (that of Odysseus, Orpheus, Conrad's Marlow, the knight errant, and so on) in order to show the male (and female) cultural roles as fictions, as constructed by culture rather than as 'natural' in any sense of the word. In *Badlands* both the male will to knowledge (and power) and its undermining are parodically presented through Kroetsch's deliberate conjunction of male story and female first-person narration.[14]

Atwood's *The Handmaid's Tale* uses parody with similar ideological and political intent. Her play with the narrative form and details of Yevgeny Zamyatin's *We*[15] (the police state; the secret agents; the subversion of authority by love; the escape; the state-regulated sexuality) is both underlined and undermined, for here women are the victims of a right-wing feminism that supports male authority in return for certain privileges. The conjunction of this kind of feminism with religious fundamentalism points to another parody (rooted in an earlier New England puritanism), that of Hawthorne's *The Scarlet Letter*. Its setting, what we might call its colour-coding, and its frame narrative, which suggests historical verification through documentation, are all present, but are also all made ironic in context: the 'Custom-House' genesis (and foreword) of Hawthorne's novel is here inverted into Atwood's epilogue, with its sexist and academic interpretations by male experts; the embodiment of shame (the illegitimate child) becomes the aim of all sex (reproduction by surrogate mothers of sorts).

Parody is a typical postmodern paradoxical form because it uses and abuses the texts and conventions of the tradition. It also contests both the authority of that tradition and the claims of art to originality. The parodic photograph by Nigel Scott used on the cover of this book offers a visual example of how the challenges of parody work. It simultaneously exploits and undercuts several recognizable traditions of the representation of women: the passive female on her pedestal is here poised for action, complete with unglamorous bathing cap; the erotic pin-up bathing beauty now refuses to engage the gaze of her (conventionally male) viewer; the Rolls Royce figure's symbolic wings are here transformed into an everyday banal bathrobe. The unevenly hung canvas backdrop calls attention to itself *as backdrop*, pointing to the entire photograph's existence as *construction*—not as reflection—of woman as subject and also as object. By recalling the texts of the past—of literature or even of history—postmodern novels similarly use parody to question whether there can ever be such a thing as a final, definitive 'inscription' of selfhood or subjectivity in fiction. Novels like *The Biggest Modern Woman of the World*, *The Temptations of Big Bear*, and

The Scorched-Wood People all re-narrate and re-conceptualize the past, both literary and historical, and thereby re-formulate the possibilities of subjectivity narrated in them. Earlier, *Beautiful Losers* had de-sacralized both the male, European, Jesuit 'inscription' of the selfhood of the female, early Canadian Indian saint, Catherine Tekakwitha, and also the equally male, American one of Hollywood stars like Marilyn Monroe. As Lorna Irvine has shown,[16] in *Blown Figures* Audrey Thomas parodies the form and imagery of the Greek epic and of *Heart of Darkness*, 'feminizing' their maleness, translating their death, war, and violence into terms of life, reproduction, and love. Similarly, Kroetsch 'Canadianizes' the American western genre as well as the Greek epic in *The Studhorse Man*. In *St Urbain's Horseman* Mordecai Richler parodically uses and abuses the Golem myth, making it recount the ironic triumph of living 'art' that helps the oppressed.[17]

All this play with the texts of the past does not, however, lead to some kind of sterile narcissism. What makes this obviously echoing form specifically postmodern is the paradoxical fact that it is precisely this intertextuality (as it is called today) that brings about a direct confrontation with the issue of the relation of art to the world outside it—to the world of those social, cultural, and ultimately ideological systems by which we all live our lives. If, as many have claimed, language is the 'absolute precondition for nearly all our social life'[18] and is inextricably bound to thought, then language and self-consciousness about language cannot but be social concerns, and not narcissistic navel-gazing. Feminists have taught us much about the importance and impact of language upon our social concepts, and novels like Atwood's *Life Before Man* and Thomas's *Intertidal Life* further study the past of language itself, through etymological word play, in order to analyze the history of woman's literal 'inscription' into language, and thus to reveal the gendered bias encoded in the language we so unself-consciously use every day. Atwood does not just 'use language in a largely referential way, providing the veri-similitude that is the staple of realist fiction and that authen-ticates the world and the word's relationship to it',[19] though she does do this; she also subverts the authority of any simple idea of a realist word/world relationship in a most postmodern—contradictory—way. Like Kroetsch, Wiebe, Bowering, and others, Atwood uses and abuses the conventions of both novelistic language and narrative in her fiction to question any naive notions of both modernist formalism (art is autonomous artifice) and realist transparency (art is a reflection of the world). This is one articulation of the postmodern paradox.

Another involves the relation of the aesthetic to the historical. The 1980 Venice Biennale, which introduced postmodern architecture (by name) to the world at large, had for its motto 'The Presence of the Past'. Twenty architects from Europe and North America constructed postmodernist façades in order to show what the street of the future (the 'Strada Novissima') might look like. What was particularly striking about this exhibition was the parodic recall of the history of architectural forms and styles in these façades. But the intent of the architects was not merely to be ironic or nostalgic or decorative. This was a critical revisiting of the entire past of humankind's relation with its built environment; it was a dialogue with what was still viable in that past; and it was a return to a critically shared vocabulary of architectural forms. All this, of course, was in reaction against those deliberately ahistorical, grey, purist monuments of 'high modernism' of the International Style that we can see all around us in our urban centres and that have brought about what Jane Jacobs calls the 'death of great American cities'.[20]

In architecture postmodernism has clearly meant a critical response to 'high modernism'—both an aesthetic and an ideological response. Here the 'post' prefix means both 'after' and 'against'. In literature, as everyone from John Barth to Terry Eagleton[21] has pointed out, the situation is not quite this clearcut. Both the self-consciousness and the parody of postmodern literature could be seen as merely more intense versions of the practice of modernism, as I have already suggested. But gone now is the modernist belief that art can really be autonomous or separate from the world. Postmodern literature situates itself squarely in the context of its own reading and writing as social and ideological actualities. For many Canadian novelists, from Timothy Findley to Audrey Thomas, the act of making fictions is an *unavoidably* ideological act, that is, a process of creating meaning within a social context. Along with the novels of Salman Rushdie, Gabriel García Márquez, Umberto Eco, and E.L. Doctorow (to name but a few), much Canadian fiction presents itself as investigating the relationship between art (and language) and what we choose to call 'reality', between the discourses of art and the structures of social and cultural power.

The 1960s saw the 'inscription' into history of those previously silenced ex-centrics: those defined by differences in class, gender, race, ethnic group, and sexual preference. And the seventies and eighties have seen their 'inscription' into fiction, in forms that vary from the 'historicity' of the Native peoples and Métis (in the fiction of Wiebe) to the 'metaphoricity' of the freaks in Quarrington's *Home Game* or the novels of Kroetsch. Female, gay, and various ethnic voices can now be heard, and the postmodern interest in the ex-centric has, I think, contributed both to this new valuing and to the challenging of all kinds of '-centrism' (andro-, hetero-, Euro-, etc.).

The sixties, for all their undeniable self-indulgence and 'presentism' (the 'now' generation), were years of a general challenge to authority that left their mark on postmodernism in Canada, as elsewhere. These were the years both of nationalist politics in Canada and of the rise of the women's movement. Not surprisingly, the fiction of those writers formed (intellectually and politically) in the sixties is often engaged fiction, dealing with issues ranging from the Canadian identity to gender politics. Many have pointed out that challenges to authority can easily lead to anarchy as well as decentralization of power,[22] but the postmodernism that grew from these roots has turned out to be less anarchic than constructively contradictory, even if seriously compromised. To offer an example, Dave Godfrey's *The New Ancestors* could be seen as both 'inscribing' the humanist individualist view of character and also challenging it with a Marxist analysis of the historical, political, and social forces that condition that individualism. The contradiction remains; the novel does not resolve it.[23] The African words symbolically remain in African; the glossary is permanently missing. Our 'natural' (that is, humanist) tendency to want to resolve difference into unity or to absorb the margin into the centre is here frustrated.

Margaret Atwood has called writers 'eye-witnesses, I-witnesses'.[24] This is why she, as a novelist with a distinct moral and political point of view, is attracted to the work of Amnesty International: 'all it does is tell stories. It makes *the story* known. Such stories have a moral force, a moral authority which is undeniable' (p. 350). This is the impulse behind a novel like *Bodily Harm* or *Life Before Man*, where the moral *is* the political, that is, 'having to do with power: who's got it, who wants it, how it operates' (p. 353). As both a Canadian and a woman, she protests any tendency toward easy passivity and naivety; she refuses to allow either Canadians or women to deny their complicity in the power structures that may subject them.

Although much of the impulse behind the postmodern has come from the sixties, those years also come under severe attack from postmodernism, which always contests as well as exploits the values that gave it birth. In the sixties the buzz-word of culture was (paradoxically) the 'natural', the authentic: flower power, rock music, sexual desire, communes, 'hanging loose'— all were manifestations of the 'natural'. What postmodernism has done is show how the 'natural' is in fact the 'constructed', the made, the social. In addition, it is never free from an intimate relation with power. Novels like *Intertidal Life* offer critiques of ideological naivety as trenchant as those of Roland Barthes. In an early book, *Mythologies*,[25] Barthes launched a series of Brechtian attacks on what is seen as 'natural' or given or common-sensical in culture, arguing that these assumptions are anything but the eternal, universal, and unchangeable values they may appear to be. Rather, they constitute what he calls ideology, the unspoken (and therefore more powerful) system of belief specific to a particular place and time. What any society calls universal 'truth' is really, therefore, socially, culturally, economically, and historically particular. Perhaps it is not surprising, then, that the art of a period that adopts an opposing notion of 'truth' might be a very self-conscious art, that its fiction might be metafiction. The critical climate of the eighties that has given us what we now label as 'poststructuralism' and 'discourse analysis' is a postmodern climate, aware of its inevitable ideological complicity with the dominant forms of culture that it wishes to challenge.

I stress the critical climate that has accompanied the postmodern in literature because I think it is no longer possible (if, indeed, it ever was) to discuss art without understanding its (and our) theoretical underpinnings. Today 'literary theory' is very much a postmodern preoccupation,[26] and this has meant that the once separate disciplines of philosophy, linguistics, history, sociology, literary criticism, and psychoanalysis have merged to form a new theoretical frame of reference within which postmodern literature is both written and read. This is a literature that questions and challenges; it is, for instance, a literature that makes non-natural all things that once went without saying in realist fiction: motivated characterization, transparent language, coherent plot structures. In Canada the literary and the theoretical have had an especially close connection because of the strong presence of a great number of important writer/theorists. We have Robert Kroetsch's novels and poetry, but we also have his interviews, his own criticism, and his unorthodox essays that challenge the borders of genre and of traditional academic argument (and its accompanying authority). The fact that Kroetsch has taught in the United States and has also been involved in editing the postmodern journal *Boundary 2* has no doubt made him aware of the positive value of his ex-centricity. Through writer/theorists Frank Davey, George Bowering, Michael Ondaatje, Stephen Scobie, Margaret Atwood, and others, Canadian criticism and Canadian literature have both felt the impact of poststructuralist philosophy, linguistics, semiotics, reader-response theory, Marxist and feminist critique. Davey's journal *Open Letter* has been receptive to postmodern ideas on both a thematic/formal level and a more ideological/political one.

The postmodern Canadian novel has developed in a manner parallel to that of the Canadian documentary long poem (as written by some of those same writer/theorists too). This mixed poetic/narrative genre has been widely studied as a postmodern form: its history from the epic to the modernist long poem has been outlined; its parodic use of narrative conventions to question the very nature of the order that narrative plot implies has been studied at length.[27] The postmodern novel has not yet been given this kind of careful and particular attention, especially the one form of it that seems to me most typical of the paradoxes that characterize the postmodern. This is the form I would like to call 'historiographic metafiction'—fiction that is intensely, self-reflexively art, but is also grounded in historical, social, and political realities: Findley's *Famous Last Words*, with its evocation of the Duke and Duchess of Windsor and the political climate of Europe before and during the Second World War, or Chris Scott's *Antichthon*, with its frighteningly modern portrayal of the consequences of differing belief in an age of ideological conformity—through the trial and death of Giordano Bruno. These works are not quite historical novels in the traditional sense, for they are also very metafictional in their attention to the processes of writing, reading, and interpreting.

They are both self-consciously fictional but also overtly concerned with the acts (and consequences) of the reading and writing of history as well as fiction. In other words, the aesthetic and the social, the present and the past, are not separable discourses in these novels. They represent a postmodern self-reflexivity that moves outward to the world beyond their borders—to history, biography, philosophy, religion, politics. This is not a modernist denial of the literary value of historical fact (in the name of aesthetic autonomy); nor is it a realist use of that fact to make the reality of the fictional world seem authentic. Instead, it is a critical counterpointing or dialogue between the 'texts' of both history and art, done in such a way that it does not deny the existence or significance of either.

The forerunner of this postmodern fiction of the seventies and eighties was Leonard Cohen's early *Beautiful Losers* (1966), a novel that places in the foreground the colonialist historical patterns of power (and subjugation) in both national and gender terms. Its unresolved contradictions (poetry/prose; body/mind; sex/spirit; French/English; Native/white; male/female) are embedded in an intensely metafictional text with parodies of texts ranging from the Bible to the Platters' songs. Cohen is the master of the postmodern cultural double bind, as Eli Mandel has argued: 'condemn him and you are on the side of a now impossible refinement; join with him and you admit your complicity.'[28] From its title on, *Beautiful Losers'* paradoxes both establish and undercut the authority of history and art; they 'inscribe' and then negate subjectivity (of the narrators and of their narrated characters); they represent and then undo representation. Cohen self-consciously offers us an accurate portrayal not of the real historical Catherine Tekakwitha, but of Edouard Lecompt's 1927 Jesuit textual 'inscription' of her in his *Une Vièrge Iroquoise Catherine Tekakwitha: Le Lis des bords de la Mohawk et du St Laurent (1656-1680)*. Cohen signals the *textual* nature of his portrait both verbally and through his description of the portrait of Catherine that forms the frontispiece of Lecompt's book.[29] The textuality of history matches that of literature: that is, the only way we can know the past today is through its traces, its texts. This is one of the lessons of the postmodern.

This is also a lesson taught by theorists of historiography in their challenging of the traditional causal, closed, linear nature of narrative history. No longer is history to be accepted as 'how things actually happened', with the historian in the role of recorder. Hayden White, Michel Foucault, Louis O. Mink, and many others have studied the implications of seeing history as a construction, as having been *made* by the historian through a process of selecting, ordering, and narrating.[30] Given this context, it is perhaps not odd that when fiction writers like Rudy Wiebe come to deal with historical personages such as Louis Riel, they should do so equally self-consciously.

Indeed, Wiebe's The *Scorched-Wood People* and *The Temptations of Big Bear* are models of postmodernist historiographic metafiction in yet another way. If the view of history as ordered and neatly closed-off narrative is now under attack, then (logically) so too should be the realist presentation of historical events and characters in fiction, for nineteenth-century historical narrative was a major model for the writing of realist novels. Jean-François Lyotard[31] has defined the 'postmodern condition' as one characterized by a distrust of 'meta-' or 'master' narratives, that is, of the received wisdom or the grand narrative systems that once made sense of things for us. Canadian novels have contributed to this distrust of everything from the state (Kogawa's *Obasan*) to religion (Scott's *Antichthon*). In a similar vein, novels today often seem to find it hard not to display their own suspicion of certain literary conventions they were once able to take for granted—basic conventions such as coherent narrative point of view. Wiebe, in telling the story of Big Bear, gives his reader multiple perspectives on his hero's actions and intentions, and then leaves us to make up our own minds. The loose ends are not tied up neatly—even when official versions of 'history' have claimed that they are (or, at least, were). In this light, of course, the recent re-evaluations of the 'history' of Riel would be part of this same postmodern process of challenge to the potentially single and closed structures of story-telling, historical or fictional.

By overtly presenting his novels as novels, while at the same time offering a variety of historical perspectives, Wiebe makes the past present in a distinctly postmodern way. He has commented on the difficulties of writing about historical events: 'Though the acts themselves seem quite clear, some written reports of the acts contradict each other.'[32] Wiebe incorporates part of this problem into the very form of his novel by contrasting the imperialist ideology of the British, who wrote those written reports, with the oral, Native tradition, whose version of events did not survive as readily as did the other. Yet the written British documents have a hollow and sterile ring to them when compared with the metaphorical and rhetorical power of Big Bear's oral speech. The formal irony of the confrontation of two languages, two worlds, two histories is paradoxically created in one language by a white, if ex-centric, Canadian.

Like Michel Foucault, Robert Kroetsch has argued that we might want to move from our usual notion of history to a new one of archaeology, which he claims 'allows the fragmentary nature of the story, against the coerced unity of traditional history'.[33] As contemporary theorists of historiography like Dominick LaCapra have underlined, we can no longer accept that the 'givens' or the 'facts' of history are eternally fixed and 'natural', and it is the self-conscious pointing to the mechanisms of historical as well as novelistic fact- (that is, fiction-) making in postmodern novels that has also helped teach us this. Historical 'fact' is the systematized, constructed version of brute 'event'; it is the past given meaning by its writers and readers. The meaning of the past is not coherent, continuous, or unified— until we make it so.

A recent show by Canadian artist John Scott, entitled 'War Artists', exposed these same formal and ideological issues in the medium of the visual arts. For example, 'The Eloquent Silence of Alex C.' (1986) is a portrait of Alex Colville, Canadian painter and once offical World War II war artist. But it is a portrait from the nose up only; it is as if the jaw has been blown away. One possible interpretation, given the title, is that war silences the artist, in the sense that no artist can effectively reveal the real horror of war through art. Perhaps too there is a suggestion of the inevitable complicity of creativity with destruction in the irony of the very concept of the war artist; it is by definition an oxymoron.

The issue of complicity that postmodernism raises is one that depends upon a recognition of the complex 'discursive' situation of literature. By this I mean that the 'discourse' of literature consists of a situation wherein the writer, the reader, and the text meet within an entire historical, social, and political, as well as literary, context. And postmodern novels themselves try to draw attention to this discursive situation: as self-conscious readers we are made to watch Demeter writing in his bathtub in *The Studhorse Man*, Becker collecting his information in *The*

Invention of the World, Findley's narrator searching the archives in *The Wars*, or his Mauberley writing on the wall in *Famous Last Words*. Both metafiction and reader-response theory have worked to make us aware of the active role of the reader in granting meaning to texts. As Geoff Hancock puts it, 'Your own memory, imagination, and wits are part of the narrative strategy.'[34] In historiographic metafiction we are lured into a world of imagination only to be confronted with the world of history, and thus asked to rethink the categories by which we normally would distinguish fiction from 'reality'. Reading becomes an act of philosophical puzzling as well as one of co-creation. In Atwood's terms, 'It is my contention that the process of reading is part of the process of writing, the necessary completion without which writing can hardly be said to exist.'[35]

Postmodern texts tend to make very self-conscious their writing, their reading, and the various contexts in which both acts take place. Atwood's narrator in *The Handmaid's Tale* anguishes over the status of her narrative: 'It isn't a story I'm telling' (in other words, she is telling the truth, not lies or fictions), yet 'It's also a story I'm telling'.[36] She acknowledges both the process of fictionalizing (or 'narrativizing') and the fact that she is telling her story *to* someone. The entire discursive context of the text is overt: 'Tell, rather than write, because I have nothing to write with and writing is in any case forbidden. But if it's a story, even in my head, I must be telling it to someone. You don't tell a story only to yourself. There's always someone else' (p. 49). Although unsure of the final receiver of her story, she sees that a 'story is like a letter. *Dear You*, I'll say. Just *you*, without a name' (p. 50). Her narrating parody of Descartes's *cogito ergo sum* is 'I tell, therefore you are' (p. 279). Atwood's narrator sees the difficulty of telling the story of history, of recasting brute experience into narrative form: 'It's impossible to say a thing exactly the way it was, because what you say can never be exact, you always leave something out, there are too many parts, sides, crosscurrents, nuances' (p. 144).

The self-reflexive epilogue of the novel is ironically entitled 'Historical Notes' and consists of the partial transcript of a symposium in which a paper is presented called 'Problems of Authentication in Reference to *The Handmaid's Tale*' (p. 312). The narrator's transcribed cassettes are not accepted here as truth or as history: the male (and sexist) historian says that she 'could have told us much about the workings of the Gileadean empire, had she had the instincts of a reporter or a spy' (p. 322). In fact she did, but what she has told us is not the kind of information the male historian wants: she has told us about women's history, a history either ignored or trivialized by the academic tradition. The historian ends his talk with this: 'As all historians know, the past is a great darkness, and filled with the obscurity of the matrix out of which they come; and, try as we may, we cannot always decipher them precisely in the clearer light of our own day' (p. 324). In his universalizing first-person plural maleness, he misses the gendered irony of his own words: 'the matrix out of which they come'—the silenced source of the selfhood of woman in the novel.

To make problematic such issues as gender, authority, facts, and subjectivity can obviously lead to a paralyzing scepticism about basic values and categories of belief in literature and in life, but it can also offer a new impetus to questioning in many areas of art and theory today. For instance, French philosopher Jacques Derrida's general project of a subversive questioning of the Western philosophical tradition and its metaphysics has opened up new areas of study that no longer take for granted such basics as the definition of 'Man' as a rational being, in control of everything. Thanks to the work of feminist writers, we are facing a new situation: exit Man, enter Humankind, including Woman. The universal (but somehow male) concept of humanist Man is giving way to a more diversified concept of experience based on *difference*. In postmodernist literature this has meant a turning to those forms that can accentuate difference, especially in the face of a mass culture that tends to homogenize or obliterate anything that does not seem to fit. In Canadian writing the two major (but by no means only) new forms to appear have been those that embody ethnicity and the female. While not all the work done in these areas has been postmodernist, some clearly has. A metafictional novel like Susan Swan's *The Biggest Modern Woman of the World* is a serious and self-consciously ironic investigation into what it means to be a woman—in both artistic and political terms. Both theory and contemporary fiction, in Canada as elsewhere, are responding to common social provocations, such as immigration patterns or the rise of feminism. And they are doing so very self-consciously in order to help us recognize that our contemporary culture is made up of events in which we participate as active agents; it is not something outside us that happens to us.

Another consequence of the postmodern valuing of the different and the diverse in opposition to the uniform and the unified is perhaps more particularly Canadian, or at least so the dominant Canadian self-image would have it. With a motto like *a mari usque ad mare* to contrast to *e pluribus unum*, Canada may like to see itself as a nation that has resisted the more American model of unification, be it geographic, demographic, or ideological. While in fact this may not be the case, the image is cherished by many. The postmodern has also translated the existing Canadian emphasis on regionalism in literature, for example, into a concern for the different, the local, the particular—in opposition to the uniform, the universal, the centralized. The emphasis is the same, but the terms of reference and context have changed. Northrop Frye,[37] Robert Kroetsch,[38] and many others have addressed the importance of both Canadian cultural disparity and local tradition. The particular and the occasional have always been important to Canadian literature's regionalist focus. Canadians have not really been attracted to the image of what Atwood once called the 'free floating . . . citizen of the world'.[39] In fact, Atwood is one of many Canadian writers who have tried to articulate the difference that defines Canada.[40] Canadian novelists have refigured the *realist regional* into the *postmodern different*: the west of Aritha Van Herk; the Maritimes of David Adams Richards; the west coast of Jack Hodgins; the southern Ontario of Matt Cohen. Robert Kroetsch writes of his desire to record and invent (a typically postmodern paradox) the Canadian west: 'That pattern of contraries, all the possibilities implied in record and invent, for me finds its focus in the model suggested by the phrase: a local pride.'[41] To render the particular concrete, to glory in a (defining) local ex-centricity—this is the Canadian postmodern.

Postmodernist 'recording' and 'inventing' are clearly processes, not products. They are not fixed, closed, eternal, and universal. Instead of feeling threatened by this un-fixing of certainties, postmodern culture tends to find it liberating and stimulating. Perhaps the loss of the modernist faith in fixed system, order, and wholeness can make room for new models based on things once rejected: contingency, multiplicity, fragmentation, discontinuity.[42] I do not mean to suggest that we should jettison one faith in order to take on board a new one. To accept responsibility as an active agent in culture is to accept that there must always be considerable open debate among writers, theorists, and readers about the value and even the meaning of these various postmodernist challenges. For example, there are writers like Kroetsch who are happy to call themselves postmodern, arguing further that the national discontinuities of Canada have made it particularly ripe for the discontinuities of postmodernism.[43] On the other hand, there are novelists like Matt Cohen[44] who argue that postmodernism lives only as a theory and not as a reality in fiction. I think the numbers are against him here, though. There are other, more internal, debates as well. Postmodern George Bowering sees, at long last, the demise of the realist novel in Canada.[45] But the numbers are against him too, I fear. What is striking and particular about Canadian postmodernist fiction is that the very real challenge to the conventions of realism has always come from within those conventions themselves. Unlike the more radical American 'surfiction' or the Québécois linguistic play, English Canadian novels have self-consciously milked realism for all its power, even while parodying and subverting its conventions. This is yet another of the paradoxes that define the postmodern.

For some critics postmodernism, by definition, 'begins at a point beyond realism',[46] but realism, like mimesis, is a convention and thus 'constitutively a social and historical phenomenon.'[47] In a polemical article entitled 'What Was Canadian Literature? Taking Stock of the Canlit Industry' T.D. MacLulich has worried about the appearance of technically innovative postmodern fiction in Canada. He feels it denigrates 'the straightforward possibilities of fiction' by which art mirrors culture.[48] But have there ever been such 'straightforward possibilities'? Or have there only been critics who choose to ignore the conventionality and complexity of realist representation? MacLulich is wrong to see postmodernist fiction as losing all desire to examine specific social conditions and particular backgrounds (ethnic, religious, regional); in fact, postmodernism merely does the same examining in a different way, challenging in the process the unexamined assumption that realism is the only convention that can undertake such an examination.

Ever since the birth of the English novel in the eighteenth century, the twin impulses of realism and self-reflexivity have vied for control of the genre. Postmodernism paradoxically tries to incorporate and to question both of these impulses. The realist novel is not dead in Canada; rather, it is the defining base upon which postmodern challenges operate. As Kroetsch says of García Márquez, 'He nips at the heels of realism and makes the old cow dance.'[49] Historiographic metafiction in particular illustrates this nipping, this internal subversion. The novels of Bowering, Findley, and Thomas both use and abuse the conventions of the realist novel. They ask us to rethink those conventions, this time *as conventions*, but also as ideological strategies. Such novels destabilize things we used to think we could take for granted when we read novels: narrative unity, reliable point of view, coherent character presentation. The once 'transparent' has now been made 'opaque'. Postmodernism in Canada has suggested a rethinking of realism, and therefore we find a situation in which realism is both challenged and taken seriously.

I mentioned earlier that realist fiction has often used historical narrative as its model. As we have seen, however, that too is no longer unquestioned and unquestionable. Like fiction, history is viewed through frames, and those frames bring only certain pre-selected things into the foreground of the reader's attention. And this is true of both public and private history. Michael Ondaatje's tale of New Orleans jazz musician Buddy Bolden, *Coming Through Slaughter*, sits not only on the border between poetry and prose, but also on the boundary between biography and fiction. In *Running in the Family* Ondaatje adds the further complication of autobiography and its conventions. One of the results of the paradoxes of postmodernism has been that its textual self-consciousness has led to a general questioning of the meaning (and value) of making firm distinctions between different forms of literature, or even between art and life. The borders between the novel and what has traditionally been considered non-fiction are constantly being crossed today. Sometimes this is done through the emphasis on what I have been calling the discursive situation of the work. The narrator of George Bowering's *Burning Water*, for instance, writes:

> When I was a boy I was the only person I knew who was named George, but I did have the same first name as the king. That made me feel as if current history and self were bound together, from the beginning.

> When I came to live in Vancouver, I thought of Vancouver, so
> now geography involved my name too, George Vancouver.[50]

Similar border challenges occur in the biographical fictions of
Joseph Skvorecky's *Dvorak in Love* or of Heather Robertson's
Willie. As Derrida has argued,[51] any genre designation both pulls
a body of texts together and simultaneously keeps it from
closing. Classifications of genres are paradoxically built upon
the impossibility of firmly defining genre boundaries.

What postmodern novels do is create the same disquiet as,
say, Magritte's various paintings called 'The Human Condition',
in which paintings are presented within paintings, and unframed
pictures within window frames represent landscapes that overlap perfectly with the landscapes of the 'reality' outside the
windows. This same self-conscious slipping between the forms
of life and those of art is what characterizes postmodernism too.
And it is the reader who must live out that slipping. In the end,
genres are defined by readers. The limits of life and art are tested
not only by fictionalizing historians, but by their readers. And,
of course, historians and biographers are themselves readers:
they find and interpret the documents (the texts) of the past.
So too do postmodern novelists.

This brings me back to the notion of 'The Presence of the Past'.
Of course, the past once existed. But we can *know* it today only
through its documents, its traces in the present. If our knowledge
of the past is something constructed (or even re-constructed),
its meaning cannot be eternal and is certainly not unchangeable.
It is this realization of the potential for change that postmodern
fiction can exploit and expose. In trying to unsettle our unexamined convictions about the status of fact and truth, it sets
up a new tension between the fictive and the historical. But it
does not do this in order to debunk or to exalt either one. Nor
does it intend to do what Truman Capote or Thomas Keneally
have done: that is, use the conventions of realism to 'novelize'
history. Historiographic metafiction questions the nature and
validity of the entire human process of writing—of both history
and fiction. Its aim in so doing is to study how we know the
past, how we *make* sense of it. The English language here happily
points to the nature of understanding (making sense) as creation
(*making* sense). Postmodern literature often turns the act of
reading into a self-conscious and active performance, and does
so by itself enacting or performing what it expounds.

It is easy to see, then, that postmodernism in its broadest sense is the name we give to our culture's 'narcissistic' obsession with its own workings—both past and present. In academic and popular circles today, books abound that offer us new social models, new frameworks for our knowledge, new analyses of strategies of power. This phenomenon does betray a loss of faith in what were once the certainties, the 'master' narratives of our liberal humanist culture. But that loss need not be a debilitating one. In postmodern literature, as in architecture, it has meant a new vitality, a new willingness to enter into a dialogue with history on new terms. It has been marked by a move away from fixed products and structures to open cultural processes and events. There has been a general (and perhaps healthy) turning from the expectation of sure and single meaning to a recognition of the value of difference and multiplicity, a turning from passive trust in system to an acceptance of responsibility for the fact that art and theory are both actively 'signifying' practices—in other words, that it is we who both make and make sense of our culture.

Notes

1 See Raymond Federman, *Surfiction: Fiction Now . . . and Tomorrow*, 2nd ed. (Chicago: Swallow Press, 1981).

2 Walter Pache, ' "The Fiction Makes Us Real": Aspects of Postmodernism in Canada', in *Gaining Ground: European Critics on Canadian Literature*, ed. Robert Kroetsch and Reingard M. Nischik (Edmonton: NeWest Press, 1985), p. 65.

3 Stanley Fogel, *A Tale of Two Countries: Contemporary Fiction in English Canada and the United States* (Toronto: ECW Press, 1984), p. 8. All further page references will appear in the text.

4 Marshall McLuhan, 'Canada: The Border Line Case', in *The Canadian Imagination: Dimensions of a Literary Culture*, ed. David Staines (Cambridge: Harvard University Press, 1972), pp. 226-48. All further page references will appear in the text.

5 Cited by Aritha Van Herk in her 'Biocritical Essay', in *The Robert Kroetsch Papers: An Archival Inventory* (Calgary: University of Calgary Press, 1985), p. xxxiv.

6 *The Family Romance* (Winnipeg: Turnstone Press, 1986), p. 15.

7 In Robert Kroetsch and Diane Bessai, 'Death is a Happy Ending: A Dialogue in Thirteen Parts', in *Figures in a Ground: Canadian Essays on Modern Literature Collected in Honour of Sheila Watson*, ed. Diane Bessai

and David Jackel (Saskatoon: Western Producer Prairie Books, 1978), p. 208.

8 *Border Crossings* 5, 3 (1986), pp. 47-50.

9 Eli Mandel and David Taras, eds (London and New York: Methuen, 1987).

10 See Lorna Irvine, *Sub/version: Canadian Fictions by Women* (Toronto: ECW Press, 1986) and Coral Ann Howells, *Private and Fictional Words: Canadian Women Novelists of the 1970s and 1980s* (London and New York: Methuen, 1987).

11 Irvine, p. 11.

12 *Home Truths: Selected Canadian Stories* (Toronto: Macmillan, 1981), p. 269.

13 Elaine Showalter, 'Feminist Criticism in the Wilderness', *Critical Inquiry* 8, 2 (1981), p. 192.

14 See Kroetsch in Shirley Neuman and Robert Wilson, *Labyrinths of Voice: Conversations with Robert Kroetsch* (Edmonton: NeWest Press, 1982), p. 97.

15 See Glen Deer, 'Rhetoric, Ideology, and Authority: Narrative Strategies in Six Innovative Canadian Novels', Ph.D. Dissertation, York University, 1987, pp. 182-3.

16 In *Sub/version*, pp. 63-5.

17 For a more traditional reading, see Chapter 10 of Wilfred Cude's *A Due Sense of Differences: An Evaluative Approach to Canadian Literature* (Lanham, Md: University Press of America, 1980), pp. 172-97.

18 Gunther Kress and Robert Hodge, *Language as Ideology* (London: Routledge and Kegan Paul, 1979), p. 1.

19 Fogel, p. 102.

20 *Death and Life of Great American Cities* (New York: Vintage, 1961).

21 Respectively, 'The Literature of Replenishment: Postmodernist Fiction', *Atlantic* 245, 1 (1980), pp. 65-71 and 'Capitalism, Modernism and Postmodernism', *New Left Review* 152 (1985), pp. 60-73.

22 Frank Davey, *From There to Here* (Erin, Ont.: Press Porcépic, 1971), p. 21; Kroetsch in Neuman and Wilson, p. 35.

23 Deer argues for transcendence of oppositions (p. 97), but this interpretation is difficult to sustain in the light of both plot and form.

24 *Second Words: Selected Critical Prose* (Toronto: Anansi, 1982), p. 203. All further page references will appear in the text.

25 Trans. Annette Lavers (London: Granada, 1973).

26 See Fredric Jameson, 'Postmodernism and Consumer Society', in *The Anti-Aesthetic: Essays on Postmodern Culture*, ed. Hal Foster (Port Townsend, Wash.: Bay Press, 1983), p. 112.

27 See, for example, Kroetsch's 'For Play and Entrance: The Contemporary Canadian Long Poem', *Dandelion* 8 (1981), pp. 61-85; Michael Ondaatje, 'Introduction' to *The Long Poem Anthology*, ed. Michael Ondaatje (Toronto: Coach House Press, 1979), pp. 1-18.

[28] *Another Time* (Erin, Ont.: Press Porcépic, 1977), p. 133.

[29] Leslie Monkman, '*Beautiful Losers*: Mohawk Myth and Jesuit Legend', *Journal of Canadian Fiction* 3, 3 (1974), pp. 57-9.

[30] For a further discussion of historiography, see Linda Hutcheon, *A Poetics of Postmodernism: History, Theory, Fiction* (London, New York: Routledge and Kegan Paul, 1988).

[31] *The Postmodern Condition: A Report on Knowledge*, trans. Geoff Bennington and Brian Massumi (Minneapolis: University of Minnesota Press, 1984).

[32] In Rudy Wiebe and Eli Mandel, 'Where the Voice Comes From', *A Voice in the Land: Essays By and About Rudy Wiebe*, ed. W.J. Keith (Edmonton: NeWest Press, 1981), p. 152.

[33] 'On Being an Alberta Writer', *Open Letter* 5th series, 4 (Spring 1983), pp. 76. See Foucault's *The Archaeology of Knowledge*, trans. A.M. Sheridan Smith (New York: Pantheon, 1972). See too Shirley Neuman, 'Unearthing Language: An Interview with Rudy Wiebe and Robert Kroetsch', in *A Voice in the Land*, pp. 226-47.

[34] 'Introduction' to *Metavisions*, ed. Geoff Hancock (Montreal: Quadrant, 1983), p. 5.

[35] *Second Words*, p. 345.

[36] (Toronto: McClelland and Stewart, 1985), p. 49. All further page references will appear in the text.

[37] *The Bush Garden* (Toronto: Anansi, 1971).

[38] 'For Play and Entrance'.

[39] *Second Words*, p. 113.

[40] For example, in *Survival* (Toronto: Anansi, 1972) or in 'What's So Funny? Notes on Canadian Humour', *Second Words*, pp. 175-89.

[41] 'On Being an Alberta Writer', p. 75.

[42] See Frank Davey's 'Introduction' to *From There to Here*.

[43] In Neuman and Wilson, p. 112.

[44] 'Notes on Realism in Modern English-Canadian Fiction', *Canadian Writers in 1984: 25th Anniversary Issue of Canadian Literature*, ed. W.H. New (Vancouver: University of British Columbia Press, 1984), p. 69.

[45] 'Modernism Could Not Last Forever', *Canadian Fiction Magazine* 32-3 (1979-80), p. 8.

[46] Gerald Graff, 'Babbitt at the Abyss: The Social Context of Postmodern American Fiction', *TriQuarterly* 3, 3 (1975), p. 311.

[47] Barbara Foley, *Telling the Truth: The Theory and Practice of Documentary Fiction* (Ithaca: Cornell University Press, 1986), p. 42.

[48] *Essays on Canadian Writing* 30 (1984-5), p. 25.

[49] In Geoff Hancock, 'An Interview with Robert Kroetsch', *Canadian Fiction Magazine* 24-5 (1977), p. 38.

[50] (Don Mills: Musson, 1980), p. 7.

[51] In 'La Loi du genre/The Law of Genre', *Glyph* 7 (1980), pp. 202-29.

Chapter 2

Caveat Lector: The Early Postmodernism of Leonard Cohen

In 1970 Michael Ondaatje asked the readers of his short book on Leonard Cohen to keep in mind, as a kind of context for the writer's past and future work, Norman Mailer's *Advertisements for Myself*.[1] Already Ondaatje had both perceived a structural constant in Cohen's work up to that point and foreseen the implications of it: the poet's self-consciousness about the artistic process had gradually begun to intrude upon the space of the texts themselves. The struggle of a very particular imagination—Cohen's—coming to grips with its materials, both thematic and formal, was an early instance of what was soon to be called postmodernist 'performance', a performance to which readers' attention was increasingly directed by the art itself. The role of the artist, his powers, his failings, were all investigated in detail, sometimes explicitly, as in the extended tale of the development of the poet Lawrence Breavman in Cohen's first novel, *The Favourite Game*, or in such isolated lines of poetry as 'I wonder how many go back to their desks / and write this down'.

That his first novel is a familiar modernist version of the romantic *Künstlerroman*, the tale of the growth of the young artist, is perhaps self-evident, as is the fact that its protagonist himself turns out to be the (ironic version of) Keats that he feels all Canadians are desperate for, the 'mild Dylan Thomas, talent and behaviour modified for Canadian tastes'.[2] The romantic roots of both the form and the content of the novel have not gone unremarked; however, there is considerable disagreement as to whether this basis constitutes the novel's limitation or its essence.[3] I should think that any decision on this point would have to take into account the very modernist irony that transforms that romanticism and paves the way for the postmodernism of *Beautiful Losers*, a novel that is, if anything, even more ironically and self-consciously aware of the artist as persona in relation to the process of creation.

The move from the modernism of the first novel to the postmodernism of the second is marked by a shift in the level of self-reference—from the content to the form of the work. *Beautiful Losers* is a relatively early example in Canadian literature of what I would call postmodern metafiction: ironic, historical, and political fiction that is also about fiction, that contains within itself a first critical commentary on its own nature as narrative and as language. As always, metafiction implicitly challenges the conventional notions of the novel genre as a realist form and does so largely by granting readers a new role. I would disagree in part with Stephen Scobie when he argues that readers of *Beautiful Losers* are not allowed to participate in the action, that we are held outside, prevented from indulging in the usual novelistic identification.[4] This would be true only if the novel as a literary genre were limited in definition to its particular nineteenth-century form: that is, to realism. Indeed I would say that the very opposite is true here: readers of the postmodern novel (like the modernist one) must *participate*, even if we do not *identify*. In *Beautiful Losers* we only run into difficulty if we insist on reading it as a realist novel, with the accompanying 'ideology' that ignores or denies the existence of formal literary conventions.

If language were not seen as a transparent medium and the novel were not considered just a limpid, realist reflection of (or means to) 'reality', such conventions would have to be acknowledged, and such an acknowledgement could not help but condition any simple psychological notion of reader identification as a one-to-one connection with those literary artifacts called characters. Postmodern metafiction, including Cohen's, implicitly posits a new role for readers: we are not simply to identify with characters, but to acknowledge our own role in co-creating the text being read. Almost like authors, readers must accept the responsibility for actively participating in the constructing of fictive worlds through words as we read.

A corollary of this participation is that, like Cohen, readers of *Beautiful Losers* thus effect a grand ironic reversal of the tradition of the Word made flesh: the novel's sexuality and even obscenity of theme and language invite us to see that here it is the flesh that is made word. In fact, without the flesh the word

might never be. The relation between the word and the flesh—
or, more generally, language and the world—is a complex and
problematized one in postmodern literature. In fact, the teasing
out of these problematic complexities of how words refer to the
world is often part of the actual content of metafiction. *Beautiful
Losers* is typical here in its ironic play with a number of levels
of reference: words openly refer to everything from themselves
to verifiable historical and political actuality. As in the traditional
realist novel, there is still a mimetic reference to the world outside
the novel (or to what can be called the extra-textual world). Also,
as in the realist novel, this is often so only in the sense that
the text has a kind of 'analogon' to the world outside it, rather
than any reductive one-to-one correspondence to it. Houses, for
instance, can exist in fiction because they exist in the world we
know; however, a particular fictional house need have no direct
'real-life' antecedent. The other customary level of reference in
all novels is that of the inner world, its fictional universe. In
contrast to the extra-textual level, this might be called the intra-
textual one. In *Beautiful Losers* the interrelations of these two
levels (inner and outer) are both thematically complex and
structurally significant.

For instance, as in the later postmodern fictions of Wiebe,
Findley, Swan, and others, parallels between extra- and intra-
textual levels reveal that the public level of reference mirrors
the private one: in other words, Canadian national crises are
made to match those of the novel's characters. In addition, these
analogies between the outer historical and political world and
the inner fictive one end up seducing us as readers into trying
to make sense of a crazy novelistic universe. What sense can
be made of the complex tale of a nameless English-Canadian
historian, his Québécois friend known simply, if evocatively, as
F., and his Canadian-Indian wife, Edith, especially when, at the
end, all the male characters merge and transform into a Ray
Charles movie projected against the sky, and all the female
characters' identities (including that of a verifiable historical
Iroquois saint, Catherine Tekakwitha) blur to form a composite
mythical Isis figure? That central bizarre triangle of symbolically
orphaned characters also allegorically acts out, of course, the
history and political destiny of the Canadian nation: of its
successive conquests (mirrored in the deaths of the Indian, Edith,

and then of the Frenchman, F.) and perhaps also its future fate (turning into an American fiction).

This simultaneous merging of inner and outer reference is confusing enough at times to thwart any attempt by readers to find a single unified interpretation of the novel, thereby enforcing, perhaps, F.'s injunction to 'connect nothing'. But what happens when explicit references to other literary and historical texts—to those by the same author or by others—are added to these two traditional levels of novelistic reference? Presumably, further complications ensue. In postmodern fiction at least two other referential levels of language are often found: an auto-referential one (in which the text refers to itself as a text or a printed page or a work of literature) and an inter-textual one (which points to the intervention of other works or artistic conventions). The result of these two additions is frequently an increased sense of 'literariness' or, perhaps, a new self-consciousness about what may be the text's only undeniably true nature: whatever its relation to 'reality', this is clearly *art*.

Certain current theories argue that this latter, intertextual kind of reference is really a basic mode of perception in the reading of all literature *as literature*: that is, through recognition of other texts readers are said to identify the structures that actually make a text a work of art.[5] Without disputing these complex and convincing theories, I should just like to note the simple fact that postmodern metafiction like *Beautiful Losers* merely brings into the foreground what is asserted to be a fact for all literature: that it relies on its relationship to other texts for its very existence *as literature*. Cohen's text openly plays on the intertextual conventions of the epistolary novel (in 'A Long Letter from F.') and the journal form (in the nameless narrator's writing in Part I). This is not so very different from the way his verse has played with the poetic tradition of imagery from Shakespeare through Baudelaire to Yeats.[6]

In an interview Cohen once admitted to a conscious inter-textual intent, since he said he wrote 'using all the techniques of the modern novel which was the discipline in which [he] was trained—so there's this huge prayer using the conventional techniques of pornographic suspense, of humour, of plot, of character development and conventional intrigue'.[7] Armed with a historical account of Catherine Tekakwitha and a 1943 Blue

Beetle comic book, Cohen claimed that he said to himself, 'if I can't write, if I can't *blacken these pages*, then I really can't do anything.'[8] And the novel's constant use both of comic-book language and advertisements and of the Jesuit chronicles of the Iroquois saint's life is the text's testimony to this intertextuality and to Cohen's success at blackening those pages. In fact, critics have enjoyed a veritable treasure hunt in the Jesuit accounts[9] and in such diverse places as the writings of Plutarch, Norman O. Brown, and Nietzsche.[10] Usually, however, they have been less quick to investigate the function of these references, especially in the light of the fact that they are often openly acknowledged in the text itself.

Frequently, for example, the erotic parts of the novel clearly set out to parody a religious text, be it the spiritual exercises of St Ignatius Loyola or the Bible itself.[11] Here the particular mode of transformation (through formal parody) of the implied spiritual values into what might be considered their opposites suggests a possible way to interpret the role of intertextuality in the novel in general: the Russian critic Mikhail Bakhtin identified this same kind of inversion of the official social and literary norms in Rabelais's work as belonging to what he called the 'carnivalesque' of the medieval folk tradition.[12] Like Cohen's postmodern metafiction, which implicates readers as active co-creators in the work, so the medieval carnival is said to exist on the borderline between art and life, making no formal distinction between actor and spectator. There are no footlights; the world is the stage. This, Bakhtin argued, creates (through an authorized transgression of the usual norms) a second, inverted world, parallel to that of the official culture.

From the perspective of Cohen's postmodern novel, what is also interesting here is Bakhtin's characterization of the 'grotesque realism' of this inverted world as both 'ambivalent' and incomplete. All (by official standards) gross or apparently negative qualities—derision, obscenity, degradation, even death—are 'ambivalent' in the sense that their opposites (frankness, freedom, regeneration, revival) are said to be implied in their very essence. In addition, the time frame of the carnivalesque, like that of nature, is cyclic, building the knowledge of renewal into dying: from one body a new one always emerges in some form or another. (To readers of *Beautiful Losers* the dead characters that reappear, transformed and merged with the living, do form but one body [for each sex]. In Catherine's uncle's words, 'I change / I am the same.') According to Bakhtin, the 'unfinished' and 'open' body is not even separated from the world around it by clearly defined boundaries; in fact, it blends with it and becomes 'cosmic'. (The novel's final figures of Isis and of the Ray Charles movie in the sky inevitably come to mind here.) In the carnivalesque the emphasis is on process, on coming into being, and in Cohen's stress on process there can be found something of the same 'incompleteness' that characterizes the grotesque.

The carnivalesque is centred on what Bakhtin's translator rather awkwardly calls the 'material bodily lower stratum'. The obsession with bodily apertures and sexual organs in the work of Cohen, as in that of Rabelais, leads to recurring images of eating, drinking, defecating, and various forms of sexual encounter (in *Beautiful Losers*, usually oral or anal). The scatological content of much of the novel has its verbal counterpart in (by official standards) the obscenity and blasphemy of the text's language. Here, again, that carnivalesque 'ambivalence' might be seen operating. This kind of language is not merely abusive, according to Bakhtin; it is also perhaps a sign of irrepressible linguistic freedom and vitality. Such obscenity, when isolated from this folk context (as it often is today), is usually perceived only as a negative. This seems to be Cohen's message in his novel too, for he goes out of his way to confront, even to try to shock, his readers in an attempt, perhaps, to get us back in touch with our bodies—and with the language of our bodies. In the early film *Ladies and Gentlemen . . . Mr. Leonard Cohen* the author remarks, 'There are no dirty words . . . ever!' With the loss of the pure 'ambivalence' of this carnivalesque bodily-centred perspective, sex (like birth, death, and other physical functions) has been rejected as proper subject matter for 'serious' literature, as well as for decorous language. Cohen, like Rabelais before him, refuses such a separation of art from the realities of bodily life.

My comparing of a medieval literary and social model with a postmodern metafictional novel here is not intended as an academic digression or even as an exotic analogy. I think that it can be argued that Cohen's world is not at all unlike that of Rabelais, at least as described by Bakhtin. For example, the carnivalesque need to invert norms felt by those living in the medieval world is said to be linked to their feelings of insecurity in the face of the stronger forces of both nature and the social order. It is, then, the fear inspired by these forces that creates (or contributes to) the essential seriousness of the official culture—and hence brings about both the need to transgress and the temporary authorization to do so in the form of the carnival (or of folk humour in general). Cohen's postmodern characters live in fear as well, ironic victims of their own natural and social 'progress'. Cities have overtaken the wilderness; plastic has replaced birchbark on canoes; movie stars have become modern saints in a celluloid heaven. In *Beautiful Losers* all the characters are said to be somehow 'mangled' in either 'ordinary' or 'eternal' machinery, depending on whether their pain is caused by material or spiritual (official) systems. F., who loves machines and preaches system, admits to failure in the end. Cohen's technological postmodern humanity is, like Rabelais's medieval equivalent, faced with a serious, even fear-inspiring universe, which at times it feels it must try to combat or defy—by obscenity, by sexuality, by exulting in the trappings of the folk (or, to use today's term, pop) culture. Comic books, popular music, videos, and movies are perhaps today's 'popular-festive forms'; however capitalist and commodified they may be, they still exist in opposition to the contemporary equivalent of Bakhtin's official formal culture. Literature, suggests Cohen, might best be opened up to the energy of 'the people', however compromised that might be.[13]

There are also in this novel, though, a number of significant departures from the Bakhtinian model. In the Russian's view (that is, Marxist—or in a concession to reigning Marxist ideology) these folk forms are basically supposed to be utopian, to look forward to the future: 'the victory of all the people's material abundance, freedom, equality, brotherhood. The victory of the future is ensured by the people's immortality. The birth of the new, of the greater and the better, is as indispensable and as inevitable as the death of the old' (p. 256). But the end of *Beautiful Losers* is a postmodern, ironic reversal of this kind of optimistic utopianism. The revolution of the 'second-chancers' fails; everyone just sits back and watches the Ray Charles movie, thankful that it is 'only a movie' and not something in 'life' that would require an active response. But Cohen's irony here could be said to be figuratively directed against the failure of the clichéd notion of the passive (or even identifying) readers of realist fiction too, against their presumed failure to engage actively in a collective process that has the potential to be socially (as well as culturally) revitalizing—the act of creating through reading.

Here lies, however, Cohen's second deviation from the Bakhtinian model. Whereas death in that model always suggests birth (because of Bakhtin's guiding perspective of 'ambivalence'), at least on the content level of *Beautiful Losers*, all of the characters are orphans; all of the sex is deliberately non-productive biologically (i.e., mechanical, oral, anal); all but one of the main characters die. In other words, birth seems to be emphatically, resolutely denied. But this would be true only on the level of realist content; in formal terms the characters are all reborn, transformed, merged together into those two final haunting figures. Defying normal realist logic, these *formal* intricacies point to the fact that rebirth is indeed implied in death, but that the only real generation or creation allowed in this particular world is the writer's—and, also, as long as we choose not to sit back and passively watch the revolution fail, the readers'.

Perhaps the most important reason for using the Bakhtinian carnivalesque as a critical concept here is that it enables a connection to be made between the social and the literary on a formal level (the inversion of norms), as well as allowing us to see the mechanics behind the linking of the act and the word, the sexual perversity of the content and the obscenity of the language.[14] Just as importantly, though, it gives a context in which to place Cohen's postmodern use of pop culture. This temporally specific (and admittedly commodified) version of the 'folk' is quite openly and ironically set in opposition to the official culture of the eternal and the serious: the Parthenon model is painted red with Tibetan Desire nail polish. (One could also argue, I think, that Cohen's turning to a career as a pop singer shows a certain respect for this tradition of the culture of 'the people'.[15]) Charles Axis (Charles Atlas), Plastic Man, Blue Beetle, 'Smack! Wham! Pow!'—these are all presented (albeit with irony) as intertextual references of comparable cultural weight to those from the Bible or Nietzsche.

Comic books, like popular songs, are 'ambivalent' in this novel: funny yet serious, transient yet perhaps also of lasting importance to those who experience them. They, along with the movies, constitute the sacred texts of a new kind of religion, a religion that indeed might be said to parody (that is, invert) the linguistic, literary, and ideological norms implied by the official one. This new religion has its martyred saints (Marilyn Monroe), its own version of the traditional genesis and exodus (the old man's flight from the treehouse), as well as its own prophets and apocalypse. But the postmodern emphasis here is always on the process, not the product, of belief. For instance, at the movies F. used to watch the projection beam (not the story it carried and projected onto the screen): 'It was the first snake in the shadows of the original garden, the albino orchard snake offering our female memory the taste of everything!'[16] But this new religion is also postmodernly paradoxical or 'ambivalent' in another sense: movies, for instance, are presented in two opposing ways in the novel. They are potentially positive forces in that they offer, through vicarious experience, the possibility of understanding things we cannot know personally. F. tells the narrator, 'You know what pain looks like, that kind of pain, you've been inside newsreel Belsen' (p. 194). On the other hand, movies can also be a new substitute for experience, a willed evasion of participation in life, as at the end of the novel (and as in the standard realist notion of novelistic identification). F. claims that the 'modern art-cinema house . . . is nothing but the death of an emotion. No marriage in these stark confines, everybody sitting on their genitals because: silver genitals on the screen' (p. 22).

This new religion, whose sacred texts belong to the realm of popular culture, turns out to be the religion of sexuality. Like the official religion of the spirit, this religion of the flesh is also systematic and therefore (in the context of the novel and of F.'s admission of failure) decidedly suspect. In a novel replete with systems, Cohen privileges these two.[17] What they are shown to share is their foundation in a body of sacred texts that act as fixed points of reference for the characters (as for readers). This postmodern 'textuality' becomes a structuring principle as well as a theme of the novel as a whole: *Beautiful Losers* parodies not only the spiritual system's Bible but also the fleshly system's sex manuals and pornographic fiction. Sexual 'perversion' (in official terms) becomes the parallel on the level of content to the perhaps shocking language on the level of form. As readers of the novel we are beleaguered, assaulted by the formal as well as the thematic challenging of our (perhaps unexamined) assumptions not only about sex, but about literature, language, and even society at large.

This challenging marks a move into yet another referential level of the text. I have been arguing that normal novelistic reference (extra- and intra-textual) is complicated here, first by an inter-textual level and then by an auto-referential one. These last two levels do not function in Cohen's text as readers of some metafiction might expect, however: they do not divert us from seeing the first two (more realist) levels of reference; they do not limit the text to some kind of narcissistic literary formalism. Instead the two more self-reflexive levels actually combine to direct readers of *Beautiful Losers* back to a version of what might be considered the most extra-textual kind of linguistic reference possible—a reference to our own process of reading—thereby completing, in a way, a kind of referential cycle. By pointing us as readers outside the text to our own reading act, these levels remind us that, although what we are reading may only be a literary artifact, a fictive universe that we are constructing in our imaginations as we read, nevertheless this act itself is really an allegory of the ordering, naming, and decoding processes that are part of our daily experience of coming to terms with 'reality'. This extra-textual level is not quite the same as the first level mentioned earlier, that is, of reference to the objects and actions of the experiential world outside the novel. Here, instead of that kind of analogy of *product*, it is an analogy of *process* that constitutes the point of reference. And it is exactly this difference that allows postmodern metafictions like *Beautiful Losers* to both use and abuse the textually ingrown or narcissistic, as well as the realist, dimensions of the novel genre. By working on the process of reading they suggest the need to examine (or even change) reading habits—and maybe also living habits.

The postmodern paradox here lies in the fact that this move outside the text is actually achieved through a moving to the inside of it. *Beautiful Losers* offers examples of both a static and a dynamic mode of auto-referential moving inside: its textual self-reference takes the form of a self-conscious parading of both the static *written* quality of the text and the dynamic *process* involved in bringing that text to life in the acts of writing and reading. At times both modes appear together, as in the results of F.'s initial pronouncement that '[p]rayer is translation. A man translates himself into a child asking for all there is in a language he has barely mastered' (p. 56). The narrator of the first part of the novel learns this lesson and later (pp. 137-42) uses the English half of a double Greek-English phrase book as a prayer book in order to ask for favours—in a language he frantically tries to master. At other times, however, it is more the static and explicitly written character of the text that is stressed. There is no other reason, for instance, for providing, in the (printed) epigraph to the (printed) novel, the ironic information that the words cited from 'Ol' Man River' are *sung* by Ray Charles.

Self-representation often interacts with the intertextual level of reference, as in the opening of the overtly written text called 'A Long Letter from F.': 'Five years with the length of five years' (p. 145) ironically and tautologically recalls Wordsworth's 'Five years have passed; five summers with the length / of five long winters!' (the opening lines of the poem usually referred to as 'Tintern Abbey'). But here the romantically ruined abbey is replaced by the Occupational Therapy room of an asylum for the criminally insane. The actual written nature of F.'s letter (that is, as a text written by hand) is ironically exploited by the *printed* text we read: those black lines reproduced in the printed novel (pp. 146, 151, 225) are supposed to have been made originally by F. with his ruler to impress the nurse; they end up impressing readers mainly with their self-conscious physical textuality, their sly literal mimesis.

F. himself is always very aware of his actual writing act and its possible results: 'I think this writing is going to ruin the baskets in O.T.' (p. 199). But he also knows what is involved (and what is lost) in the transferring of the experience of life to the page of art: writing of his favourite movie stars, he begs them to '[l]ie down on my paper, little movie flesh' (p. 206). This part of the novel ends with F. 'finishing the joyous letter' he had promised (p. 226) with the words 'Yours truly, Signé F.' The formal closure of the written letter, however, appears to deny the section's rejection of closure (on the content level): F. is supposed to have escaped the asylum from which he writes— and signs—the letter in which we read his account of his escape.

F.'s letter is self-conscious in yet another way. He announces to his reader/friend (and here, by our act of reading, we become formally identified with that intended receiver) that '[t]his letter is written in the old language and it has caused me no little discomfort to recall the obsolete usages' (p. 153). As he writes of history and revolution, he fears: 'I've gone too deep into the old language. It may trap me there' (p. 163). Later F. invokes history again in this 'old style' (p. 188), and then 'in the middle style', which turns out to be the jargon of the junkie. But, paradoxically, he accompanies this street jargon with ironically contrasting academic-style footnotes to explain the terminology, complete with all the scholarly etymological trappings. F. is very aware of the reader of his letter: he still wants to teach, to influence his friend and, by extension, us. However, it is also interesting to note that in the earlier novel, *The Favourite Game*, the major metaphor for artistic creation was masturbation, a metaphor that suggests more a solipsistic than a didactic impulse. But once again, this would be true only if we remained on the level of realist content; on the level of form or process the seeming onanism is turned outward, back to the reader. This ironic reversal is made clear in the emblematic scene in which F. reads a book to Edith on 'Auto-Erotic practices' (pp. 168-9). The part read aloud to her contains two separate remarks about how surprised and shocked 'the average reader' will be to discover how abnormal the tastes of the seeming innocent, normal person really are. The final effect of the act of reading on F. is a kind of allegory of the effect that reading *Beautiful Losers* might have on the reader: 'The texts had got to me' (p. 169). Cohen often parodies pornography in order (allegorically, once again) to reinforce this extra-textual connection with the reader on the level of process. And he achieves this kind of link between art and life through intertextual and auto-referential metafictional techniques that would, like masturbation, appear on the surface to be narcissistic in the extreme. But it is by these very means that the postmodern text can 'get to' its reader.

In the film *Ladies and Gentlemen . . . Mr. Leonard Cohen* the writer is seen watching and commenting upon himself as he takes a bath on screen. The Cohen in the bath writes on the tiles beside the tub: 'Caveat lector'. Ever self-conscious, Cohen has never, obviously, been totally devoid of the 'con'. *Beautiful Losers* itself also often approaches its textual self-consciousness in a similarly overt and ironic manner. The narrator, for example, suddenly askes: 'O Reader, do you know that a man is writing this? A man like you' (p. 102). This ironic kind of postmodern identification on the level of process is necessary to the second part of the novel, for it is as much to us as to the narrator that F.

cries, 'interpret me, go beyond me' (p. 158). Manipulating all who read his words, F. tells us all to continue reading his letter if we want to know the end of the story of Catherine Tekakwitha's life; however, we are also told, 'Read it with that part of your mind which you delegate to watching out for blackflies and mosquitoes' (p. 188). The story that follows begins, 'She wandered through the leafy woods . . . .' But suddenly F. interrupts to explain: 'I have to start you off with fiction, such is your heritage' (p. 195).

Such interpolated remarks are frequent in the novel and serve to trip us up as readers, to bring us back to the realization that we are both reading a text and being manipulated by its writer(s). In section 17 of the first part, for instance, the narrator slips this auto-referential sentence into the middle of a strange capitalized prayer: 'I Am A Creation In Your Morning Writing A Lot Of Words Beginning With Capitals' (p. 54). And F. later asserts: 'All of my arabesques are for publication' (pp. 151-2). In the third part of the novel, entitled 'Beautiful Losers: An Epilogue in the Third Person', a little boy asks an old man: 'Aw, tell me one of those Indian stories that you often swear you're going to turn into a book one day' (p. 232). The old man then proceeds to list a (written) chart of names—Indian, English and French equivalents, which we, as readers, have already read in this book (pp. 5, 7). The third-person voice of this final part is deliberately and symbolically hard to locate by normal narrative logic, but it is as self-conscious as the others: 'The old man had commenced his remarkable performance (which I do not intend to describe)' (p. 241). However, this narrator cannot resist, and proceeds to describe in detail.

From the reader's point of view, of course, for the narrative voice to *describe* is, in effect, for it to *create* the scene. The narrator of the early part of the novel is obsessed with the idea of creating, but specifically with the idea of creating a system (a notion he picked up from F.). The teacher, F., once saw himself as a Dr Frankenstein in the middle of a car crash. Armed with a needle and thread, he had tried to put dismembered human parts back together: 'I had an idea of what a man should look like, but it kept changing' (p. 175). F.'s nightmare becomes an allegory, a kind of *mise en abyme*[18] of the novel's entire process of characterization, wherein all of the characters (including F.) merge: 'sometimes I found I'd run the thread right through my own

flesh and I was joined to one of my own grotesque creations—
I'd rip us apart—and then I heard my own voice howling with
the others, and I knew that I was also truly part of the disaster'
(p. 175). As readers, unable perhaps to identify in the traditional
realist manner with the novel's rather aberrant characters, we
find ourselves included here instead, along with the creator(s).

There is yet another formal allegory of this kind that functions
in much the same way for readers. An ironic version of the
process of creation is presented in the self-reflexive motif of
naming. The nameless narrator sees that to name is to control:
'The French gave the Iroquois their name. Naming a food is one
thing, naming a people is another' (p. 6). Reacting against this
nominalist imperialism, he protests the change from the descrip-
tive name 'The People of the Long House' ('Hodenosaunee') to
the French 'Iroquois'—derived, significantly, from *hiro* (a
phatic—'like I said') and *koué* ('a cry of joy or distress' usually
added to help interpret *spoken* words to a listener [pp. 7-8]). Here,
then, the oral gives way to the written, the Indian legends to
the French Jesuit chronicles. The English, of course, continued
this imperialistic naming process when they gained political and
military control. Individuals are seen to suffer the same fate as
their people: Tegaigenta becomes Marie-Thérèse, and the Indian
Kateri turns into Catherine, the virginal Christian saint. Names
are not just appearance, though; they are destiny. F. ironically
mentions in passing: 'There is love on Rue Ste Catherine,
patroness of spinsters' (p. 186).

In *Beautiful Losers* F. is the major theorist of the naming process:
'Into the world of names with us. F. said: Of all the laws which
bind us to the past, the names of things are the most severe.
. . . Names preserve the dignity of Appearance. F. said: Science
begins in coarse naming, a willingness to disregard the particular
shape and destiny of each red life, and call them Rose' (p. 40).
The narrator here is, significantly, a man without a name, hence
linked by implication to Catherine's Indian uncle's perception
of the 'one true face which was the same and which was a thing
without a name which changed and changed into itself over
and over' (p. 131). Like F.'s sewing image, this non-controlling
non-naming acts as a *mise en abyme* of the novel's formal method
of characterization: the collective male subject, the old man at
the end, also has no fixed name.

F. informs us as well that, according to Père Cholenec,

Catherine Tekakwitha died 'en prononçant les noms de Jésus et de Marie' (p. 209). F.'s version of this story contains a significant variant: she died *mis*pronouncing the divine names, stumbling over them. He proceeds to berate the French chronicler for not recording her exact sounds: 'She was playing with the Name, she was mastering the good Name, she was grafting all the fallen branches to the living Tree' (pp. 209-10). As if to save us the bother, F. makes the obvious link with the Tetragrammaton and the name of God. Yet it was F. who had prayed, 'O Father, Nameless and Free of Description' (p. 178) and invoked the apocalyptic Orphan who, like the narrator, lacked 'the flaw of naming in his eye' (p. 188).

In *Beautiful Losers* the process of naming is also related to those of translating and praying. And the languages of prayer here, as we have seen, are Greek and English. Sometimes we are given only the stilted English as translated from the Greek phrase book (pp. 137-41); sometimes we are given both (p. 142). Twice, however, we are given only the Greek—which we are left to translate on our own. Early on, F. compares the Canadian Indians to the ancient Greeks (p. 9) and, in order to account for the apocalyptic[19] nature of the dinner scene in which Catherine's spilled wine stains the universe (!), the narrator provides a lengthy explanation of the Greek etymology of the word 'apocalypse' (p. 98). Both of these incidents prepare the reader for Edith's Isis speech (p. 183), an important (and untranslated) Greek text, echoed later by the blonde, moccasined girl in the car at the end of the novel (p. 235). The lack of translation here might appear at first to provide a formal link with the other systems of one-way (that is, faulty) communication in the novel: the radio and the movies. Yet to translate would theoretically be to enable understanding, to complete the circuit of communication whose metaphor in the novel is not sex but the Telephone Dance. Unlike the Canadian Indians who put their fingers in their own ears to block out the myth-destroying words of the European Jesuits (pp. 81-2), the French F. and the Indian Edith connect with each other, just as readers must connect with the text in actually translating the Greek into English.

This circuit or circle of communication is, however, a postmodernly paradoxical or 'ambivalent' image, in Bakhtin's sense of the word. For readers it has a positive value, connecting as it does the extra-textual (ourselves) to the textual, to its 'necklace of incomparable beauty and unmeaning'. But in the intra-textual world of the novel any circle images turn out to be definitely suspicious: once again, this may suggest that only creators (and readers) are allowed to connect (and only outside the text). Within the novel's world the necklaces that appear are those circles made of burning tomahawks around the neck of Brébeuf or those made of heavy teeth around the necks of the Indian women (which F. later compares to their 'pre-baptismal sins [that] hung about their necks' [p. 193], and induced great orgies of self-mortification). Catherine's aunts sing to her a marriage song about the '[e]ternal wreath, this necklace of teeth'. The traditional folkloric associations of the circle or ring as a symbol of both eternity and the female sexual organs[20] are here coloured somewhat by the potential negativity of the wreath image. Catherine herself is then made to display, through the narrator's imagery, both attraction and repulsion toward the young brave intended as her husband: 'She felt in her imagination the circle of his hunter's strong brown arms, the circles he would force through the lips of her cunt, the circles of her breasts pressed flat under him, the circle of her bite marks on his shoulder, the circle of her mouth in blowing kisses' (p. 50). Such is her imaginary, wish-fulfilling version; the reality, however, comes to be perceived (thanks to her new religious faith) in terms of the circles of whips, thongs, fangs: 'A burning circle attacked her cunt and severed it from her crotch' (p. 51). The Christian religion is here presented as a closed system, that is, as a potentially destructive circle. The text/reader (like the text/author) circuit is the only positive circling allowed. Creating, non-naming, translating—all these activities become allegories of the acts of writing and reading the text itself.

There are also other, less extended mirrorings of these processes in the novel. One begins as a prospective[21] or foreshadowing play in which the language, seemingly casually, prefigures the entire final apocalyptic[22] scene of the transformation of the old man into the Ray Charles movie. Earlier F. sits in the System Theatre watching not the film, but the projection beam—the process, not the product on the screen: 'the unstable *ray changed and changed* in its *black* confinement' (p. 223, emphasis added). F. then wonders what will happen when (not if) the newsreel escapes into the feature. The newsreel is said to be like Boulder Dam (placed strategically between 'life' and art); when the dam breaks later in the novel, the old man ceases to see the film, for he has become the newsreel (or its postmodern equivalent, the television news). He escapes into the feature. The dividing line between fact and fiction, 'life' and art, breaks with the dam. The Ray Charles movie gets projected against the sky, not just against a screen. The race of the performer recalls that in death, F.'s skin turned black—just as Catherine's had turned white. The common auto-referential *mise en abyme* of the black and white printed page here appears not in any static form, but as a dynamic force. The act of turning colour—blacking pages—itself becomes the paradoxically marginal centre of attention.

On the very last pages of the novel there is a sudden, oddly italicized first-person plural address that specifically suggests the inclusion of the readers as co-creators: *'we submit this document, whatever its intentions, as the first item in a revived testimonial to the Indian girl'* (p. 306). This complicity is then made inviting, even seductive: 'Welcome to you who read me today' (p. 307). The intertext is pretty obvious, but there is none of the hostility of 'Hypocrite lecteur, mon semblable, mon frère'—Baudelaire's famous Prologue to his *Fleurs du mal*; nor is there any of the aggression of Eliot's modernist recalling of it in *The Waste Land*. The writer of postmodern metafiction wants to lure readers into the act of meaning-making, to tantalize us with our own expectations—if only then ironically to thwart them.

Cohen's postmodern sensibility, his delight in complicity as well as critique, is already evident in *Beautiful Losers*. His subsequent writing confirms it, playing as it does even more explicitly with auto-referentiality, reader expectation, language, and generic boundaries (novel/lyric poem). In all his later texts the consistent obsession with things sexual is still connected to Cohen's obsession with creation—and its failure. The textual self-consciousness also works to show that, *pace* his critics, Cohen's other obsession is not so much with Leonard Cohen the man as with Leonard Cohen the creator. And, as all postmodern creators seem aware (if in varying degrees), it is ultimately through the co-operation of readers that writers can make themselves and their texts both live and live on. The borderline between 'life' and art, between the newsreel and the feature: this is the fine line Cohen has trod, the tight-rope upon which he has balanced his postmodern creations. Echoing Bakhtin's description of the carnival, Cohen's *Death of a Lady's*

Man asserts: 'There is no more stage. There are no more footlights. You are among the people.'[23] This is not an assertion of realism, of the transparency of art in relation to 'life'; this is life in art— as postmodern process. Narcissus does not drown in the text's self-reflecting pool; it is we, the voyeuristic readers, who save him—as the postmodern novelist had planned all along. *Caveat lector.*

Notes

[1] In Ondaatje, *Leonard Cohen* (Toronto: McClelland and Stewart, 1970), p. 56.

[2] *The Favourite Game* (London: Secker and Warburg, 1963), p. 104.

[3] At the negative pole, see Ed Kleiman's review in *Alphabet* 9 (1964), p. 78 and Douglas Barbour, 'Down with History: Some Notes Towards an Understanding of *Beautiful Losers*', *Open Letter* 2, 3 (1974), p. 59. The more positive view is held by Stephen Scobie, *Leonard Cohen* (Vancouver: Douglas & McIntyre, 1978), p. 73 and Patricia Morley, *The Immoral Moralists: Hugh MacLennan and Leonard Cohen* (Toronto, Vancouver: Clarke, Irwin, 1972), pp. 56-60.

[4] *Leonard Cohen*, p. 125.

[5] See the early theory of Julia Kristeva in *Sēmēiotikē: recherches pour une sémanalyse* (Paris: Seuil, 1969), p. 255, and, more recently, the work of Michael Riffaterre, especially *Semiotics of Poetry* (Bloomington: Indiana University Press, 1978), p. 110; *La Production du texte* (Paris: Seuil, 1979), pp. 9, 90, 97; 'Intertextual Representation', *Critical Inquiry* 11, 1 (1984), pp. 142-3; 'Syllepsis', *Critical Inquiry* 6, 4 (1980), pp. 626-7.

[6] In *Leonard Cohen*, Scobie traces Cohen's allusions in *Let Us Compare Mythologies, The Spice-Box of Earth* and *Flowers for Hitler* (pp. 24, 35, 47ff.).

[7] In Ondaatje, p. 45.

[8] In Michael Harris, 'Leonard Cohen: The Poet as Hero: 2', *Saturday Night* June 1969, p. 29, emphasis added.

[9] See Leslie Monkman, '*Beautiful Losers*: Mohawk Myth and Jesuit Legend', *Journal of Canadian Fiction* 3, 3 (1974), 57.

[10] Dennis Lee, *Savage Fields* (Toronto: Anansi, 1977), pp. 67, 122-3, 123n, 125.

[11] See, respectively, D. G. Jones, 'In Search of America', *Boundary* 2 3, 1 (1974), p. 236, and Linda Hutcheon, '*Beautiful Losers*: All the Polarities', *Canadian Literature* 59 (1974), pp. 43-4, 48 and 'The Poet as Novelist', *Canadian Literature* 86 (1980), pp. 8-10.

[12] Mikhail Bakhtin, *Rabelais and His World*, trans. Hélène Iswolsky (Cambridge, Mass: MIT Press, 1968), pp. 1-58, 94-5. These pages form the basis of the discussion to follow immediately; any later page references

will appear in parentheses in the text. It is impossible today to discuss the carnivalesque and parody without acknowledging the important impact of Bakhtin's insights on current theory.

[13] Cf. Eli Mandel, 'Cohen's Life as a Slave', in *Another Time* (Erin, Ont.: Press Porcépic, 1977), pp. 127-8, where he identifies pop culture with anti-literary, anti-humanist impulses in Cohen's work.

[14] Various critics have approached this language issue from the perspective of realism: the characters *need* the obscenity either to reveal their manias or to establish their protest against rationality. See Ondaatje, p. 49 and D. G. Jones, *Butterfly on Rock* (Toronto: University of Toronto Press, 1970), p. 78.

[15] In the light of this career I find it hard to agree with Scobie, who claims that pop culture represents banal, cheap, accessible emotion and is used satirically by Cohen. See his *Leonard Cohen*, pp. 115-16.

[16] *Beautiful Losers* (Toronto: McClelland and Stewart, 1966), p. 223. All further page references will appear in parentheses in the text.

[17] Critics concur on the existence of this system-obsession, but there is little agreement as to whether systems can be, should be, or actually are, broken down in the text. See, in the one camp, Scobie, p. 101 and Jones, *Butterfly on Rock*, p. 78; and in the other, Lee, p. 88 and Hutcheon, '*Beautiful Losers*: All the Polarities', pp. 49-55.

[18] There is no convenient English equivalent for this word, short of simply 'mirroring' (a term that is not quite accurate). However, a familiar example of the phenomenon would be the cover of the Quaker Oats box picturing a Quaker holding a Quaker Oats box, picturing a Quaker holding . . . and so on. See Lucien Dällenbach's exhaustive study of the history and modalities of the *mise en abyme* in his *Le Récit spéculaire* (Paris: Seuil, 1977).

[19] Here I intend 'apocalyptic' in the biblical sense of the word. Compare this scene to Revelations 6:12, where the full moon becomes like blood.

[20] See Bakhtin, p. 243.

[21] See the discussion of prospective and retrospective *mises en abyme* in Dällenbach, pp. 89-94.

[22] Again, the intertext is Revelations, this time 1:7: 'Behold, he is coming with the clouds, and every eye will see him.'

[23] *Death of a Lady's Man* (Toronto: McClelland and Stewart, 1978), p. 197.

Chapter 3

The Postmodernist Scribe:
The Dynamic Stasis of Contemporary
Canadian Writing

Like the various descriptions of postmodernism offered by today's cultural commentators, those of modernism, from whatever perspective, seem to find it impossible not to take into account the fact that there is a paradox at its very core too: that revolutionary novelty of form was in part, at least, the result of a renewed questioning—by each of the arts—of the past traditions that had engendered it. In literature the work of Joyce and Eliot, to mention only the most obvious, focused attention on the creative process involved in the transformation of the old into the new. What, then, would be the difference between this kind of radicalized harking-back to tradition and that of someone like Cohen or Kroetsch or John Barth today, writers who also look into what Barth has called the 'treasure-house' of past literature, in order to discover the new, the novel? Barth has claimed that his infamous early label for postmodernism, the 'literature of exhaustion', should more accurately be renamed the 'literature of replenishment'.[1] But what is at times striking about this literature (whichever label should eventually stick) is not so much a departure from modernist techniques as an intensification and expansion of them. I have been arguing that many of today's postmodern novelists seem to delight in exploring not just the authorial process of their texts' creation, but also that parallel and equally necessary process of the texts' recreation in the mind of the reader. Textually self-conscious about their medium (as language and as narrative), postmodern metafictions are also overtly aware of the twin processes involved in their production: their creation and their reception.

This same kind of self-reference, this acknowledging of conditions of existence, if you like, is also characteristic of other art forms of our time, including (as Stanley Cavell has argued)[2] film.

But film is the offspring of an earlier but equally self-aware medium: photography. And if, as many claim, self-reflexivity does lead to a general breakdown of conventional boundaries between art forms, then we should not be too surprised to find novelists today looking to the visual media for new inspiration— both technical and metaphorical. But why have so many *Canadian* writers, in particular, turned to the notion of taking photographs for their analogue of *literary* production? This self-conscious recourse to photography, which many have seen as a fixed and fixing medium, as a metaphor for creation is all the more surprising because of its often negative connotations: it is as if writing fiction were to be considered—by analogy—an act of petrifying into stasis the dynamics of experience. But what could be the reason for the Canadian preoccupation with this particular metaphor? What in our culture has provoked its popularity?

Perhaps it is to the novels themselves that we should look to learn the answer: in constituting its own first level of self-commentary, metafiction (in Canada, as elsewhere) proves to be a most didactic genre. It makes clear, for instance, that there are new metaphoric equivalences available today for the written text, drawn from new media (often visual and aural): the stability (and fixity) of the photograph, the (illusory) kinesis of the moving picture, the (deceiving) orality of the tape-recording. These images are habitually used in Canadian literature today to suggest something distanced, frozen, even dead, in a sense. The act of their creation is, paradoxically, a death-dealing one: the reduction of dynamic process to static product. But our actual experience of the same literature, despite this often thematized murder, is quite the contrary. There is also, the novels teach us, a reactivating, a resurrecting, process and this is the act of reading.

Yet we do not really literally *read* photographs, do we? Why, then, the insistent recourse to that analogy in the work of Timothy Findley, Robert Kroetsch, Alice Munro, and so many others? For postmodern metafiction writers who are obsessed (as they all are) with both the power and the limitation of the printed word to invoke the absent object, film and especially photography provide obvious sources of a certain kind of image: objects in movies and photos are also inherently self-referential in the sense that their presence literally refers to the absence of that to which they refer.[3] If we believe Susan Sontag, photography marks man's second—*un*fortunate—fall into abstraction; the first came with the advent of the printed word.[4] For Sontag there is a set of paradoxes at the heart of photography, and the very ambivalence in recent novelists' use of both cinematic and photographic contexts may reflect their awareness of the appropriateness of these paradoxes to their particular postmodern projects. After all, the camera records and justifies, yet it also imprisons, arrests, and thus falsifies the fleeting moment. Taking pictures is a way of both certifying and refusing experience, both a submission to reality and an assault on it. 'Cameras are the antidote and the disease,' writes Sontag, 'a means of appropriating reality and a means of making it obsolete.' Cameras can engender in the photographer both aggression and a passivity born of impotence. Yet they also make both the taker and the viewer into potential artists, as the last section of Munro's *Lives of Girls and Women* suggests.[5] Called 'Epilogue: The Photographer', it tells the story of the protagonist's vocation as a writer.[6]

These inherent paradoxes of both medium and result can, then, be as easily exploited in fiction as in film or photography themselves. To offer another, earlier example, in Cohen's first novel, *The Favourite Game*, the hero uses cinematic imagery to describe the safely distanced, controlled recording of the events of his life, events he *must* distance in order to transmute them into art. However, the same imagery is also connected to that of irresponsible power and to that of leaving scars, so obviously this (albeit perhaps necessary) creative distancing is far from innocent. Similarly, as we saw in *Beautiful Losers*, movies are potentially both an important source of vicarious experience and a deliberate and suspect means of avoiding 'real life'.

Even more common than this kind of ambivalence in Canadian literature today, however, is an almost Sontag-like indictment of photography for what it does both to the people and to the objects involved. In *The Collected Works of Billy the Kid* Michael Ondaatje uses photography as the controlling metaphor for perception and (even more problematically) for artistic production.[7] Billy tries to perceive reality in a detached, framed, camera-like way; only prophetic flashes forward to his own death are allowed to break this control (as new organic images invade the predominantly mechanical ones). Ondaatje's physical presentation of the book as a kind of static verbal and visual picture album is, however, premised upon one important underlying caveat: appearances lie. Photos are single and static; life is not. Motion frozen into form comes to be associated with the fixity of madness, though Billy does fight this by dynamic attempts at real understanding: he recomposes, retakes, replays scenes of trauma, but always as an attempted means of control.

One could argue that there is, of course, an implicit aggression in any use of the camera. Think of the verbs we use to talk about it: we load, aim, shoot a camera. Margaret Atwood has perhaps been the Canadian writer who has most openly acknowledged the paradoxical non-interventionist violence of photography. The protagonist of *The Edible Woman* not only comes to fear her hunter/photographer fiancé, but also makes an important connection between photography and acquisition: fostering a consumer relationship to events and experience, photography can be seen as a mode of surrogate possession. Taking movies, as in *Surfacing*, is just as destructive: its kinesis, its active component, is an illusion. It remains an act of arresting, seizing, killing. Like Ondaatje, however, Atwood is also aware that her own art could theoretically be defined in much the same terms: as a verbal (that is, static and limiting) fixing of experience. In *Coming Through Slaughter* Ondaatje investigates more fully this particular view of literary art, but there he associates it explicitly with a photographer: the historical E.J. Bellocq, of more recent *Pretty Baby* fame.

In this novel Bellocq's picture-taking (of New Orleans prostitutes) becomes the measure of his impotence, even his aggression; certainly it is his form of sexual voyeurism. Photographs here not only turn women into (literally) two-dimensional objects that can be symbolically possessed, but also provide inexhaustible opportunities for speculation and fantasy. In the novel, images of mirrors and the glass plates of windows are directly connected with the camera's framing, and, significantly, both are repeatedly smashed by Buddy Bolden, the jazz musician. The seductive, dynamic immediacy of Bolden's free-form music is set in opposition to the sterile, static distancing of Bellocq's photos. But Ondaatje is not naive; nor is he unambivalent in his response to those two art forms. Bolden's personal and public fate was madness and silence: no recordings of his music exist. Bellocq's photos, on the other hand, remain— even the one of Bolden used at the start of the novel. Near the end of the book the narrator enters in person to recount his researching into Bolden's life, an act that even repeats Bellocq's taking of pictures. The printed novel, like these photos, remains; the jazz lives on only in the written descriptions of its power in that novel. As pure oral 'process' it cannot be fixed; nor can it be repeated. You had to be there.

Ondaatje's awareness of the difference between the auditory and the visual, or, by analogy, the oral and the written, is acute, and (as we shall see in Chapter 5) it is an awareness he shares with many other postmodern writers. For instance, in *Coming Through Slaughter* he presents tape-recorded interviews with people who knew the real Buddy Bolden. Yet that is not quite true: what he gives us, in fact, are written versions of oral interviews. As readers, of course, we *hear* nothing. We even have to take the author's word for it that these people existed, let alone that they said the particular words transcribed. Ondaatje is also very aware of the impossible paradox of conserving the oral, in any sense, in written form. However, we must ask ourselves how much more complex, then, the situation is in Timothy Findley's *The Wars*, where we read the tape transcripts of the narrator's interviews with Lady Juliet d'Orsey. Here the so-called 'speaker' is not a real historical personage, but a fictional character. Obviously, one of the new conventions of novelistic realism these days involves a kind of double or even contradictory movement—one, first, towards authenticated immediacy and authenticating recording (visual or aural); but by this very act of recording (and its subsequent transposition into print) a double distance is obviously created. Not surprisingly, we have returned to one of the paradoxes of photography outlined by Sontag: the implication of instant access to the 'real' is what results in a distancing from the 'real'. The tape-recording (like the camera) has provided an obvious but problematic mimetic device for literary realism. While it records, it also frames[8] and automatizes. By definition, it is exclusive: it excludes the recorded object from the presence of the replaying (except in the capacity of listener), but it also excludes the receiver from the presence of the 'reality' *when* it was being recorded. Yet when critics discuss a novel such as *The Wars* they speak of the 'evidence' of taped conversations, of photographs, of diaries and letters,[9] and they do so with none of the novelist's own self-consciousness either about the distancing, the marking of absence, that these new realistic trappings entail, or about the fact that this 'evidence' is many times removed from any historical 'reality'. There are no photographs in *The Wars*; there are only *descriptions* of photos, imaginary ones at that. There are also only printed versions of tape transcripts—of imaginary interviews. And yet in the criticism we find statements such as:

> Findley's 'writer' or 'narrator' demands a great deal from his relationship with the reader, commanding him to look and listen simultaneously: the story of Robert Ross is shown as a series of photographs or pictures (with which we can do nothing, if not *look* at them); but at the same time, the narrator is busy telling us about the archives, the archivist, his progress as a researcher, his methodology, his interviews with Marian Turner and his taping sessions with Juliet D'Orsey, all of which we must *listen* to.[10]

As we read this remark we look at it—just as we would look at a page of Findley's novel—but we *hear* nothing, *listen* to nothing, in either case. All we see are black marks on a white surface, and that is literally the only mode of actual perception open to the readers of *The Wars*. We do not *hear* Juliet d'Orsey; we only read the transcript of her (imaginary) words. We do not *look at* photographs in that novel either. What the narrator tells us about one scene in the novel should, in fact, provide us with our general model for interpretation: 'There is no good picture of this except the one you can make in your mind.' The static quality of print can certainly be seen as an analogue of the fixity of photography, but there is also a significant difference in the reception of the two art forms: in the act of reading, those static black marks are not permanently dead. Somehow they are activated.

How? By whom? By that generalized, englobing 'you' that Findley's narrator repeatedly addresses. In the canon of nineteenth-century realism the object observed could be (even, had to be) separated from the subject. According to postmodern metafiction's new set of realistic conventions, the object *cannot* be separated from the observer. 'You' become part of that which 'you' behold. 'You' become the source of the (literally) life-giving power that transmutes the fixed illusion of print into the fluid reality of literary experience. The act of writing, as Cohen, Atwood, Munro, Ondaatje, and other postmodernists realize, is like taping a conversation or shooting a picture in at least one way: it is an act of reducing open, imaginative immediacy to framed form. Form in itself, they suggest, is potentially sterile and dead. It takes a reverse, dynamizing process to resurrect that creative immediacy.

As we saw in the last chapter, this positive view of the act of reading has been presented within the novels themselves, and I think this is partly what has led to the re-evaluation of the role of the reader in literary theory today. But the critical rise of hermeneutics and reader-response theory has been met by an even stronger (or more fashionable) trend in criticism underlining instead that more negative side of the act of writing that we have seen as a theme in postmodern metafiction. It has become a truism of one kind of poststructuralist thought that writing has traditionally been viewed as that which ossifies, petrifies, and blocks, and that the written is that which is finished, alien, divorced from its phonetic and therefore social context.[11] Of course, this idea is not new; nor is it purely a theoretical abstraction set up as a straw man by the critics we now label as 'deconstructionists'. Canadian novelists such as Rudy Wiebe, Jack Hodgins, and Robert Kroetsch have been extremely self-conscious about the postmodern paradox of their looking, in their written novels, for new, specifically oral narrative forms that would grant both more immediacy and a broader social context to their work. The same is true in the African writings of Dave Godfrey and Margaret Laurence, where the vital, oral, ancestral African past meets the more static, print-oriented 'European' present. In *The Diviners* Laurence makes this opposition even clearer: she sets up the oral Scottish narratives and Métis songs against Morag's writing—and, implicitly, her own.

This theme of the privileging of the oral over the written, this idea of the voice as the metaphor for communal truth and existential authenticity, is exactly what deconstructionists, led by French philosopher Jacques Derrida,[12] have been trying to combat. The 'phonocentric' bias of Western metaphysics, argues Derrida, devalues writing, demoting it to a mere representation of speech, a second-order reality of communication. Although Derrida himself does not go into the historical implications of this devaluing in specifically literary terms, there is obviously, on a very basic level, an inherent romanticism in the idea of the oral as more expressive, even instinctive. And it is no accident that many of the Canadian writers mentioned in this chapter were 'formed' (intellectually and ideologically) in the neo-romantic sixties. During those years the (rather romantic) revival of interest in 'the natural' sparked a return to viewing folk traditions as spontaneous literary utterances. This view was combined with a perhaps naive concept of folk memory that suggested a communality, a sense of community in time (as well as space) as art forms were passed down orally from one generation to the next.[13]

Then along came the sixties' prophet of the new folk orality in the electronic global village: Marshall McLuhan, Canada's own contribution to Derrida's 'phonocentric' conspiracy. For McLuhan, as for Innis before him, in the 'Gutenberg Galaxy' the presence or absence of writing was the single most important factor in the development of cultural and indeed psychological forms. With literacy and writing came the increased power and extension of the visual—that is, of the detached and, hence, the alienated. McLuhan elaborated from this thesis a set of contraries:[14] the written (the visual) was cool, indifferent, causal, civilized. It was private and static. On the other hand, the oral (the auditory) was hot, empathetic, magical, mythic. It was public and dynamic. These oppositions are not at all foreign to readers of the works of contemporary Canadian novelists who—despite themselves, I suspect—are McLuhan's true spiritual heirs. They too come out of the contradictory, neo-romantic, anti-establishment sixties that gave us both earthy communes and the excesses of exotic introspective mysticism. With considerable irony, McLuhan once wrote:

> Until writing was invented, we lived in acoustic space, where all backward peoples still live: boundless, directionless, horizonless, the dark of the mind, the world of emotion, primordial intuition, mafia-ridden . . . a goose quill put an end to talk, abolished mystery, gave us enclosed space and towns, brought roads and armies and bureaucracies. It was the basic metaphor with which the cycle of civilization began, the step from the dark into the light of the mind.[15]

When reading these words, of course, it is hard not to be aware of another irony: that of the way McLuhan has chosen to get across his message of retribalization, of the need for the reinstatement of the visceral, oral culture: he used *print*. It is tempting to say that Gutenberg undercuts him even here.

That the ironic struggle goes on, and, fittingly, does so on the battlefield of the printed page, is something that Canadian postmodern metafictionists are acutely aware of, even if their critics are not. In looking, often desperately, to auditory models for metaphors of the immediacy of artistic process, they are not guilty of what Derrida might see as a resurrecting of the myth of the authenticity of the spoken word. Rather, what they set up and investigate is an unresolved and unresolvable dialectic between the written and the oral, or, as we have seen, more generally, between the static and the dynamic, always aware of the similar double nature of their texts' very production: the experience-fixing act of writing (like that of photographing or taping) and the reactivating one of reading. And, as we shall see time and time again in this study, it is Gabriel García Márquez's *One Hundred Years of Solitude* that acts as the postmodern prototype or even paradigm of this oral/written dialectic:[16] for all it may seem to be part of the oral narrative tradition of Latin America, it is literally ended when we—together with a character—finish reading a specifically written text. In Canadian metafiction this postmodern contradiction is often explored by polarizing, and then privileging, one of the poles in order to investigate the space in between. Therefore we tend to find two separate models: one that takes its form and modality from oral gossip and communal (mythic) memory, and another that is modelled on the historical chronicle and the individual need to record in writing.

The oral model of communal gossip is tied to myth, legend, fairy stories, and the fanciful imagination of the tall tale; the written one is linked instead to the cause-and-effect rationality and realism of historical narrative. It is here that we most often find those new technological trappings of literary realism—tape-recording transcripts, photographs, movies, historical archives: Findley's *The Wars* or Wiebe's historiographic metafictions. On the other model, however, instead of this serious earnestness we find the carnivalesque or Rabelaisian scatology and obscenity of, to some extent, Cohen's *Beautiful Losers* or, more obviously, Kroetsch's *The Studhorse Man* and *What the Crow Said*, with their emphasis on animal (and animal-like) noises, folk legends, and, in general, the traditions of story-telling (*story* in the sense of a lie, as well as a narrative). All of these oral modes are opposed to what one character in *What the Crow Said*—himself a printer—calls the 'Gutenberg conspiracy'. In that novel Kroetsch creates a wonderfully absurd allegory of McLuhan's prophecies for the fate of 'typographical man'. He begins by taking literally the gender form of McLuhan's general label: it is his *men* who are print-oriented, who are therefore maimed and destroyed by their need to imprint themselves in a visual manner on their place and time. His women, earthy and fecund, exist in another world, one closer to the natural yet ritualized continuity of folk traditions. In Québec today some feminist writers have come to a similar conclusion. They argue that a truly female writing would be modelled not on linear, rational, male discourse (which they call 'phallocentric'), but on gossip, 'bavardage'—closer to the oral texture of conversation, with its fragments and silent pauses.[17]

There are a number of Canadian postmodern novelists who are acutely aware of both these models, however. Their works reveal an attempt to come to terms with the potential for stasis and the need for kinesis implicit in the written/oral opposition. In *The Temptations of Big Bear* Rudy Wiebe sets himself a series of challenging novelistic tasks. First, how to capture and create *in print* a historical character, Big Bear, whose essence was his *voice*. Second, how to convey the rhetorical and ritualistic power of this Cree speech in the English language. And third, how to present, powerfully and convincingly, the historical fact of Big Bear's oral presence when no records (much less recordings) of his speeches have survived. These are three seemingly impossible problems that Wiebe has solved very ingeniously. Making us—and his characters too—very self-conscious about the inadequacies of translation, Wiebe then invents, fictionalizes, a set of lyrical, heavily metaphorical speeches (for, in English, metaphor is the only way left for us to connect verbally with nature). He does not *tell* us of the impact of these speeches; he *shows* us their supra-rational effects on Indians and whites alike, thereby inviting the reader to participate imaginatively in their legendary magic. The prophetic truth of these words he then contrasts to the arid factuality of the British treaties and documents that, though written and therefore permanent, turn out to be lies.

The theory of language implied in Wiebe's novel is related

to that articulated by Northrop Frye in *The Great Code*.[18] What I have here been calling an oral modality is a *metaphorical* conception of language, whereby the word evokes the thing, and where there is no clear separation between subject and object, for they are linked by a common energy, by a concept of a plurality of gods, or of embodiments of nature. Big Bear's theology, as well as his oratory, is based on such a view of the connection of language to nature. After Plato, argues Frye, language becomes more and more individualized, more of an external expression of inner thoughts. In this *metonymic* conception of language, subject and object are now unifiable only by recourse to a monotheistic God-figure, a transcendent reality that verbal analogy can point to. Oral communality and continuity give way to the single, written authority of the Word.

The biblical epigraph of *The Temptations of Big Bear* very clearly illustrates this theory. It is from St Paul to the (pagan) Athenians:

> God who made the world and all that is
> in it, from one blood created every race
> of men to live over the face of the whole
> earth. He has fixed the times of their
> existence and the limits of their territory,
> so that they should search for God
> and, it might be, feel after Him, and find Him.
> And indeed, He is not far from any of us,
> for in Him we live, and move,
> and have our being. (Acts 17)

Big Bear's belief in the Great Spirit would put him in agreement with the first and last sentences here. It is only the middle one ('He has fixed the times of their existence and the limits of their territory, so that they should search for God and, it might be, feel after Him, and find Him') that would bother him, for it reveals the fundamental source of the novel's conflict between concepts of language, and thus between entire cultures. Like the imperialistic British in Canada, asking the Indians to select their one square mile each of land on a reservation, the Christian God has set territorial limits in space and time. But, according to Big Bear: 'No one can choose for only himself a piece of land of the Mother Earth. She is. And she is for all that live, alike.'[19] For the Indian, acknowledgement of human limitation and subsequent self-denial cannot be the ways to a God that is omnipresent and omnipotent. The authority of the Word of the transcendent

Christian God, however, is posited on these exact human 'virtues'. And it is so written by humanity itself in what we actually call the *Script*ures. Big Bear's authority, on the contrary, derives from nature and remains a natural (and spoken) one. In the end he lies down to die or, as he puts it, 'to finish the long prayer to The Only One that was his life' (p. 414). He becomes part of nature, that is, of the Great Spirit. The final words of the novel are these: 'Slowly, slowly, all changed continually into indistinguishable, as it seemed, and everlasting, unchanging, rock' (p. 415). But the immortal fixity of rock is not that of the Word. As Big Bear explained earlier in the novel to the white girl, Kitty (and, of course, to us), 'rock gives us the pipe by which we pray to The First One, for rock is the grandfather of all, the first of all being as well as the last' (pp. 314-15).

Yet while Wiebe is obviously and seriously exploring the oral/written opposition, he cannot escape one final, anti-McLuhanesque irony, and he knows it. Although poetry may keep a metaphoric conception of language alive today, as Frye has indeed claimed, the novel—that long, resolutely written form—belongs to another linguistic order: Big Bear's dynamic oral presence can be conveyed to us today only in static print; the oratorical power that goes beyond words can be recounted only in words; and perhaps the truth of historical fact can be presented only in novelistic fiction.[20]

In the *Sophist* Plato made a distinction between 'icastic' imitation (the search for what we today would call photographic realism) and 'fantastic' imitation (the realm of imaginative fantasy). If Wiebe's fiction belongs to the first category, that of Jack Hodgins surely belongs to the second, as the title of his first novel suggests: *The Invention of the World*. But that same final irony haunts the articulation of the static/dynamic here too, though in a very different way.

In this novel a certain Strabo Becker, sitting amid the chaos of his scrapbooks and cassettes, tries to reconcile the factual history and the exaggerated legend of one Donal Keneally, founder of the (fictional) Revelations Colony of Truth on Vancouver Island. He literally shows us, however, the so-called historical raw materials of his story: the newspaper clippings, the transcripts of his tape-recorded interviews, and other odds and ends of 'facts'. He disclaims any fictionalization; he is not the story's creator. What he has done, instead, is only gather 'its shreds and fragments together from the half-aware conversations of people around me, from the tales and hints and gossip and whispered threats and elaborate curses that float in the air like dust'.[21] The factual and the legendary come together. So too do the written and the oral: Hodgins' narrator begins the tale with 'Becker tells you this'—*to tell* being a verb that can conveniently work for either mode of articulation.

One of the models for this novel is the Irish oral narrative tradition. We find its formal influence in the circular and doubling structures of the plot and characterization. Even more obviously, we find ourselves in the Celtic world of giants and supermen fathered by bulls, led on by prophetic dreams, and finally slain in true sacrificial, symbolic sytle. This invented, formulaic world traditionally has lived on through the orally transmitted words of the bard. But in Hodgins' novel we are asked to distrust the accuracy of any oral transmission. Various interviewees tell Becker that the very presence of a tape recorder elicits lies, not truth. Recording (like writing) distances and alienates. One character explains to Becker: 'I just talk like me until I start talking into that machine and start thinking about what I'm saying, and then it doesn't sound like me talking any more. Maybe it's because I can see it, laid out on a page, when you get at it with that typewriter of yours' (p. 251). The alienating fixity of the written tape-transcript, like that of the photograph, is both a record of 'reality' and, as Sontag argued, a falsification of it. Legend and history have equal access to the truth of the past: that is, they both can lie. This particular lie, however, we call myth. In Becker's words: 'Myth . . . like all the past, real or imaginary, must be acknowledged. . . . Even if it's not believed. In fact, especially when it's not believed' (p. 314).[22]

The novel's title, *The Invention of the World*, sets up an implicit and explicit opposition between *invention* as the making (by humanity) out of given raw materials and *creation* as the 'genesis ex nihilo' (by divinity). Becker, we are told, speaks only with 'borrowed words'; he is only a 'caretaker god', the only kind possible in a fallen world, that is, a world fallen into print, as McLuhan and Sontag have lamented. Becker may remain just a history-obsessed scribe at the end of the novel. He may miss the unrecordable, un-scriptured revelation of truth on the Irish hill-top, a revelation that transforms the lives of his companions. But Hodgins has not missed it, and he too is, in a sense, only a scribe. In one of Plato's dialogues, the *Phaedrus*, Sophocles delivers a strong oral defence of the spoken word, but it is a defence we today know only in written form, because Plato too was a scribe of sorts. There always seems to be an irony underlying the exploration of the static and the dynamic, and it is an irony that postmodernism revels in.

At the very end of *The Wars*, Findley's narrator tells us of a final photograph: 'Rowena seated astride the pony—Robert holding her in place. On the back is written: "Look! you can see your breath!" And you can.' That 'you', like the 'you' addressed in *The Invention of the World*, is called upon not to see the breath, but to breathe the life into the static fixity of that photograph. Furthermore, since what 'you' do is not merely *look at* any photograph, but read its description, construct its only reality in 'your' imagination, 'you' already have provided the necessary dynamic breath. In other words, it is not just oral literature that must be defined by its actualization in performance. What postmodernist fiction, in Canada and elsewhere, has been trying to teach us is that even the most written of forms, even the novel, needs that 'you'. 'Typographical man'— and woman—'you' may be, but the hope is that it will still be books (and not, *pace* McLuhan, only television) that will save 'you' from what the electronic prophet called the alienation of the fragmented, desacralized world in which we live.

Notes

[1] See Barth's two famous essays, 'The Literature of Exhaustion', *Atlantic* August 1967, pp. 29-34 and 'The Literature of Replenishment', *Atlantic* January 1980, pp. 65-71.

[2] This is the major premise of Cavell's *The World Viewed: Reflections on the Ontology of Film* (enlarged ed; Cambridge, Mass.: Harvard University Press, 1979).

[3] See Cavell, p. xvi.

[4] Susan Sontag, *On Photography* (New York: Farrar, Straus and Giroux, 1977), p. 4. My debt to this work will be clear throughout this chapter. The one quotation below is from p. 179.

[5] This comparison, however, is not without its problematic aspects. Del explains that he was not a popular photographer, for the pictures he took turned out to be 'unusual, even frightening', for they revealed images that transcended time—and illusion. She compares this to her

own novel, based on images of the real town ('All pictures') yet different from it: 'The main thing was that it seemed true to me, not real but true, as if I had discovered, not made up, such people and such a story, as if that town was lying close behind the one I walked through every day' (*Lives of Girls and Women* [Toronto: McGraw-Hill Ryerson, 1971], p. 206).

6 Metaphorically, this book's very form might be said to reveal a constant tension between the reading and the (figurative) viewing process, the active and the more passive. The individual chapters are more like short stories—or individual photographs; as a whole, they become a kind of novel, but the novel as photo album. We turn the pages and see isolated, framed tales/pictures, which only cumulatively present a kind of narrative progression and continuity of theme and action.

7 For extended studies of this theme, see T. D. MacLulich, 'Ondaatje's Mechanical Boy: Portrait of the Artist as Photographer', *Mosaic* 14 (1981), pp. 107-19; and Anne Blott, '"Stories to Finish": *The Collected Works of Billy the Kid', Studies in Canadian Literature* 2 (1977), pp. 188-202.

8 See Seymour Chatman, *Story and Discourse: Narrative Structure in Fiction and Film* (Ithaca, NY: Cornell University Press, 1978), p. 96, on film's power to frame.

9 For instance, Eva-Marie Kröller, 'The Exploding Frame: Uses of Photography in Timothy Findley's *The Wars', Journal of Canadian Studies* 16 (1981), pp. 60-74.

10 John F. Hulcoop, '"Look! Listen! Mark My Words!" Paying Attention to Timothy Findley's Fictions', *Canadian Literature* 91 (1981), pp. 38-9; italics are the author's.

11 An archetypal statement of this view would be Julia Kristeva's in *Desire in Language*, trans. Thomas Gora, Alice Jardine, and Léon S. Roudiez (New York: Columbia University Press, 1980), p. 58: 'For the phonetic consciousness—from the Renaissance to our time—writing is an artificial limit, an arbitrary law.' She points out the (postmodern) paradox of a written form—the novel—being based on 'the devalorization of writing, its categorization as pejorative, paralyzing, and deadly'. There is also a strain of sociological Marxist criticism that takes a similar stand. See V. N. Volozinov [M. M. Bakhtin], *Marxism and the Philosophy of Language*, trans. Ladislav Matejka and I. R. Titunik (New York, London: Seminar Press, 1973), p. 73.

12 See Jacques Derrida, *Of Grammatology*, trans. Gayatri Chakravorty Spivak (Baltimore: Johns Hopkins University Press, 1974) and *Dissemination*, trans. Barbara Johnson (Chicago: University of Chicago Press, 1981).

13 An interesting study of this naïve interpretation of oral 'folk' literature is to be found in Ruth Finnegan, *Oral Poetry: Its Nature, Significance and Social Context* (Cambridge: Cambridge University Press, 1977).

[14] This list is gleaned from *The Gutenberg Galaxy* (Toronto: University of Toronto Press, 1962).

[15] Marshall McLuhan, *Counterblast* (London: Rapp and Whiting, 1970), pp. 13-14.

[16] For open avowals of the influence of this book, see Robert Kroetsch, *The Crow Journals* (Edmonton: NeWest Press, 1980), pp. 11, 18, 29; and Jack Hodgins, in an interview with Geoff Hancock, *Canadian Fiction Magazine* 32/3 (1979/80), especially pp. 39, 62, 63.

[17] See Suzanne Lamy, *d'elles* (Montréal: l'Hexagone, 1979). The theory behind much of this can be found in views such as those of Kristeva in 'D'une identité à l'autre' (*Tel Quel* 62 [1975], pp. 10-27), where she contrasts the (male) homogeneous 'symbolic' forces of language to the heterogeneous 'semiotic' ones—the rhythm, nonsense, etc. of infantile, psychotic, and poetic discourse. This latter she links to the pre-mirror stage (in Lacanian psychoanalytic terms) and thus to the instinctual and the maternal.

[18] Northrop Frye, *The Great Code* (Toronto: Academic Press, 1982). See, in particular, pp. 6-25.

[19] Rudy Wiebe, *The Temptations of Big Bear* (Toronto: McClelland and Stewart, 1973), p. 28. All further references will appear in parentheses in the text. For a related and most interesting reading of Wiebe's *The Scorched-Wood People* in the light of Harold Innis's *Empire and Communications*, see Stan McMullin, 'Wiebe, History, and Fiction', *Journal of Canadian Fiction* 28-9 (1980), pp. 249-52. McMullin shows how this novel (like *Temptations*, I would argue) illustrates the way literate cultures can command territorial space in different ways than oral cultures can, because centralized power (made possible by bureaucracy) is more easily brought into being with writing. The clash of the two cultures leads to a loss of tradition and stability for the oral one.

[20] Wiebe recounts an even more obvious progression from written historical fact to oral legend (ballads) to prose fiction in his telling of the tale of Albert Johnson, the 'mad trapper'. See 'The Death and Life of Albert Johnson: Collected Notes on a Possible Legend', in *Figures in a Ground*, ed. Diane Bessai and David Jackel (Saskatoon: Western Producer Prairie Books, 1978), pp. 219-46.

[21] Jack Hodgins, *The Invention of the World* (Toronto: Macmillan, 1977), p. 69. All further references will appear in parentheses in the text.

[22] Julius Champney, in the novel, reverses Becker's process. As a former mapmaker (an activity associated with the written imposition of a false and limiting order upon nature), now a poet, Julius enacts the oral/written and fiction/fact contradictions by imagining the voices of real history. He hears and sees in his mind, in detail, a scene he knows only in broad outline from the history of the region.

Chapter 4

Historiographic Metafiction

In Chapters 1 and 2 I argued that today's metafictions—those novels that, by definition, are self-referential or auto-representational—suggest that the mimetic connection between art and life (by which we still seem to want to define the novel genre) has changed. It no longer operates entirely at the level of *product* alone, that is, at the level of the representation of a seemingly unmediated world, but instead functions on the level of *process* too.[1] We as readers make the link between life and art, between the processes of the reception and the creation of texts: the act of reading participates in (and indeed posits or implies) the act of textual production too. The focus here is not on the reader and author as individual, real, historical agents or on the text as the product of action, but on the processes involved in what French linguistic theory calls the *énonciation*, or what I earlier called the discursive context of the writing and reading of the text.[2]

In his book *The Discourse of Modernism* Timothy J. Reiss claims that it is precisely this process, or 'discursive activity', that has been suppressed by our present dominant cultural model: the model that provides 'the conceptual tools that make the majority of human practices meaningful'.[3] Since the seventeenth century, Reiss argues, this model has been what he somewhat awkwardly calls an 'analytico-referential' one that has functioned equally powerfully in science, art, and philosophy. In all these domains the process (and the agents) of the act of *énonciation* have been ignored—for example, in the name of scientific objectivity and universality, or in the name of novelistic realism or critical, anti-romantic formalism. In Reiss's view, however, any such suppressed 'discursive practice' will gradually resurface and subvert the reigning dominant model. It will do so by creating (or revealing) such conflicting internal contradictions in that model that it will itself soon be called upon to form the replacement, the new tools of analysis. This, I suspect, is what we have been witnessing in the rise of reader-response criticism over the last fifteen years: at least one of the agents of the *énonciation* is being recognized as part of our accepted analytic model. But, as Constance Rooke has argued in responding to Roland Barthes's 'The Death of the Author':[4] 'the reader has been exalted at the expense of the writer; the author has had to die so that the reader may live. This revolution seems to me unnecessarily bloody in one sense and bloodless in another.'[5] Indeed, if literary (as well as critical) practice were heeded, as we have been seeing, then we would have to take into account not just the reception of the text but also its production, since both are thematically part of most metafictional texts.

Witness the narratorial/authorial voice in George Bowering's *Burning Water*, explaining to the reader the conditions of his writing: 'We cannot tell a story that leaves us outside, and when I say we, I include you.'[6] In order to write of George Vancouver off the West Coast of Canada, 'George Bowering', the narrator, self-consciously goes in the opposite direction, eastward to Trieste. His story alternates between the narration of the process of writing or preparing to write (in the present tense) and the telling of Vancouver's past trials and exploits. Through his meditation on art and life he sees the difference between himself as novelist and Vancouver as namer, as the one who wanted to write 'all over the globe' and to 'be a famous story' (p. 62). Until his story is *told* by someone, though, Vancouver remains a man who can chart and name, but who cannot become a true 'man of imagination' (p. 75), despite his claim that the work of the imagination is not the opposite of his search for facts: 'The imagination depends upon facts, it feeds on them in order to produce beauty or invention, or discovery' (p. 155).

Gradually the controlling and obtrusive narrative voice is silenced and the story for a while appears to tell itself, just as in the 'good old days' of the realist novel for which the narrator has earlier been yearning (p. 23). But here there is a difference: 'as the voyage grew longer and the book got thicker he felt himself resting more and more on his faith in the readers: would they carry him, keep him afloat? He thought so' (p. 173). The difference is that this narrative voice, wondering about its reader, is 'thematizing' or allegorizing, in a sense, the act of *énonciation*, the interaction of textual production and reception, of writing and reading. Reading this is not unlike looking at Velázquez's famous painting of *Las Meninas*, another inscribed allegory of *énonciation*: we look at a painting of a painter looking at us. Yet the real subjects of the work *being painted* (rather than *being viewed* by us) are the historical king and queen situated in our position but perceived by us only in a background mirror. *Las Meninas*—like *Burning Water*—is a work of art that presupposes the viewer's presence and then plays ironically with it; it also includes a representation of the producer at work.

There is clearly little attempt in this novel to attain even what Barthes called the 'effect of the real'.[7] As Bowering once wrote:

> A realist fiction was intended to produce a window on the world. Hence the value of invisibility, or more properly of transparency. One did not so much read the novel as read through it to the world. Post-modern novels, on the other hand, are in a way decorative. If they are windows they are stained-glass windows. . . .[8]

And the maker of the window—and its viewer—are often figured within it. As we have seen in Chapter 2, or as Bowering (again writing as critic) has put it:

> In the post-modern novel you do not identify with the characters. If you are to identify with anyone it is likely to be the author, who may lay his cards on the table & [*sic*] ask for your opinion or even help in finishing the book. In any case you are offered a look at the writer writing, not left in the dark waiting for the stage lights to be lit upon the scene for you and left there for your imagined occupation.[9]

As in the Bakhtinian carnival, in the postmodernist novel there are no footlights separating art and audience.

In a novel like Timothy Findley's *Famous Last Words* the situation is both the same and significantly different: Mauberley, the producer of part of the text within the text, is a writer whose 'whole and only ambition' in life, we are told, has been 'to describe the beautiful'.[10] Yet what he chooses to inscribe on the walls of the Grand Elysium Hotel is, as we shall see, anything but beautiful. The artist as aesthete is, in the end, only a voyeur; fittingly, if horribly, he dies with an ice-pick in his eye, a silver pencil in his hand. Readers too, however, are also in a sense voyeurs, though here ones whose vision of the protagonist's text, at least, is quite literally controlled by another character within the novel, Quinn. We only read Mauberley's inscriptions as Quinn does; we too watch. As complicitous voyeurs we cannot be exempt from the implications of the novel's theme of culpable voyeuristic silence and the responsibility of action. Just as the sceptic, Freyburg, punches Quinn in the stomach (and then denies the act) in order to teach him a lesson about the falsity of the recording of history, we too are made to feel almost viscerally the enormity of the consequences of the historical events recounted. However, more subtle than the overt Brechtian technique of *Burning Water*, the self-consciousness of *Famous Last Words* points as well to reading as more than voyeurism, as an act in itself, an act that brings to life words on a wall or a page (and through them, their writer); through reading, the word is figuratively made flesh. This collaboration of receiver and producer, as allegorized in the relation of Quinn to Mauberley and his text, situates the novel's *énonciation*, its context of the joint creative acts of reading and writing . . . and of their potential ideological consequences.

Both of these novels are, however, more than just self-consciously fictive constructions that thematize their own 'discursive processes', in Reiss's terms. Both are also examples of what I have been calling historiographic metafiction, and both are concerned with the reader as much as with the writer.[11] The 'messages' of both their form and content are even intended to apply to more than just the single individual. In other words, they complicate what Robert Harlow's *Scann* asserts: ' . . . there is no such thing as history. There is only individual consciousness expanding.'[12] In historiographic metafiction the collective often balances the individual, just as the portrayal of reading balances that of writing. In contrast, however, to the case with documentary fiction (such as that of Thomas Keneally or of the New Journalists, as they were known in the sixties), the entire act of *énonciation* itself is never suppressed: in many of these novels there is a clearly defined and precisely situated narrating voice that overtly addresses a reader. There is none of the authorial self-effacement characteristic of *cinéma vérité* or of some non-fictional novels—a suppression of the agent of textual production that Reiss sees as typical of 'analytico-referential discourse'.

The other narrative technique used by this kind of historical metafiction is not to have one overt narrating voice (Pierre Falcon in *The Scorched-Wood People*), but many (as in Skvorecky's *Dvorak in Love*). Readers of Rudy Wiebe's *The Temptations of Big Bear* are left to pull together the various and fragmentary points of view we have been offered and, like the jury at the end of the novel, we (also at the end of the novel) must make an evaluation and interpretation of all we have been told. Similarly, in Chris Scott's *Antichthon* the narrative perspective on Giordano Bruno's life and death is constantly changing (as are the time and place co-ordinates), as new testimony is established, then cancelled out, then re-established, only to be put in doubt once again. Yet all points of view are ultimately united in and by the text's readers, who in this case resemble the protagonist, who says to himself: 'A man should know his own mind, Giordano. And I do, Cardinal, I do. For I am you; and Fra Giovanni, the French King and the Holy Roman Emperor; friend Zuan and my lord Archbishop Priuli; I am Michel de Castelnau and Francis Walsingham, Pope Clement and the angel Michael (even she!), the one and the many, a unity and a diversity—myself!'[13] Readers have a second surrogate in the novel as well—Kaspar Schopp—who shares with us both a certain foreign distance from the complex Italian proceedings and a keen desire to learn the 'truth' about the circumstances leading up to the death of Bruno. When, in Chapter 8, he pieces together the puzzle of the *real* reason why Bruno must die, within a few pages readers do as well. We, like Kaspar, have been manoeuvred by the text into the proper position from which to see what we might call an anamorpho-sis[14]—the death's head that has always been visible, but could be understood only from one particular perspective.

What is perhaps most interesting about this emphasis on the complex situation of the *énonciation* is the way this kind of metafiction thematizes its own interaction both with the historical past and with the historically conditioned expectations of its readers. If, as these texts suggest, language in a sense constitutes reality, rather than merely reflecting it, readers become the actual and actualizing links between history and fiction, as well as between the past and the present. They do so not in the mode of traditional historical fiction (where history is meant to authenticate fiction on the level of *product* or representation), but in a new (or at least newly articulated) mode. It is not just a matter of life and art both being fictive, as Borges and Nabokov taught us. Historiography, claims historian Hayden White,[15] is a poetic construct; fiction, suggest Bowering, Wiebe, Scott, Findley, and others, is historically conditioned. Therefore to write history (or historical fiction) is (equally) to narrate, to re-present by means of selection and interpretation. History (like realist fiction) is *made* by its writer, even if events are made to seem to speak for themselves. For example, as Dennis Duffy has noted, the effect of reading in fragmented form about the thematized archival researching process in Findley's *The Wars* is to make us aware that stories 'do not tell themselves. They do not come to us with beginnings, middles, and ends waiting to be bevelled neatly against each other. They come from scraps and tags, and we order them according to our notions of meaning rather than out of a certainty that it had to have been this way.'[16]

What historians call 'narrativization'—making experience into a story—is a central mode of human comprehension. As Fredric Jameson argues, it is one of the ways we impose meaning and formal coherence on the chaos of events.[17] Narrating solves 'the problem of how to translate *knowing* into *telling*'.[18] Such statements as these are possible only in the context of yet another attack on the empirical, positivist assumptions of 'analytico-referential discourse'. 'The traditional devices for constructing a comprehensive view of history and for retracing the past as a patient and continuous development must be systematically dismantled,' challenged Michel Foucault.[19] If these devices have not yet been totally dismantled, they have certainly been granted intensely self-conscious attention recently—both by historians and by Canadian novelists.[20]

Hayden White, for instance, sees the link between the novelist and the historian in their shared 'emplotting' strategies of exclusion, emphasis, and subordination of elements of a story, but he feels that the difference in their tasks lies in the historian's confrontation with 'a veritable chaos of events *already constituted*'.[21] Yet as Foucault and Jameson have repeatedly stressed, in a very real sense history, while it had a real 'referent' once upon a time, is accessible to us now only in textualized form, that is, through documents. Therefore postmodern historiographic metafictionists, who also deal with 'events *already constituted*' but who self-consciously signal this textual nature within their novels, are perhaps in an even more complex position than the historian: they are constrained by the demands of narrative fiction as much as by those of historical events. They must deal with literature's intertexts as well as history's documents.

Joseph Skvorecky's authorial acknowledgement is typical and revealing of this complicated state of affairs:

> Dvorak in Love is my first attempt at writing a historical and biographical novel. It is not a scholarly life of Antonin Dvorak, and therefore I have used poetic licence where historical reality really does not rule out historical possibility, and I have been inspired by many works which space does not allow me to acknowledge. To those interested in an exact factography, I would recommend the standard biographies of Dvorak, and in particular John Clapham's Dvorak (1979).[22]

This novel, however, contains within itself a wonderfully apt metaphor (actually a *mise en abyme*) of the difference between history as 'factography' and historiographic metafiction. The Buffalo Bill Wild West Show, intended to acquaint the American public with 'the mighty drama of American civilization' (p. 202), consists of a series of tableaux vivants portraying everything significant from 'The Primeval Forest of America before Its Discovery by the White Man' to 'Sitting Bull Defeats General Custer'—in which Sitting Bull himself plays the title role, thereby creating 'through a daring piece of casting . . . a unity of the truth of the imagination and the truth of reality, of reality and history' (p. 202). This 'effect of actuality wedded to poetic vision' is the result of what is called a 'new form of art' brought about through 'compromises in fine art necessitated by the uncontrollable elements of the human actor in drama' (p. 203). The 'individual voice' of the historical 'human actor' becomes subsumed, however, into 'the total harmony of elements' orchestrated by a single narrating historian.

Foucault claimed, in *The Archaeology of Knowledge*, that we can never describe our own archive, our own discursive history, because we always speak from within it. Yet it is also true for Foucault that the historicizing of the historian's consciousness is a condition of historical study. That this same insight has not yet had an impact in literary studies (at least, in what Stanley Fish calls our particular 'interpretive community') can be seen by the fact that there was such an outcry a few years back at D.M. Thomas's (acknowledged) incorporation of a historical, eye-witness account of Babi Yar in his novel *The White Hotel*. For weeks, accusations of plagiarism littered the Letters to the Editor column of *The Times Literary Supplement*. Yet no one, to my knowledge, sought to chastise the 'parasitic' novelist for his fictional parody of a Freudian case-history. Perhaps this marks only a certain willingness today to recognize the place of fiction and interpretation in psychoanalysis, a place we may seek to ignore in our 'analytico-referential' view of historiography and biography, as if these forms of writing have somehow been granted some more direct and unmediated access to 'reality', or as if they are more objective and, in the end, more 'scientific'.

Many metafictional works investigate this 'ontological' issue of what exactly can be said to constitute fact and fiction—or life and art. They challenge what Wolfgang Iser once dismissed as 'the basic and misleading assumption . . . that fiction is an antonym of reality'.[23] And often this challenge is made operative through the novels' use of intertextuality. For example, Bowering works entire sections of George Vancouver's *A Voyage of Discovery* into the textual fabric of *Burning Water*, but this does not stop him from playing fast and furiously with the known 'facts' of Vancouver's voyage (and, in general, his life—and death).[24] At one point the narrator finds just the word he wants in Vancouver's journal. Using the third person he tells us: 'When he found those things he knew a book was going well . . . it was happening to itself rather than waiting around for him to think of it' (p. 145). At another point, after directly citing the formal prose of the historical Menzies, the narrator self-consciously reminds us of both the distance and the illusion of nearness evoked by such intertextual authenticity: 'In the eighteenth century they were fond of Latinate abstractions' (p. 101). While at times aiming for historical accuracy of detail and tone, the novel often deliberately rejects any realist pretence. An Indian is made to say, 'In the winter it rains all the time, but we always say that at least you don't have to shovel it' (p. 141).

While a book like *Famous Last Words* appears to attempt a more consistently accurate evocation of a particular historical period, it too relies on intertextuality to signal both its oblique relation to historical fact (that is, through documents or texts) and its essentially literary nature. Findley mixes the historical and the fictive in various complex ways: some characters are pure fiction (Paisley); others are fictive but their associates are verifiably real (the fictional Loverso and the historical Matteotti); many others are somewhat fictive versions of known historical personages (Pound, the Duke and Duchess of Windsor, von Ribbentrop, Schellenberg, Hess, Lindbergh, Sir Harry Oakes).[25] The added complication is that some events as well as characters (including Mauberley himself) are *literarily* (rather than historically) verifiable—through intertexts that range from Pound's 'Hugh Selwyn Mauberley' sequence to the Bible's Book of Daniel, via Dante's *Inferno* and even Matthew Arnold's poem 'The Last Word' (1867), where we read of the protagonist's fate:

> Charge once more, then, and be dumb!
> Let the victors, when they come,
> When the forts of folly fall,
> Find thy body by the wall.

In fact, the text's complex interrelations between fact and fiction are given a formal (and almost moral) *mise en abyme* within the novel itself. Mauberley recounts that, one evening, 'Wallis told the story of her life and left out China. I was very hurt. Then the Duke told the story of his life and left out having abdicated. Wallis was very pleased. Nonetheless these stories told the temper of the times and the motto we had adopted: *the truth is in our hands now*' (p. 177). Of course, readers of the novel may well recall Mauberley's remark about his own writing on the wall: 'All I have written here is true; except the lies' (p. 59).[26]

The relation of fiction to historical fact in novels like this is made even more complex than any simple binary opposition between fact and fiction can suggest, because of the textual role of the *énonciation*. For instance, *Antichthon*'s title at once suggests (meta)fictive rather than historical dimensions because the strange word actually signifies 'a world opposite to our own'. Yet the novel itself purports to tell the tale of the real historical heretic/martyr Giordano Bruno. In doing so, however, it calls into question the nature and value of so-called historical fact, even of eye-witness accounts (and of their place in the production and reception of the text). Kaspar Schopp tries to render facts as accurately as possible: as readers we are provided with letters, transcripts of conversations, and other documentation revealing Kaspar's belief that the human heart, if not the mind, could be 'a great fabricator of lies, and it was important for the correct historian to maintain the distinction between fact and fiction' (p. 142). Yet, as one character cynically proclaims, 'Truth and falsehood are what men believe them to be, neither more nor less' (p. 223). Schopp's own integrity as a clerk who records history accurately is undermined when an ecclesiastical authority, after washing his hands of Bruno's fate ('I've done all I can, the record will show'), adds: 'The record, what's that? Posterity, that makes sinners of wise men and saints out of fools. We pay our clerks to write it, pay them according to the need. Ours is spiritual, theirs material. This German now, Scioppius [a.k.a. Schopp], he's in Rome. We're watching him, expecting some promise there' (p. 181). This 'promise' inevitably becomes, for readers, 'compromise'.

This relationship between historical fact and the act (and permanence) of writing is, as we have seen, a common theme in historiographic metafiction: in *The Temptations of Big Bear* the fixed permanence and arid factuality of written treaties and of newspapers (not to mention of the aptly named Scriptures) of the white world are pitted against the oral, unrecorded, and thus undefendable discourse of the Indian world. In *The Scorched-Wood People* Wiebe continues to probe these same issues.[27] Louis Riel, as a Métis, is caught between these same two worlds: 'his people mere pemmican-eaters, not a word about them necessary anywhere in the libraries of the world, while their words crowded upwards in him until he felt his head would burst! He *must* write their words down, the persistent sound of their words rising, vanishing with the grass, the fading buffalo; and who would hear them if he did not speak, did not write, write?'[28] Part white (and trained by the Church), Riel feels the need to write, but the culture he will record lives on in an oral tradition of legends and songs that exist 'to help you remember' (p. 38), as in the world of Big Bear. The desperate need to give a recorded voice to the 'voiceless, unheard of' Métis (p. 106) is what drives Riel at the end of his life. Although 'magnificently tireless with talk' (p. 190), Riel was also madly writing: 'words to fill the leather suitcase, to give his unwritten people a place on paper before the frozen earth closed them away one by one and no one would hear them, the words they cried to each other lost like the cry of gulls turning trackless over the river, words to be used against him, for every written word called to judgement' (p. 245).

As we saw in the last chapter, this permanence is rarely accepted without ambivalent responses: Riel seeks it for his people, and yet he knows its negative power only too well ('The words crouch black on pale paper, unchangeable and deadly' [p. 170]). He is careful to have Schmidt read aloud to the people all the written declarations, but *we* read them as written text, as we do the entire 'song of Riel', granted to and narrated by the Métis singer Pierre Falcon, a song we read in English, of course:

> So, even [Riel's] vision I can only offer in the words which he so clearly borrowed from the Bible he read both in Latin and French: and sometimes, desperately, in English. . . . For the violent and silly acts of our people I received songs; for this, our greatest vision and commitment to a hard road, nothing. I must leave the words to stand in all their unmemorable bareness: their unearthly power will have to be seen in the effect they had on Riel, on our people, and on Canada during those *last* ten years. (pp. 140-1)

Added to the metafictional self-consciousness about language and its relation both to fact and to narrative in this passage is something else: an awareness of the potential *power* of language, and of written language in particular. McDougall, the 'paper man', arrived to act against the Métis armed with 'a sheet of paper and two boxes of guns' (p. 28); and since the paper 'would prove everything' (p. 16), *it* was actually the more dangerous. The narrator, however, presents only as ironic 'fact' Sir John A. Macdonald's politically opportunistic interpretation of Riel's situation and its usefulness to him:

> . . . [Macdonald] smiled his patented double House of Commons smile which in one expression could contain regret for the sorrow of mothers and wives and children weeping their dear hearts out when men are called to arms and at the same time the blessed relief that finally something drastic had been perpetrated and even the dullest voter will comprehend that now guns can provide their simple, direct solution. . . . And the political capstone: no Opposition would now dare vote against the last gigantic loan which could complete the financing of the Canadian Pacific Railway for the massive benefit of Canada from Sea to Sea and, quite incidently, for the benefit of CPR shareholders. Riel had created the catastrophe, an outbreak worthy for Conservative purposes of elevation to rebellion, as the Prime Minister would explain carefully to the Governor General as soon as the fighting was over. . . . (pp. 246-7)[29]

Historiographic metafiction, therefore, in a very real sense, is ideological fiction, taking ideology as meaning 'those modes of feeling, valuing, perceiving and believing which have some kind of relation to the maintenance and reproduction of social power'.[30] To write either history or historical fiction is equally to raise the question of power and control: it is the story of the victors that usually gets told. And, as Hayden White has remarked, 'the very claim to have discerned some kind of formal coherence in the historical record brings with it theories of the nature of the historical world and of historical knowledge itself which have ideological implications.'[31] The creator or discerner of that formal coherence is in a position of power too—power over facts, clearly, but also power over readers. We come back to the metafictional reinstating of the *énonciation*, then, but this time to look at its potential for ideological manipulation.

That this is a potential inherent in the writing itself of both history and fiction is evident in a novel like *Famous Last Words*. The name of the protagonist, Mauberley, is an intertextual marker of fictionality from the start,[32] yet this fictive character offers as 'fact' some events that we know to be historically accurate, intricately linked to others that are clearly invented. In the context of the novel as a whole, however, this fact/fiction relation also operates on an ideological level: although directly (if peripherally) involved in great political events and moral issues of his age, Mauberley falls victim to his own aestheticism, his life of aesthetic contemplation and absorption in subjective impressions of beauty. His culpable silence, his hesitations and procrastinations, are paid for with that final ironic testimony and confession written on the walls before his death.

Hayden White sees this 'condition of Irony' as the true content of the current 'crisis of historicism',[33] a state that I think defines the postmodern. For White, though, irony, seen as a basis for an absurdist world view, is a negative. In his words, it 'tends to dissolve all belief in the possibility of positive political actions', because it 'tends to engender belief in the "madness" of civilization itself and to inspire a Mandarin-like disdain for those seeking to grasp the nature of social reality in either science or art'.[34] But Findley's novel turns against Mauberley's 'Mandarin-like' attitudes, sceptically turning its irony against irony itself in order to reinforce its didactic message about the ideological consequences of the refusal of political action.

Chris Scott's *Antichthon* is yet another example of historiographic metafiction that addresses political issues through its questioning of the relations between fact and fiction, between truth and imagination. It is a novel about the fear of the subversive power of the visionary. Not unlike F. in *Beautiful Losers*, Giordano Bruno is presented here as a threat, not because of his doctrines (false or true) but, as one character explains, because 'he could show men what they wanted to see, enticing them on with their reflections until they were captivated. He was oblique and evasive like a mirror, a dealer in illusions, not false so much as superficial' (p. 21). Mirrors usually reflect some reality, however. Yet Bruno himself constantly insists that he is speaking 'as a philosopher', by which designation he means 'speaking figuratively' (p. 35). We are told that he speaks the 'language of allegory' (p. 36), a language that is not to be taken literally. Nevertheless Bruno is executed by those in power who are themselves not above using blackmail, spying, and finally torture to assert their authority over the 'truth': 'Question not the Word, Giordano' (p. 184).

Obviously, this kind of metafiction represents something beyond a post-colonial Canadian need to reclaim the past,[35] because it is not necessarily Canada's past that is always sought out: witness Scott's Bruno or Skvorecky's Dvorak. Instead, postmodern novels appear to signal another need: the need to investigate the ontological nature as well as the function both of their literary products and of the processes that created them and keep them alive. The institution of literature is comprised of writers and readers, producers and receivers of texts, and also of the 'circumstantially dense interchange'[36] between them, an interchange that has social, historical, and ideological dimensions. The narrator of *Burning Water* addresses the reader: 'We are making a story, after all, as we always have been, standing and speaking together to make up a history, a real historical fiction' (p. 9). The placing of these last two terms in apposition is not so much a teasing contradiction as a kind of affirmation of the common nature of both history and fiction: both are discourse, and by 'discourse' I mean here language as active *énonciation*, and not as fixed and static text. With that affirmation comes an awareness of the potential for ideological manipulation of readers—through rhetoric or through the power of language and of the vision it can create. And with this awareness comes, too, the realization of the possibility, if not the permissibility, of evasion through silence of the responsibility implied in the act of *énonciation*.

What the apparent paradox of this notion of historiographic metafiction brings to the fore might really be a characteristic of all novels: the fact that a work of fiction is never only an autonomous structure of language and narrative, but is always also conditioned by contextual forces (such as society, history, and ideology) that cannot or should not be ignored in our critical discussions. The (formalist) critical move away from history has recently come under serious attack.[37] And it is clear from postmodern metafiction that the strongest force operating within the art itself to establish our awareness of the 'wholeness' of the literary context (besides that of the *énonciation*) is its overt historical and political determination. In different ways, in novels as diverse as Joy Kogawa's *Obasan* and Heather Robertson's *Willie*, fictional and traditionally non-fictional genres interpenetrate in this paradoxical metafictional form through our realization (as readers) of their shared identity: both are discourse, that is, language in operation. We owe to Roland Barthes the strong formulation, if not the concept, that language is always fascist and that power is involved in even the most subtle mechanisms of social exchange.[38] Literature is no exception to this rule; and neither is Canadian literature. And, *pace* Robin Mathews, it knows it.[39]

Notes

[1] For a fuller explanation, see Linda Hutcheon, 'Process and Product: The Implications of Metafiction for the Theory of the Novel as a Mimetic Genre', in *Narcissistic Narrative: The Metafictional Paradox* (1980; rpt. London and New York: Methuen, 1984), pp. 36-47.

[2] A standard, clear definition of *énonciation* would be that of Tzvetan Todorov in *Les Genres du discours* (Paris: Seuil, 1978), p. 48 (my translation): 'A discourse is made not of sentences, but of enunciated sentences, or more simply, of *énoncés*. Now the interpretation of this *énoncé* is determined on the one hand by the sentences enunciated, and on the other, by the *énonciation* itself. This *énonciation* includes a speaker who enunciates, a listener whom one addresses, a time and a place, a discourse that precedes and follows; in brief, a context of *énonciation*. In still other terms, a discourse is always and necessarily a speech act.'

3 Timothy J. Reiss, *The Discourse of Modernism* (Ithaca, NY: Cornell University Press, 1982), p. 11.

4 'The Death of the Author', in *Image Music Text*, trans. Stephen Heath (New York: Hill and Wang, 1977), pp. 142-8.

5 Constance Rooke, 'Fear of the Open Heart', in *A Mazing Space: Writing Canadian / Women Writing*, ed. Shirley Neuman and Smaro Kamboureli (Edmonton: Longspoon/NeWest Press, 1986), p. 258.

6 George Bowering, *Burning Water* (Don Mills, Ont: Musson, 1980), p. 9. All further references will appear in parentheses in the text.

7 Roland Barthes, 'L'Effet de réel', *Communications* 11 (1968), pp. 84-9.

8 *The Mask in Place: Essays on Fiction in North America* (Winnipeg: Turnstone Press, 1982), p. 25.

9 *The Mask in Place*, p. 30.

10 Timothy Findley, *Famous Last Words* (Toronto: Clarke, Irwin, 1981), p. 5. All further references will appear in parentheses in the text.

11 In modernist texts the writer tends to be the main focus of self-reflexivity; in postmodernist ones the reader is added.

12 Robert Harlow, *Scann* (Queen Charlotte Is.: Sono Nis Press, 1972), p. 87.

13 Chris Scott, *Antichthon* (Montreal: Quadrant, 1982), pp. 126-7. All further references will appear in parentheses in the text.

14 The allusion here is to Holbein's famous anamorphosis in his portrait of the 'Two Ambassadors', specifically as used as an allegory by Hubert Aquin in his novel *Trou de mémoire*.

15 Hayden White, *Metahistory: The Historical Imagination in Nineteenth-Century Europe* (Baltimore: John Hopkins University Press, 1973), p. ix: history is 'a verbal structure in the form of a narrative prose discourse'.

16 'Let Us Compare Histories: Meaning and Mythology in Findley's *Famous Last Words*', *Essays on Canadian Writing* 30 (1984-5), p. 190.

17 Fredric Jameson, *The Political Unconscious: Narrative as a Socially Symbolic Act* (Ithaca, NY: Cornell University Press, 1981). See also Hayden White, 'The Narrativization of Real Events', *Critical Inquiry* 7 (1981), pp. 793-8; Louis O. Mink, 'Narrative Form as Cognitive Instrument', and Lionel Gossman, 'History and Literature: Reproduction or Signification', in *The Writing of History: Literary Form and Historical Understanding*, ed. Robert H. Canary and Henry Kozicki (Madison: University of Wisconsin Press, 1978), pp. 129-49 and 3-39 respectively.

18 Hayden White, 'The Value of Narrativity in the Representation of Reality', *Critical Inquiry* 7 (1980), p. 5.

19 Michel Foucault, 'Nietzsche, Genealogy, History', in his *Language, Counter-Memory, Practice: Selected Essays and Interviews*, trans. Donald F. Bouchard and Sherry Simon (Ithaca, NY: Cornell University Press, 1977), p. 153.

20 See Stephen Scobie, 'Eye-Deep in Hell: Ezra Pound, Timothy Findley,

and Hugh Selwyn Mauberley', *Essays on Canadian Writing* 30 (1984-5), pp. 212-13: 'Canadian writers especially, in both prose and poetry, have been fascinated by the documentary style, in which historical events and personalities are used as a framework, or set into a complex dialectical relationship with the writer's imagination and subjectivity.'

21 White, *Metahistory*, p. 6n.

22 Joseph Skvorecky, *Dvorak in Love: A Light-hearted Dream*, trans. Paul Wilson (1983; Toronto: Lester and Orpen Dennys, 1986), unpaginated acknowledgements page. All further references will appear in parentheses in the text.

23 Wolfgang Iser, *The Act of Reading: A Theory of Aesthetic Response* (Baltimore: Johns Hopkins University Press, 1978), p. 53.

24 Ian McLaren has suggested to me that Bowering has amusingly generated a homosexual relationship between Vancouver and Don Quadra out of mere innuendo in Vancouver's description of their brief contact as 'very friendly intercourse'.

25 For verification many texts can be consulted. See, for example, the Duchess's autobiography called *The Heart Has Its Reasons* (1956; New York: Fawcett, 1957); Walter Schellenberg's *The Schellenberg Memoirs*, ed. and trans. Louis Hagan (London: Andrew Deutsch, 1956); James Leasor, *Who Killed Sir Harry Oakes?* (London: Heinemann, 1983); the autobiography of Charles Lindbergh, *Autobiography of Values* (New York and London: Harcourt, Brace, and Jovanovich, 1976); James Douglas-Hamilton, *Motives for a Mission* (London: Macmillan, 1971).

26 Stan McMullin, in 'Wiebe, History, and Fiction' (*Journal of Canadian Fiction* 28-9 [1980], pp. 249-52), has made the same link between what I am calling historiographic metafiction and the issue of lies (and fictions) in the work of Rudy Wiebe: 'The inherent Mennonite fear of the fiction, of the lie, which seems to be the essence of creative writing, has led Wiebe to evolve his own distinctive genre' (p. 249).

27 In 'Rudy Wiebe's Approach to Historical Fiction: A Study of *The Temptations of Big Bear* and *The Scorched-Wood People*' (in John Moss, ed., *The Canadian Novel: Here and Now* [Toronto: NC Press, 1978], pp. 182-200), Allan Dueck offers a stronger formulation. He sees Wiebe as rejecting 'the common conception that historical facts are knowable and objectively verifiable by reference to historical data. In his view, the objective rendering of an historical story is impossible because both those who initially recorded the "facts" and those who subsequently interpret them are biased' (p. 182).

28 Rudy Wiebe, *The Scorched-Wood People* (Toronto: McClelland and Stewart, 1977), p. 80. All further references will appear in parentheses in the text.

29 It is interesting, by way of context here, that Wiebe once wrote: 'It should not be surprising to central Canada that in the prairie fictions

of the Sixties and Seventies Sir John A Macdonald (born in Scotland) becomes a conniving bastard . . . and Riel a saint. For telling our story on the prairie *is* different from telling our story in the Maritimes or Ontario or British Columbia.' (In *A Voice in the Land: Essays By and About Rudy Wiebe*, ed. W. J. Keith [Edmonton: NeWest Press, 1981], p. 211.)

30 Terry Eagleton, *Literary Theory: An Introduction* (Oxford: Basil Blackwell, 1983), p. 15.

31 White, *Metahistory*, p. 21.

32 See Scobie, 'Eye-Deep in Hell', pp. 206-27 for a fuller treatment of this.

33 White, *Metahistory*, p. 41.

34 Ibid., p. 38.

35 See Graeme Gibson's 'Gothic Shocks from History: The Birth of a New Novel', *Globe and Mail* 4 June 1983, p. E17.

36 Edward W. Said, *The World, the Text, and the Critic* (Cambridge, Mass.: Harvard University Press, 1983), p. 45.

37 Besides the recent works cited above of both Said and Eagleton, perhaps the best-known attack on anti-historicism is that of Frank Lentricchia in *After the New Criticism* (Chicago: University of Chicago Press, 1980).

38 Roland Barthes, 'Inaugural Lecture, Collège de France', trans. Richard Howard, in *A Barthes Reader*, ed. Susan Sontag (New York: Hill and Wang, 1982), pp. 461, 459.

39 See Mathews, 'Literature and Politics: A Canadian Absolute', in *Journal of Canadian Fiction* 35-6 (1986), pp. 44-55. Mathews makes a very common—if undefended and indefensible—claim that the (never defined) postmodern is apolitical and ahistorical (p. 46) and does not see that things like 'sexual politics' (which he denigrates) are directly linked to what he calls 'real politics' (p. 54). See Chapter 6, below.

Chapter 5

The Postmodern Challenge to Boundaries

It has rapidly become a cliché of postmodern criticism that the literary text's self-reflexivity has led to a general breakdown of the conventional boundaries between the arts.[1] But it is also clear that other boundaries are being challenged too, including those between genres, and even those between art and what we call life or 'reality'. Magritte's paintings could perhaps stand as a visual model for this kind of challenge. The various ones I mentioned earlier called 'The Human Condition' are paintings within paintings, unframed pictures (which stand within window frames) whose pictured landscapes overlap perfectly with those of the world outside the windows. This slippage between the image and what it refers to (all happening within a painting, we must recall) provides what Robert Hughes has called the source of modernist disquiet.[2] This is one of the many things postmodernism inherited from modernism. In postmodern fiction the same art/life slipping occurs within a similar self-reflexive framework, but in fiction this marks a new move beyond the modernist novel's need to assert its supreme independence and autonomy *as art*.[3] Life can now (more or less safely) be let in again.

In the theory and criticism of postmodernism today it is also almost a truism that women's writing in particular has led the way in the new explorations of (and against) borders and boundaries.[4] While the next chapter will show that I think this is indeed the case, I am also curious about what effect—on this formal level—feminism might have had on male postmodern writers, perhaps even without their being fully aware of it. Let me take as an example Clark Blaise's *Lusts*, a novel about the complex interrelations of men and women, and (not incidently) also of fiction, biography, and autobiography—or, in more straightforward terms, of art and life. And what form is better equipped to portray those personal and literary tensions than that of the epistolary novel? But this particular version of that canonical letter/novel form actually *enacts* the changing shape of that female/male and life/art relationship. The initial exchange of letters between Rosie Chang, a professor of English at Berkeley who is the biographer of the deceased poet Rachel Isaacs, and Rachel's husband, Richard Durgin, gives way (in part one) to an autobiographical account of Durgin's life. However, it is an account (and a life) divided into novelistically shaped chapters. The second section begins with a letter from Rosie, but the direct reply from Durgin is entitled 'Chapter 7'. The third and longest part of the novel opens with the title 'Chapter 14', but this time Rosie's letter to Durgin announcing her arrival in Faridpur, Rajasthan, India, where the novelist-cum-autobiographer now lives, forms all of section four. The epilogue—in the third person—reads as if it might be from the Isaacs biography *or* from a new novel by Durgin; in either case, it would mark a new start in *life* through *art*—for both correspondents, male and female. There are early[5] hints of this meeting of the past and the future beyond the book's end, and a literary reference in Rosie's first letter foreshadows it: 'I'll stand at the end of the pier, waiting your installments with all the anticipation of the French Lieutenant's woman' (p. 6). Like the heroine's fate in Fowles's novel— also a novel about the interaction of men and women, life and art, reality and imagination—Rosie's destiny lies outside the novel's boundaries.

The main narrator of *Lusts* is Durgin, a (failed?) writer, forced to examine his own life as both man and artist in the light of the suicide of his wife Rachel, a gifted poet who suffered from what Durgin calls 'a reality confusion that functioned as art' and that killed her: 'She was a reality junkie, and she died of an overdose' (p. 28). Durgin, the working-class American, had sought escape from reality through dreams, while his cosmopolitan wife had wanted raw American reality. This she found in him—all ego and brash innocence. The titular lusts refer to Durgin's lust for life and for women (presented in a fairly positive way), but also to the 'industrial lust' of Pittsburgh, his not-so-innocent 'blood-lust' for knowledge, and that something 'related to desecration' that sealed his first brief and lethal marriage. These twin connotations of the title cohere around two vital and oddly related symbolic incidents of Durgin's youth: the memory of the stone he coldly threw (as a boy) at the perfect stag protecting its does, and that of looking at his own sperm under a microscope in biology class in high school: 'From that day on, my version of the ultimate fiction . . . would have a strongly sexual bent' (pp. 20-1). Having cast that first stone against the male protector-figure and having given in to that 'ultimate fiction', Durgin can only retire from his lusts after the death of his third wife. It is as if only then can he learn that temperance of which Plato's Agathon speaks in the *Symposium*: 'the power to control our pleasures and our lusts, and none [such control] is more powerful than Love'.

Nevertheless, the text we read reconfirms his earlier claim that he had always put his faith in 'blind, undiminished life', something Rachel 'didn't have and couldn't get' (p. 46). Her identification with victims led her to write of death, of the horrors of the Holocaust, a topic whose brutality, according to Durgin, is beyond all art and all language (pp. 80-1). This is a novel about differences: in sensibility (perhaps between male and female); in writing from 'things' vs. writing from 'feelings'; in choosing fiction vs. poetry. For Durgin, the novelist, art must 'extend reality': 'A novel should be a living cell of an entire social and individual organism' (p. 81). Rachel's poems lacked this living quality of being composed 'from life itself'.

However, in Durgin's view Rachel could not, in the end, be the genius her admirers wish her to be: 'Geniuses bend us to their world, they see the world whole and they are aggressive in creating it' (p. 216). Rachel's pain instead remains 'disembodied' (p. 208) until Durgin gives it flesh through his prose account of his own suffering: in the postmodern, things and feelings, fiction and poetry meet. The woman with 'page-white' skin (p. 160), the 'animal of words' (p. 179) who hates her own body for its unaesthetic qualities (p. 177), regards her husband's lust (and love?) as 'low animal heat' (p. 178). Always willing to 'trade moral sanity for aesthetic perfection', Rachel, after death, must suffer her life and death to be shaped and interpreted by others. Unlike art, life 'refuses to assume a predictable shape', and Durgin, like a tragic Tristram Shandy, asks, 'what is the art—what is the name—for such a contingency?' (p. 45).

Caught in the tension between art and life, Durgin postpones writing to Rosie about Rachel's death—it would be like 'killing her all over again' (p. 120)—preferring to deal with the details of the painful past 'the way I've recreated them' (p. 144). But eventually he must account for his (and their) failure to keep life, love, and art alive. Rachel's cosmopolitan, cultured European background left her 'ignorant of America' (p. 27), the very America her husband represents. This is the real America and cannot be allegorized away and distanced, as she wished it could be: even its most trivial impinging upon her is presented as the cause of her identification with the victims of the Holocaust. In her poem 'Roaches', for example, her husband is named Adolf because he exterminates the New York cockroaches he has trapped under cups—one of the couple's 'bell-jar tricks'.

These overt references to Sylvia Plath, another young suicide, another gifted poet married to an artist and obsessed with her father, serve to highlight difference as much as sameness. Plath was the archetypical American woman that Rachel would never have understood. However, their modes of suicide, while different, are linked: Rachel bakes bread and it cooks in the oven as she slits her wrists. An earlier reference in the novel to Bloomsbury and to Virginia Woolf's suicide and madness (pp. 50-1) adds another literary historical echo to Rachel's act. In the case of both intertexts here, it is a matter of what Durgin, in another context, calls 'equivalence of disparate experience' (p. 93) rather than any novelistic imitation.

This is not a modernist *Künstlerroman*, despite its portrayal of the ordinary extraordinariness of the growth of the male artist. This is a postmodern version, playing with and contesting the boundaries between men and women, but also between art and life, fiction and autobiography. Blaise is not alone in this kind of challenging: recent works by Robert Kroetsch, Margaret Atwood, Susan Swan, Rudy Wiebe, Timothy Findley, and, perhaps most obviously, Michael Ondaatje attest to the attraction of boundaries and margins as sites of novelistic investigation. And the issue of gender often enters the discussion, as we shall see again later. Ondaatje has, in fact, been described as a writer fascinated with borders,[6] including those between art and reality. But he has combined his challenge to the life/art boundaries with a defiance of the limits of conventional literary genres. *The Collected Works of Billy the Kid* is a series of poems with a narrative structure, based on a real historical personage. *Coming Through Slaughter* is a fictionalized biography of the real Buddy Bolden, told in fragments that force the reader to enact the processes of aesthetic ordering and imagining that constitute the narrator's own process of writing the fiction. But *Running in the Family* is one of the most complex of Ondaatje's postmodern challenges to boundaries: its fragmented collection of memories, research, poems, and photographs works to reconstruct a more immediate and personal history—the writer's own familial past in what was then called Ceylon. But, as we have seen, to write of anyone's history is to order, to give form to disparate facts; in short, to fictionalize. Ondaatje's self-consciousness about this inevitable process becomes part of the very subject of this postmodernist work.

Of all the Canadian poets who have turned to fiction in the last few decades (Cohen, Atwood, Kogawa, Musgrave, and so on), Ondaatje is the one who seems most aware of generic borders, and of how thay can be usefully trespassed. (Indeed, a number of his poetic and prose works have been transformed into dramatic productions.) Other writers have played about with the borders between the novel and the short story and even poetry and fictional prose, but Ondaatje takes such play one step further than does, for example, Blaise: he takes it outside the boundaries of what we conventionally accept as *literary* genres (i.e., fictional) and into the discourses of history and biography, even autobiography.

In Chapter 4 we saw that the actual writing of history has come under considerable scrutiny in the past few years and that it is history's link to fictional narrative that has been the main focus of attention. The work of Hayden White, Fredric Jameson, and others has challenged the way in which we draw the borders between history-writing and fiction-writing. The new scepticism, also taught to us in part by historiographic metafiction, brings to the fore the fictionalizing (as well as ordering and selecting) processes involved in any attempt to reconstruct the past. This is not the only context into which Ondaatje's challenge to the conventions of genre should be placed, however. In the critical wake of poststructuralism's emphasis on 'textuality', distinctions between genres have been radically destabilized: poetry, fiction, biography, history, criticism, theory—all can be seen primarily as *texts* and therefore can be read as such, that is, with suspicion. Ondaatje's self-aware acknowledging of the textual nature of the past (the past as we can know it today, as it comes to us through books, archives, records, even memories) places *Running in the Family* in the critical poststructuralist context as well as the literary postmodernist one. And what is common to both is the importance granted to the role of the interpreting reader. The boundary between textualized life and textual art is bridged not only by (inevitably fictionalizing) historians, but by their readers. Ultimately, it is readers who define genre.

Jonathan Culler has argued against the definition of literary genre as a set of taxonomic categories into which we force works that happen to share certain pre-defined features, and in favour of one that makes the reader central to decisions about genre distinctions. Genre can then be redefined as 'a set of expectations, a set of instructions about the type of coherence one is to look for and the ways in which sequences are to be read'.[7] Literature that does not fit into already known genres, therefore, becomes a way of resisting this forcing or co-opting and a way of challenging the reader to make new sense of it. The best example of such literature for Culler would be one that uncompromisingly rejected both traditional representation and any notion of human intentionality. Yet Ondaatje's work never does this; it is compromised—that is, it is both historical and 'performative'. In other words, it indeed does seek to represent a reality outside literature, and one of the major connections between life and art is the performing narrator, whose act of searching and ordering forms part of the narrative itself. Nevertheless, I would argue that this kind of postmodern writing— precisely because it is compromised (and thus accessible)—is a more effective mode of challenge to genre limits than the more radical texts (of the *Tel Quel* group or even of Derrida) that Culler has in mind.

Whatever the form, this transgression of generic boundaries has been responsible for an important *critical* refocusing on the process of production or writing in literature. In its anti-romantic formalism, modern critical writing had come to find *texts* less problematic to deal with than *authors*, reading and reception safer to talk about than writing and production.[8] But postmodernist texts like Ondaatje's and Blaise's have reintroduced production in their stress on performance. In one critic's words, in the postmodern '[s]igns of the artist's or poet's presence are demanded in the published work. . . . The personal presence is an instance . . . of localization, of a growing concern with particular and local definitions.'[9] One of the motives behind such 'localization' is the postmodern desire to situate even the most self-reflexive of its performances within history.[10] As we read of the narrator's search for both the content and the form of what we know as *Running in the Family*, we not only watch the historiographic and fictionalizing impulses at work, but also participate in them. As in *The Collected Works of Billy the Kid* and *Coming Through Slaughter*, in this bio- or historio-graphic meta-fiction we experience that postmodern performance (which Ondaatje had seen in Cohen's work) in our act of reading the fragmented text.

Though the fragment is clearly another of the inheritances of modernism, the later work of Roland Barthes[11] probably contributed most to making it one of the major postmodernist forms.[12] The process of reading a fragmented text is such that readers can be implicated directly in the challenge to the boundaries both between genres and between 'real life' and art. As Barthes wrote: 'Is it not the property of the real to be unmasterable? And is it not the property of the system to master it? How can one proceed, faced with the real, if one refuses mastery?'[13] Barthes's own reply was to dismiss all the apparatus of 'system' (such as genre and traditional form) and let in 'dissemination', the free play of open language. But this is not Ondaatje's response, though he too turns to the fragment in his transgression of the limits of given literary forms.

From the more traditional poetic narrative form of *The Collected Works of Billy the Kid*, Ondaatje moved to the equally poetic narrative of *Coming Through Slaughter*, but the use of prose unavoidably introduced the conventions of the novel, conventions that are subsequently challenged by both the historical nature of the subject and the fragmented form of the work. Again Barthes offers one possible explanation: 'When one places fragments in succession, is no organization possible? Yes, the fragment is like the musical idea of a song cycle: each piece is self-sufficient, but is never more than the interstice of its neighbours.'[14] If Billy is more overtly a poetic song-cycle, *Coming Through Slaughter* (the story of a jazz musician whose unwritten and unrecorded music lives on ironically in Ondaatje's printed fragments) is also appropriately structured in this musical way. *Running in the Family* carries even further the fragmented presentation of what Barthes elsewhere calls 'biographemes',[15] or units of biography and history. Here it is even more clearly we as readers who participate in the act of organizing the past that constitutes the focus of this book.

Like Ondaatje as narrator, we become a kind of first-level link between life and art, and therefore the most direct challenge to the border between them. The author's strategy of presentation by fragments suggests the same postmodernist parallel we have been seeing between the acts of reading and writing the text. For example, the section labelled 'April 11, 1932' begins with the words 'I remember the wedding . . .'[16] (of Ondaatje's parents). But reader expectation (of a description of the remembered event) is immediately disappointed, since the wedding remains a textual gap, never to be described. The subsequent section, entitled 'Honeymoon', again leads us to expect an account of at least what followed the absent wedding, but once again we get only a lacuna. What we are offered instead is a listing of things going on at the time, both in Ceylon and elsewhere. These are not really randomly selected, however. The wedding couple may not appear, but things that impinged upon them do: from the price of beer to the ideal of feminine beauty at the time. It is only much later in the text that the gap is partially filled: the section is called 'Photograph', and in it we are told, by the narrator, about 'the photograph I have been waiting for all my life. My father and mother together. May 1932. They are on their honeymoon' (p. 161). We too have been waiting, if not all our lives, at least for 135 pages of fragments, for this look at the couple. But Ondaatje is not finished playing with his readers' expectations. Only after verbally describing the photo in detail does he actually reproduce it. By then, of course, it is redundant: words can be as real as photographic images.[17]

The relation of language to the representation of reality is an important issue in this book as a whole. One of the reasons for this is the number of problems it raises for the process of reading, as well as that of writing. As we saw in Chapter 2, when we read a novel we assume (because of the conventions of the genre) that what the text's language refers to (the referent) is a fictive universe rather than our 'real' one,[18] however much it may be made to resemble the real. I have argued that the case is somewhat more complex in historiographic metafiction, specifically because the fictional nature of the referent is repeatedly stressed (by the text's overt self-consciousness), while its historical nature is also constantly being implied: Chris Scott's Giordano Bruno in *Antichthon* both is and is not the real historical Giordano Bruno. In writing of both Billy the Kid and Buddy Bolden in the self-consciously metafictional way he does, Ondaatje too chooses this middle ground of reference, creating what we might call a 'historiographic' referent. Unlike the historical (or real) referent, this one is created in and by the text's *writing* (hence, historio*graphic*). The referent here is doubled; it partakes of two 'realities.' In *Running in the Family* Ondaatje adds one further element to this linguistic tension between art and life by making the history a personal one, subject to his *own* fictionalizing memory as well as that of others.

History, like narrative, becomes therefore a process, not a product. It is a lived experience for both reader and writer. In *The Collected Works of Billy the Kid* Ondaatje literally inserts himself into Billy's textual world in the final photograph of himself as a child in a cowboy outfit; in *Coming Through Slaughter* he enters Bolden's New Orleans to interview those who had known the musician and to photograph the places where he had been. Here the processes of recording and narrating history become part of the text itself. In *Running in the Family* Ondaatje is not only the recorder, collector, organizer, and narrator of the past, but also the subject of it, both as an Ondaatje whose tale will be told and as the writer who will tell it. Only the initial prefatory section uses the third-person point of view for the narrator; from then on, the 'I' of the text is a constant presence, the one who is 'running'. We are always being made aware of even his physical presence as he writes: 'The air reaches me unevenly with its gusts against my arms, face, and this paper' (p. 23). He reads and copies information about his family from stone inscriptions, church ledgers, old news clippings. As he soon realizes, 'I witnessed everything' (p. 70). And so too do we—through him. This is another form of that postmodern challenge to the formalist refusal to deal with the process of literary production that we have been seeing in other Canadian novels.[19] Performance is as much a part of the very content of this book as it was of *Beautiful Losers*.

To write the history of one's own family is to enter the realm of autobiography as well as biography. But lately, in all forms of narrating the past, the realization of the essential bias or subjectivity of the entire enterprise has come to supplant any former positivist faith in the possibility of objective representation: the idea of the invention of reality through language, or even of the creation of the self through language, no longer seems to upset some historians and (auto)biographers. And, of course, it has never really upset novelists, even those most attuned to naturalistic representation. Canadian writers have often teased the life/art borders of self-consciously autobiographical fiction: David Young's *Incognito* and most of the work of Audrey Thomas come to mind, for both use photographs in much the same way Ondaatje's texts do: as supplements and as lures. But Ondaatje has perhaps been the most consistent and thorough in his interrogation of both the inner and outer boundaries of art.

Michel Foucault once claimed that '[t]he frontiers of a book are never clear-cut: beyond the title, the first lines, and the last full stop, beyond its internal configuration and its autonomous form, it is caught up in a system of references to other books, other texts, other sentences: it is a node within a network'.[20] The network of *Running in the Family* includes intertexts of all kinds, both literary and historical. One section, for example, is entitled 'Historical Relations' (p. 39). It is a fragment about Ondaatje's family past, so we might construe the title to mean the 'relations' or 'relatives' of his own 'history'. It is only later in the book that we discover that *An Historical Relation* is the name of a memoir by Robert Knox, a man who was held captive in Ceylon for twenty years, and that it constitutes one of Ondaatje's major sources of historical information about the land and its traditions. The pun on 'historical relations' as 'connections with history' (which Ondaatje is constantly making) and as 'relatives from the past' underlines the inevitable meeting between the chaos of actual historical facts and the ordering processes of the one who writes history. Some of the other intertexts are personal memories of Ondaatje and his family, memories he spends his time 'trying to swell . . . with the order of dates and asides, interlinking them all'. In this way, we are told, 'history is organized' (p. 26).

The writing of history also involves a process of interpretation, for the facts must be given meaning in a particular context, whether they be the dates in a church ledger or the complex personal interactions of the people involved. The latter turn out to be the most difficult: 'I still cannot break the code', the writer laments (p. 53). He comes to realize that '[t]ruth disappears with history and gossip tells us in the end nothing of personal relationships' (p. 53). Although he questions his own motives in invading the privacy of the past in this way, he admits that he still wants to know that 'lost history', because it too is part of the reality of his past. After offering us a number of people's memories of his father, the narrator concludes: 'There is so much to know and we can only guess. Guess around him. To know him from these stray actions I am told about by those who loved him' (p. 200). Therefore his own book will forever remain 'incomplete' as a history: 'In the end your children move among the scattered acts and memories with no more clues' (p. 201). If the self can be created in words, it can also be evaded by the same means. Language has power, but it is not a supreme power: the past can (and does) escape articulation. The past is the ultimate intertext whose significance is both intensely desired and constantly deferred.

The network of texts that makes up *Running in the Family*, however, also includes more manageable intertexts, and one of them is certainly, once again, that most influential of postmodernist novels, Gabriel García Márquez's *One Hundred Years of Solitude*.[21] Any book that opens with references to ice, a dream, and time cannot help but recall the famous opening of that novel: 'Many years later, as he faced the firing squad, Colonel Aureliano Buendía was to remember that distant afternoon when his father took him to discover ice.'[22] Throughout Ondaatje's text the syntax of certain sentences will recall this opening: 'Years later, when Lalla was almost a grandmother, she was standing in the rain . . .' (p. 42). In both books the writer is from the world he writes of (and creates) and yet outside it, both present and absent in the writing. These two generational tales—of the Buendías and the Ondaatjes—share too a similar setting. Ceylon, conveniently, has a city called Colombo, but even without it Ondaatje's island bears many resemblances to García Márquez's Colombian Macondo: the extremes of heat, drought, and flood; the exuberant vegetation; the incessant insect activity; the almost mythically exaggerated inhabitants—all culminating, in Ondaatje's case, in Lalla's 'magic ride' to her death on the flood. Ceylon itself is described as an almost mythic place, which throughout its history has 'seduced all of Europe'. Its name was constantly being altered to fit the language of the latest invader, just as its shape on maps (based on sightings of the island) grew 'from mythic shapes into eventual accuracy' (p. 63). Not surprisingly, the people of this land have developed their own set of myths— both national (the thalagaya tongue as key to verbal brilliance) and familial (the grey cobra as the shade of Mervyn Ondaatje).

Just as Macondo was torn apart by internal dissension but also had to deal with imperialistic foreigners, Ceylon too has been split by insurrection and, more importantly, has spent most of its history coping with the foreign 'Karapothas'—the beetles that crawl over the land but see nothing (pp. 73-5). It is interesting that the political dimension in both historiographic metafictions is always tied to the aesthetic. In *Running in the Family* a Ceylonese poet is cited: 'to our remote / village the painters came, and our white-washed / mud-huts were spattered with gunfire' (p. 86). Ondaatje answers the poem with a poem, not about painters coming from outside, but about the people of the land itself: the 'toddy tapper' whose beverage the narrator had spent his mornings drinking, literally making it into a part of himself. He is not one of the destructive foreigners; he is no alien.

As we saw earlier, *One Hundred Years of Solitude* is a novel that has all narrative energy and tone of the oral traditions of South American storytelling, but we are never allowed to forget that it is as a written text that we experience it: the novel ends when Aureliano Babilonia completes his reading of Melquiades' parchments. Our reading, in other words, ceases with his. All this oral-seeming tale had, in fact, been foretold, we learn, and foretold in writing. One of the ways in which Ondaatje deals with this same duality of the oral gossip and tales to be transformed into written history is to turn to poetry, arguably the most oral of written literary forms. The first poem in the book is self-consciously about orality: its epigraph is a quotation about the Sinhalese being the least musical people in the world, with no sense of pitch, line, or rhythm (p. 76). What follows is a poem about a voice without music, but it is a poem with a very fine sense of pitch, line, and rhythm. It is one of those poems that deny their own denying subject, like Coleridge's 'Dejection: An Ode' or, closer to home, Leonard Cohen's entire collection *Energy of Slaves*.

This is not the only way in which Ondaatje's text is self-reflexively postmodern, of course. The two epigraphs of the book point to two other major metafictional obsessions: writing and language. Ondaatje is very present in the text as physical writer of it. But as a boy he associated the act of writing only with the punitive writing-out of lines in school: 'The only freedom writing brought was as the author of rude expressions on walls and desks' (p. 84). He points to the writing on the walls of prison camps as further testimony of this transgressive kind of freedom through writing. But the other examples he gives—of ancient graffiti poems—are subsequently made into images in his own poem (pp. 92-4), thereby implying, perhaps, that poetry in general partakes of this same transgressive freedom, that all writing potentially forms this kind of connection between art and life.

This self-consciousness about the act of writing (on the first page we read: 'Half a page—and the morning is already ancient' [p. 17]) is matched by an equally evident concern for language. After an epigraph suggesting that language conditions perception, the narrator tells us why he wants to write the history of the people of his familial past: 'I wanted to touch them into words' (p. 22). In order to do so he has to journey to the island whose own history is one of invasions by many nations, all claiming 'everything with the power of their sword or bible or language' (p. 64). He has to realize that the Dutch spelling of his own name is just a 'parody of the ruling language' (p. 64), but that nevertheless it is his name, a name he shares with many others.

Kneeling in the church by the gravestone of an ancestor, he reflects that 'to see your name chiseled in large letters . . . in some strange way removes vanity, eliminates the personal. It makes your own story a lyric' (pp. 65-6). The physicality of language, its concrete letters, is a recurring motif in the text. As a boy in school he had learned to love the curls and curves of the Sinhalese alphabet. Like a Stephen Dedalus entranced with form, the five-year-old Ondaatje related the shapes of the letters to those of the small bones of the human body: 'How to write. The self-portrait in language' (p. 83).[23]

But it is also true that the act of reading is as important to this book as that of writing. Ondaatje lays claim to two different family traditions of reading: 'my father swallowed the heart of books and kept that knowledge and emotion to himself. My mother read her favourite poems out loud, would make us read plays together and acted herself' (p. 168). From the former he inherited his sense of secrecy; from the latter, his sense of the dramatic. But Ceylon and the Ondaatje past would seem to demand more of his mother's 'recording by exaggeration', more of her mythologizing impulse—even in a historical narrative. Again, perhaps this reflects the impact of both García Márquez and postmodern performance.

In Ondaatje's life it was his mother who offered a model of the way the boundaries of life and art could be crossed: 'Whatever plays my mother acted in publicly were not a patch on the real-life drama she directed and starred in during her married life' (p. 171). But for readers another model is provided. A section like 'Dialogues', with its different voices and different stories, is a microcosmic version of the structure of the entire text: the fragments of the past that Ondaatje works to put together are mirrored in the fragments he offers his readers. His use of the inclusive first-person plural in the section following 'Dialogues' underlines his desire to implicate the reader (as 'we') in his own process of interpreting and ordering the fragments of experience: 'During certain hours, at certain years in our lives, we see ourselves as remnants from the earlier generations that were destroyed. So our job becomes to keep peace with enemy camps, eliminate the chaos at the end of Jacobean tragedies, and with "the mercy of distance" write the histories' (p. 179). The writing and reading of the text are both acts of ordering and granting meaning: just as we are shaped by our past, so the past is shaped by us as we 'eliminate the chaos'.

As the book draws to a close, these various postmodernist concerns for language, writing, memory, fact, and fiction all converge in the author's attempt to come to terms with his father. After expressing his worry about the power of language ('Words such as *love, passion, duty,* are so continually used they grow to have no meaning—except as coins or weapons' [p. 179]), he addresses his father directly: 'I am now part of an adult's ceremony, but I want to say I am writing this book about you at a time when I am least sure about such words' (p. 180). 'Give the word,' he begs. Readers then get a bizarre mythic story, which Ondaatje claims he is unable to deal with. But what follows is even more important: the narrative perspective changes from Ondaatje the writer's to that of his father. The first-person narration shifts to third-person, except for one telling sequence in which 'he' reaches for a whiskey bottle and the 'I' drinks from it (p. 188). This identification of the two men (through language) has been prefigured on the previous page through the father's offering a ride to the scented cinnamon-peeler, a scene that had inspired (or been inspired by) a poem that the son had written and that we had read over ninety pages earlier (p. 95). In the third-person narrative about his father, though, Ondaatje imagines him trying to deal with his separation from his wife and children. He follows him home and watches him look for a book he has been reading. He finds it in the bathroom, being attacked by ants who are carrying the 'intimate print' away one sheet at a time. At this moment the ants—like readers of Ondaatje's book—have reached page 189! Directly linking the 'white rectangle' of the disappearing page with the bathroom mirror whose 'company' his father feared, Ondaatje cements the identification with a recall of those earlier questioned words: love, passion, duty. Here the father watches the ants move the page away: 'Duty, he thought. But that was just a fragment gazed at by the bottom of his eye' (p. 189). He surrenders the page to the ants, as we surrender it to the narrative and pass on.

At the end Ondaatje returns to the actual act of writing with which he opened the text, but this time he makes clear that, as a process, writing or creating is part of the larger processes of nature: 'At midnight this hand is the only thing moving. As discreetly and carefully as whatever animals in the garden fold brown leaves into their mouths, visit the drain for water, or scale the broken glass that crown the walls. Watch the hand move. Waiting for it to say something, to stumble casually on perception, the shape of an unknown thing' (p. 190). Along with the text's producer, we watch that hand move as it tries to write of that which will finally make sense of the past. Ondaatje is forced to conclude, however, that his father will always be 'one of those books we long to read whose pages remain uncut' (p. 200). Since the only other books with uncut pages mentioned in this book are novels, this may well be an affirmation of the final fictional status of any attempt to capture the past. And the author's acknowledgements at the end of the book reinforce this view. After thanking all the people who helped him garner the facts for the work, he adds: 'While these names may give an air of authenticity, I must confess that the book is not a history but a portrait or "gesture". And if those listed above disapprove of the fictional air I apologize and can only say that in Sri Lanka a well told lie is worth a thousand facts' (p. 206).

Though moving from Ceylon to Toronto in setting *In the Skin of a Lion*, Ondaatje here continues his exploration of the boundaries between fact and fiction, life and art, and, even more explicitly, men and women. But this time he adds another dimension: a confrontation between the conventions of the realist novel (and so-called objective history-writing) and the self-reflexivity of postmodern metafiction. The opening disclaimer announces, 'This is a work of fiction and certain liberties have at times been taken with some dates and locales.' We might add that certain fates have been imagined where the historical record is conveniently silent: the end, for instance, of famous Canadian missing person Ambrose Small. The second of two epigraphs of the novel also points us to the metafictive orientation of the text: 'Never again will a single story be told as though it were the only one.' This comes from John Berger, one of the most powerful of the historiographic metafictionists and politically oriented critics (of both verbal and visual art) writing today. In fact, Berger's own novels contain the same mix of class commentary, political analysis, play with the conventions of realist narrative, and textual self-reflexivity as does *In the Skin of a Lion*.

While this too is a somewhat fragmented novel in its form, it also both uses and abuses, exploits and subverts the conventions of realist fiction in a way that is very postmodern, though different from Ondaatje's earlier prose works. The frame tale of this novel situates the narrative as being told (orally) in a car driving to Marmora, Ontario. The car's occupants are not named and the reason for the trip is not clear until the end of the novel. But what is important is that it is a frame concerned primarily with the telling of stories. The language used to talk of that telling, however, is an odd one: it is a story to be 'gathered'; 'he picks up and brings together various corners of the story',[24] as if it were a palpable thing, and particularly, a literal frame. Readers are thus alerted early to the kind of physicality that will characterize the lives of the characters and the history of Toronto in this book.

The first full narrative chapter opens, once again, elliptically, but more in the mode of realist fiction. 'The boy' watches 'the men'—immigrant loggers going to work in the small town of Bellrock. They are exotic to him, as are the maps of the world in the geography book he loves so much: *'Caspian. Nepal. Durango'* (p. 9). In conformity with the conventions of realism, the text finally names 'the boy', but that gesture is here robbed of its realist authenticating power and made intensely, metafictively allegorical: he is named in the same paragraph in which he himself gives 'fictional names' to the insects he is studying. While it is true that '[e]ven the real names are beautiful' (p. 9), they are clearly secondary. This theme of naming, both fictive and real, is central to this story about historical Toronto as lived in by both real and fictive characters. The protagonist, Patrick, not only is fictional, but comes from a place 'which did not appear on a map until 1910, though his family had worked there for twenty years and the land had been homesteaded since 1816' (p. 10). In the school atlas his place is 'green and nameless'— like Atwood's progressively insane pioneer's.[25]

But it is not just geography that leaves things nameless; history too shares in this silencing of that which does not fit into its customary mapping techniques. The history that survives, as the novels of Rudy Wiebe have so powerfully shown, is the official history of written documents and of photographs of the *men* deemed central to the prevailing power. So we know of the rich Ambrose Small and the powerful R.C. Harris, the city commissioner; but history has not necessarily recorded the names of the (unofficial) women of the rich (here, Clara Dickens) nor of the anonymous workers who built the structures commissioned by Harris. Class and gender relegate some to the position of outsiders, ex-centrics, a position that this novel uses as its paradoxical (and very postmodern) centre. Patrick may belong to the central racial and gender group that controls Canadian life, but he is working-class, from the country, the son of an 'abashed man' who was an outsider even within his profession of logging (he was the dynamiter). Patrick also actively works to alienate himself as well, of course, distancing himself emotionally and expressively ('[t]he unemotional tongue' [p. 19]), and the novel is the tale of his re-insertion into community and connection.

This ex-centric first comes to find a place among the other outsiders who populate the city of Toronto in the first four decades of this century. We meet the nameless immigrants who build the Bloor St Viaduct (1915-18), labouring in difficult and dangerous situations in order to build another's dream. As they symbolically claim the completed bridge for themselves (before the official, recorded historical opening), they walk across it with torches 'like a wave of civilization, a net of summer insects over the valley' (p. 17). This image is both ironic and accurate: these people do constitute the future civilization of this particular city and also, in many ways, they are indeed like 'summer insects'— part of the nature that the officials are trying to overcome, to conquer. These officials, however, are the named, the male public figures that history has recorded. These are the ones with the vision: 'Before the real city could be seen it had to be imagined, the way rumours and tall tales were a kind of charting' (p. 29). The metafictive position of the writer here is an ambiguous one: he too is the one with the vision, the male who will be recorded in history. But, unlike the officials in the story here, this writer will not forget the others, will not leave them un-named.

In a scene worthy of García Márquez—or *Running in the Family*—the uncompleted Bloor Viaduct becomes the dangerous site of wind meeting resistance: here in the unlikely (but 'visually' astounding) form of a group of nuns. One of these is blown off the bridge and assumed dead, though her body is never found. In reality she is saved by one of the few named workers on the bridge, the dare-devil Nicholas Temelcoff, hanging from the bridge on a rope. Neither the saviour nor the saved ever tells of the salvation. The nun leaves her habit and habits behind and vanishes into the world to redefine her identity as a woman from scratch, outside of history. Nicholas himself has never had any firm sense of *his* identity, partly because he is an invisible immigrant, even to himself: 'He never realizes how often he is watched by others. He has no clue that his gestures are extreme. He has no portrait of himself' (p. 42). Even his language, one of the methods by which we define our selfhood, is not his own. He learns it from the radio and from popular songs: 'As with sight, because Nicholas does not listen to most conversations around him, he assumes no one hears him. . . . He loves his new language, the terrible barriers of it' (p. 43). For immigrants language and identity are connected: '[i]f he did not learn the language he would be lost' (p. 46).

The narrative then switches back to the protagonist, Patrick Lewis, who arrives in Toronto and finds that, despite his gender and his Anglo-Canadian background, he is also an outsider or ex-centric, that the rural and the working-class (even if male) are also nameless in the city. But there are degrees of ex-centricity: Patrick has the power of self-naming, if not much more. Arriving by train, '[h]e spoke out his name and it struggled up in a hollow echo and was lost in the high air of Union Station. No one turned. They were in the belly of a whale' (p. 54). By 1924 Patrick appears to have named some identity for himself, even if it is an ironic one: he becomes a 'searcher' for the historical Ambrose Small, a millionaire who disappeared in 1919. He decides that Small's mistress is the key to the disappearance, but his encounter with her leads to his own entrapment. He falls in love with Clara Dickens, but she later leaves him to join Small in hiding. He eventually finds them both again and is almost killed for his effort.

When we find him again he is working on another of the projects of the city commissioner, Harris—this time, the tunnel into Lake Ontario to bring water into the water-filtration plant being constructed in Toronto. Echoing and inverting Harris's Bloor Viaduct, this tunnel goes under, not over, water, but is just as dangerous for the anonymous men building it. The text here is dense with historical (and ironic) detail, for capitalist history has recorded—if not the names of the workers—at least the names of the companies who participated in the building (p. 109). Patrick's self-alienating ex-centricity is clearer than ever. To his capitalist bosses he is just another worker; to his ethnic neighbours he is a stranger: 'The southeastern section of the city where he now lived was made up mostly of immigrants and he walked everywhere not hearing any language he knew, deliriously anonymous. The people on the street, the Macedonians and Bulgarians, were his only mirror. He worked in the tunnels with them' (p. 112). This distanced sense of community seems all he is capable of. And this particular community is made up of only ex-centrics. Gradually they get through to him with their friendship, and something breaks in Patrick: 'He looked up and saw the men and women who could not know *why* he wept now among these strangers who in the past had seemed to him like dark blinds on his street, their street, for he was their alien' (p. 113). It is in this state that he once again makes the acquaintance of an actress friend of Clara's, named Alice Gull.

But the circumstances of their meeting are crucial to the

political arena in which the rest of the novel takes place. The immigrant workers gather illegally for secret theatrical performances in Harris's prized waterworks. Patrick accompanies them to watch an allegorical play in which all the pain and fear of the immigrant are dramatized. The protagonist of the play is made up as a clichéd immigrant, is subjected to insult and assault by the authorities, and, throughout, embodies 'his' powerlessness through silence, through lack of speech and the ultimate frustration of injustice unspoken, unspeakable. The person playing the 'hero' here turns out to be another ex-centric—Alice Gull, a woman with no history but with strong politics. A single mother, raising Hana, the child she has had by a murdered revolutionary activist, Alice calls herself a 'mongrel'—like Patrick. It is Alice who sets up one of the major image networks in the novel: unlike the officials who want to go under or over water, Patrick is said to be '[l]ike water', for he 'can be easily harnessed' (p. 122). She sees danger in this, for Patrick has power he does not know about, but which fuels the rest of the plot.

At first, despite his romantic involvement with Alice, Patrick remains cool to her revolutionary activism, but gradually he comes to see that, though not an immigrant or a woman, he too is an outsider and powerless and that he must 'name the enemy' (p. 124)—here, 'the rich'. For both Patrick and Alice it is the plight of the immigrant workers (such as those in the tanneries) that most clearly illustrates the class distinctions that they too live out. Alice tells him: 'the smell of the tanning factories goes into their noses and lungs and stays there for life. They never get the smell off their bodies. Do you know the smell? You can bet the rich don't know it. It brutalizes. It's like sleeping with the enemy. It clung to Hana's father. They get skin burns from the galvanizing process. Arthritis, rheumatism. That's the truth' (p. 124). This is the world of work into which Patrick now enters, yet he still attempts to distance himself from it, this time by imagining a painting of the multicoloured bodies of the hide dyers:

> If he were an artist he would have painted them but that was false celebration. What did it mean in the end to look aesthetically plumaged on this October day in the east end of the city five hundred yards from Front Street? What would the painting tell? That they were twenty to thirty-five years old, were Macedonians

mostly, though there were a few Poles and Lithuanians. That on average they had three or four sentences of English, that they had never read the *Mail and Empire* or *Saturday Night*. . . . That they would die of consumption and at present did not know it. (pp. 131-2)

Social commentary challenges the separatist aestheticism of art that denies history and human pain—but, in a typically postmodern paradox, we learn this through art, that is, through Ondaatje's novel.

These tannery workers are not quite as nameless as the bridge and tunnel workers, but they do not have the power of self-naming: 'the labour agent giving them all English names. Charlie Johnson, Nick Parker. They remembered the strange foreign syllables like a number' (p. 132). When they do name themselves, it is by nationality: '*Hey Italy*'—and to Patrick, '*Hey Canada*', for even a Canadian can be ex-centric here. Patrick is still wilfully alien, relishing his inability to understand the foreign languages among which he lives, relying on Alice for communication. He withdraws: 'He himself had kept his true name and voice from the bosses at the leather yard, never spoke to them or answered them' (p. 136). But this state, while self-protective, has its consequences. Patrick is like a 'stroke victim' (p. 138) and is contrasted with that other, much more verbal, contemporary ex-centric, Joseph Conrad. It is her reading of a Conrad letter that provokes Patrick to tell Alice that the 'trouble' with ideology 'is that it hates the private. You must make it human' (p. 135). It is Alice's death, however, that causes him to feel true human sorrow and to (in the words of the title and the first epigraph to the novel) 'wander through the wilderness in the skin of a lion'.

Before this, however, Patrick tries to recover Alice's history, her silenced past. Once a searcher for the disappeared, he becomes a re-searcher for the re-appeared. Trying to piece together the few documents of history that Alice's daughter, Hana, possesses, Patrick has only three photos, a rosary, and a sumac bracelet with which to work. But in the library archives he learns of Nicholas Temelcoff's role in building the Bloor St Viaduct (he had thus far been known to him only as a friend who ran a bakery) and puts it together with the many stories he knows: 'He saw the interactions, saw how each one of them was carried by the strength of something more than themselves' (p. 144), and figures out that Alice *Gull* is the (flying!) nun who was blown off the unfinished viaduct. It is at this moment that he realizes the essentially narrative and plural quality of life:

> His own life was no longer a single story but part of a mural, which was a falling together of accomplices. Patrick saw a wondrous night web—all of these fragments of a human order, something ungoverned by the family he was born into or the headlines of the day. A nun on a bridge, a dare-devil who was unable to sleep without drink, a boy watching a fire from his bed at night, an actress who ran away with a millionaire—the detritus and chaos of the age was realigned. (p. 145)

And that realignment is this novel, the narrative that we too, as readers, have been piecing together.

But Patrick's research in the library foregrounds more than just the private history of the characters; it makes him aware of the configurations of public history as well. As the novel has already emphasized, those who worked on the monuments of public history are the anonymous. As with Maxine Hong Kingston's portrayal of the equally anonymous Chinese builders of American railways in *China Men*, pictures do exist of these workers, but their names are unrecorded: 'Official histories and news stories were always soft as rhetoric, like that of a politician making a speech after a bridge is built, a man who does not even cut the grass on his own lawn' (p. 145). These photos are contrasted with those of Lewis Hine, the American who documented 'trapper boys in coal mines, seven-year-old doffer girls in New England mills' (p. 145). Then a narrator who is clearly not Patrick intervenes, perhaps acting as the Lewis Hine of the narrative: 'But Patrick would never see the great photographs of Hine, as he would never read the letters of Joseph Conrad. Official histories, news stories surround us daily, but the events of art reach us too late, travel languorously like messages in a bottle' (pp. 145-6). It is art, this historiographic metafiction teaches, that can make order of the 'chaos and tumble of events': 'The first sentence of every novel should be: "Trust me, this will take time but there is order here, very faint, very human." Meander if you want to get to town' (p. 146).

As readers we then watch a narrator struggle with expression: 'She could move like . . . she could sing as low as. . . . Why is it that I am now trying to uncover every facet of Alice's nature for myself?' (p. 147). Whose voice is this? We might think it Patrick's, except that the next sentence reads, 'He wants everything of Alice to be with him here' (p. 147). As in John Berger's novel G. (and the epigraph from Berger is not unrelated here), the narrative voices of the writing artist-figure and the memory-ridden protagonist merge; memory and creation are more closely related than we might like to think: 'All these fragments of memory . . . so we can retreat from the grand story and stumble accidentally upon a luxury one of those underground pools where we can sit still. Those moments, those few pages in a book we go back and forth over' (p. 148).

Patrick learns Alice's past; he learns the irony of her self-naming—for she takes her name mockingly from the parrot in the Macedonian cafe that is her first stop in her new life after the fall (literally and—if with irony—symbolically). In restoring Alice's past to himself and to us, he also restores memory to Nicholas Temelcoff, the man who saved Alice's life:

> This is what history means. He came to this country like a torch on fire and he swallowed air as he walked forward and he gave out light. Energy poured through him. That was all he had time for in those years. Language, customs, family, salaries. Patrick's gift, that arrow into the past, shows him the wealth in himself, how he has been sewn into history. Now he will begin to tell stories. (p. 149)

Patrick too learns that there is a private history to match the public: 'He knew now he was the sum of all he had been in his life since he was that boy in the snow woods' (p. 152).

It is fitting that Alice, the ex-nun, should choose to be an actress, for in the theatre not only could she constantly relive her re-naming, but she could also unite art and life in a self-conscious way. It is fitting too that Patrick be a self-distanced re-searcher, for he 'has always been alien' (p. 156). Though 'born in this country', he 'knows nothing of the place' (p. 157): 'He was a watcher, a corrector. He could no more have skated along the darkness of a river than been the hero of one of these stories' (p. 157). Yet something happens that changes all of this, that teaches him a new role as actor—acting out history: 'Each person had their moment when they assumed the skins of wild animals, when they took responsibility for the story' (p. 157).

His skin is a lion's skin, and Alice's death causes him to face his responsibility, to cease being 'nothing but a prism that refracted' the lives of others (p. 157). That her death coincides with his learning of the past of Canada, of the union battles of workers silenced by history, is not unrelated to his radical-ization. Alice's mysterious death is directly connected to her naming: as Patrick calls her name, she dies. The source of identity is now associated with death and permanent loss of self. But this act also makes Patrick name himself as the revolutionary who will continue her cause (just as she had continued her lover Cato's). Alice's hatred of the exploiting rich is translated into Patrick's torching of the Muskoka Hotel and his flight into the water—'[u]nhistorical' (p. 172) (in the sense of being fictive as well as unrecorded). True to Alice's prediction—she once told Patrick she knew she could never make him hurt someone—he is careful that no one is injured in the fire. But the act is a revolutionary one that lands him in prison.

There he again meets Caravaggio, an east-end Italian thief he has met earlier. Just as it was Alice's violent death that jerked him out of his passivity, it is Caravaggio's throat-slitting (to cries of 'Fucking wop! Fucking dago!') by prisoners 'who have evolved smug and without race' (p. 185) that breaks the self-imposed, protective silence to which Patrick has again retreated. No society seems to be free of its prejudice; the revolution must be not only against the rich but against the bigoted. And not all the rich are evil, as Caravaggio learns upon his escape from prison, though they are always different. He watches a rich woman (and her gender is probably not insignificant) trying to write a poem, trying 'to discover what she was or what she was capable of making' (p. 198), but Caravaggio, despite his name, 'would never leave his name where his skill had been' (p. 199).

The last full chapter of the novel takes place in 1938, after Patrick's release from prison. The opening section recalls the opening of *Ragtime*, another novel of class, immigration, politics, and injustice. In Doctorow's novel we find an opening portrait of the year 1902: 'Everyone wore white in summer. Tennis racquets were hefty and the racquet faces elliptical. There was a lot of sexual fainting. There were no Negroes. There were no immigrants.'[26] A page later, we are told that Emma Goldman teaches a different version: 'Apparently there *were* Negroes. There *were* immigrants.' Ondaatje's chapter portrays 1938 in similarly contradictory terms, and in a tone and syntax that recall *Ragtime*: 'Everyone tried to play the Hammond Organ. "Red Squads" intercepted mail, teargassed political meetings. By now over 10,000 foreign-born workers had been deported out of the country. Everyone sang "Just One of Those Things"' (p. 209). The ironic juxtaposition of details here is self-commenting and powerful.

The newly liberated Patrick is a different man. No longer solitary, he will live life for and with another: Alice's daughter, Hana. He rejects his earlier silence that denied communication, realizing that his main link with Alice is through the living real, not the dead remembered. It is at this point that Clara Dickens returns to his life, first as a voice on the telephone, calling him after Ambrose Small's death. The frame narrative at last begins to make sense: the two figures in the car are Patrick and Hana, going to Marmora to pick up Clara. But before the frame can be neatly cornered, so to speak, one more story must be told: that of Alice's death. In order to do so, the narrative flashes back to Patrick's and Caravaggio's plot to blow up Harris's water-filtration plant.

It is a plot that involves acting (in the sense of theatrical play as well as political action) with and against the paranoid rich in a context of union crackdowns and communist fear ('the events in Spain'). It is also a plot about power, literal (dynamite) and allegorical. Harnessing the energy that Alice saw as dangerous, Patrick literally 'infiltrates' the filtration plant from the outside tunnel he had earlier helped blast out of rock. He wires the entire structure and then confronts Harris, who has taken to sleeping in his beloved waterworks. Their initial words situate the theme. Harris says, 'How dare you try to come in here!' and Patrick replies, 'I'm not trying this, I've done it' (p. 235). His grievance is clear. He tells Harris that *he* and other workers built that building, not Harris, but that Harris forgot them (p. 235). To Harris's 'I fought tooth and nail' for the luxurious waterworks, Patrick replies: '*You* fought. *You* fought. Think about those who built the intake tunnels. Do know you know how many of us died in there?' (p. 236). Harris's reply is historically damning: 'There was no record kept.' In an attempt to save his life and his plant, Harris lectures Patrick on power: 'You don't like power, you don't respect it, you don't want it to exist but you move around it all the time' (p. 236). That there is some truth to this accusation is ironically conditioned by the fact that Patrick is at that moment carrying a blasting-box in his hands.

This discussion of power comes to be tied to the notion of imagination and creation in a paradoxical postmodern way. Harris tells of dreams he had, dreams that turned out to be dreams of plans of places that could have existed in Toronto, but have been rejected: 'These *were* all real places. They could have existed' (p. 237). When Harris continues, we realize that the rich city commissioner has been granted the vision that is a *mise en abyme* of this entire novel's mixing of history and fiction and its focus on class politics:

> You must realize you are like these places, Patrick. You're as much of the fabric as the aldermen and the millionaires. But you're among the dwarfs of enterprise that never get accepted or acknowledged. Mongrel company. You're a lost heir. So you stay in the woods. You reject power. And this is how the bland fools—the politicians and press and mayors and their advisers—become the spokesmen for the age. (p. 238)

The responsibility for the silencing of history lies not only with the rich and the powerful, the text suggests. This is part of Alice's legacy to Patrick, and it is fitting that it is now we learn of the circumstances of her death—killed by a mistake, a clock bomb hidden in a bag she carried by accident, a bomb that Patrick himself likely had created.

The tale of 'Maritime Theatre' (the chapter title) ends in anti-climax: Patrick falls asleep; Harris has the blasting-box defused and medical aid brought to his 'captor'. He understands why Patrick chose him: 'he was one of the few in power who had something tangible around him. But those with real power had nothing to show for themselves. They had paper' (p. 242). So too, of course, does the novelist. This is the power to change how we read history and fiction, to change how we draw the lines we like to draw between the real and the imaginary. The ex-centric, those on the margins of history—be they women, workers, immigrants (or writers?)—have the power to change the perspective of the centre, and that power is given voice in *In the Skin of the Lion.*

Like *The Collected Works of Billy the Kid, Coming Through Slaughter,* and *Running in the Family,* this too is a book about ex-centricity and its power through naming and language. As the work of

Michel Foucault has shown, power is an ambivalent force, neither negative nor positive. It can build as it can destroy; it can be used to combat injustice as easily as to induce complacency. Literalized as actual dynamite in *In the Skin of a Lion*, power allows the conquering of nature in the name of civilization and yet also brings about the destruction of human life. The creative power of the novelist, however, the power to name the unnamed of history, may offer a less ambivalent model for yet another kind of power.

Notes

[1] See the introduction to Part IV, 'Patterns and Consequences of Self-Reflective Art', in *The Discontinuous Universe*, ed. Sallie Sears and G.W. Lord (New York: Basic Books, 1972), pp. viii-ix.

[2] *The Shock of the New* (London: BBC, 1980), p. 247.

[3] After Mallarmé, according to Michel Foucault, literature 'breaks with the whole definition of genres as forms adapted to an order of representations, and becomes merely a manifestation of a language which has no other law than that of affirming—in opposition to all other forms of discourse—its own precipitous existence; and so there is nothing for it to do but to curve back in a perpetual return upon itself, as if its discourse could have no other content than the expression of its own form; it addresses itself to itself as a writing subjectivity . . . .' In *The Order of Things* (London: Tavistock, 1970), p. 300.

[4] See, for instance, Louise Dupré, 'From Experimentation to Experience: Québécois Modernity in the Feminine', in *A Mazing Space: Writing Canadian / Women Writing*, ed. Shirley Neuman and Smaro Kamboureli (Edmonton: Longspoon/NeWest Press, 1986), p. 358, on women's challenges to generic and formal boundaries.

[5] *Lusts* (Garden City, NY: Doubleday, 1983), p. 45. All further references will appear in parentheses in the text.

[6] By Sam Solecki, entry on Ondaatje in the *Oxford Companion to Canadian Literature* (Toronto: Oxford University Press, 1983), p. 620.

[7] 'Towards a Theory of Non-Genre Literature', in *Surfiction*, ed. Raymond Federman, 2nd ed. (Chicago: Swallow Press, 1981), p. 255.

[8] For one explanation of this process, as discussed in Chapter 4, see Timothy J. Reiss, *The Discourse of Modernism* (Ithaca, NY: Cornell University Press, 1982), and a related review article: Linda Hutcheon, 'A Poetics of Postmodernism?' *Diacritics* 13, 4 (Winter 1983), pp. 33-45.

[9] Jerome Rothenberg, 'New Models, New Visions: Some Notes Toward

a Poetics of Performance', in *Performance in Postmodern Culture*, ed. Michel Benamou and Charles Caramello (Milwaukee, Wisconsin: Center for Twentieth Century Studies, 1977), p. 14.

[10] This aesthetic practice would disprove Herbert Blau's (and many others') accusation that postmodernism represses history, that it is 'disinherited, apolitical, vain'. See his 'Letting Be Be Finale of Seem: The Future of an Illusion', in *Performance in Postmodern Culture*, p. 66.

[11] For instance, in *Le Plaisir du texte* (Paris: Seuil, 1973), translated as *The Pleasure of the Text*, trans. Richard Miller (New York: Hill and Wang, 1975); *Roland Barthes par Roland Barthes* (Paris: Seuil, 1975), translated as *Roland Barthes by Roland Barthes*, trans. Richard Howard (New York: Hill and Wang, 1977); *Fragments d'un discours amoureux* (Paris: Seuil, 1977), translated as *A Lover's Discourse: Fragments*, trans. Richard Howard (New York: Hill and Wang, 1978).

[12] See Reda Bensmaia, 'From Fragment to Detail: Roland Barthes', *Enclitic* 5, 1 (1981), pp. 66-97. Barthes himself called the fragmental text the matrix of all genre. See 'Colloque international sur le genre', *Glyph* 7 (1980), p. 235.

[13] *Roland Barthes by Roland Barthes*, p. 122.

[14] Ibid., p. 94.

[15] *Sade/Fourier/Loyola* (Paris: Seuil, 1971), p. 14.

[16] *Running in the Family* (Toronto: McClelland and Stewart, 1982), p. 36. All further references will appear in parentheses in the text.

[17] Another way in which Ondaatje plays with readers' perception of photographs is to show the picture first, with no context, and then to discuss it later. In one case, a nearly blind woman describes the photo with the eyes of memory, and the author writes that the picture 'has moved tangible, palpable, into her brain, the way memory invades the present in those who are old' (p. 112). Since we too have actually seen the photograph, it is also tangible and palpable in a literal way for us.

[18] This distinction is that of Georges Lavis, 'Le Texte littéraire, le référent, le réel, le vrai', *Cahiers d'analyse textuelle* 13 (1971), pp. 7-22.

[19] This refusal is ruefully acknowledged within a critical context by Frank Kermode in *The Genesis of Secrecy* (Cambridge, Mass.: Harvard University Press, 1979), p. 45: 'Even now, when so many theories of interpretation dispense in one way or another with the author, or allow him only a part analogous to that of the dummy hand at bridge, the position is not much altered; the narrative inhabits its proper dark, in which the interpreter traces its lineaments as best he can.'

[20] *The Archaeology of Knowledge*, trans. Sheridan Smith (New York: Harper and Row, 1976), p. 23.

[21] Another Canadian novel openly drawing on this text is Jack Hodgins'

The Resurrection of Joseph Bourne: Or a Word or Two on those Port Annie Miracles (Toronto: Macmillan, 1979).

22 *One Hundred Years of Solitude*, trans. Gregory Rabassa (1970; New York: Avon, 1971), p. 11.

23 This alphabet image reappears a number of times: in the black boar's 'wet alphabet of tusk' that could bring death (p. 142) and in the change in his mother's handwriting, as if she 'forced herself to cope with a new dark unknown alphabet' (p. 150).

24 *In the Skin of a Lion* (Toronto: McClelland and Stewart, 1987), p. 9. All further references will be in parentheses in the text.

25 The intertext here is Margaret Atwood's poem 'Progressive Insanities of a Pioneer', which opens with, 'He stood, a point / on a sheet of green paper / proclaiming himself the centre' and ends with, 'the green / vision, the unnamed / whale invaded'.

26 *Ragtime* (New York: Bantam, 1976), p. 4.

Chapter 6

'Shape Shifters': Canadian Women Writers and the Tradition

In the first chapter of this book I mentioned the temporal conjunction of postmodernism and feminism, but stressed that they could in no way be equated, mostly because the particular political agenda of feminism makes it substantially different in intent from the more complicitous questioning of the political (that is, usually without any final answers) that characterizes postmodernism. I should also say that I think we can no longer talk of feminism in the singular, but must talk of feminisms in the plural, for there are as many kinds of feminism as there are kinds of women: white, black, Asian, Indian; Anglo- or French, native, 'ethnic'; lesbian, heterosexual. Those ex-centrics outside the 'mainstream' (white, Anglo-/French, heterosexual) have often been the ones whose split identities—as Japanese- or Italo-Canadians, for instance—have made them feel closer to the postmodern concerns for difference and multiplicity rather than sameness and single identity. These women writers live as well as write their doubled sense of self. So too do native women, doubly colonized by history and by gender.[1] Their own cultural traditions (mostly oral) and their personal past often become the focus of works that cannot escape that postmodern irony we saw in Chapter 3, because they are in fact written, not oral. These writers also tell us as much about their people as themselves. History, autobiography, and metafictional self-reflexivity meet, for instance, in the opening of Maria Campbell's *Halfbreed*:

> I am not very old, so perhaps some day, when I too am a grannie, I will write more. I write this for all of you, to tell you what it is like to be a Halfbreed woman in our country. I want to tell you about the joys and sorrows, the oppressing poverty, the frustrations and the dreams.[2]

The fact that postmodernism values difference and ex-centricity is due in great part to the fact that feminisms (along with studies of post-colonial racism, Marxist class analysis, and gay theory, of course) pushed it in that direction. Feminists noticed that, in theory at least, poststructuralist challenges to the bastions of liberal humanism, especially to the notion of universal 'Man', had not necessarily led to the discovery of Woman, as we have seen. The modernist avant-garde too, for all its aesthetic radicalism and political utopianism, had not been very ideologically aware of its representations of women. Postmodernism, thanks to feminisms, now is.

These two forces have come together today in their related challenges to the canon (to the 'eternal' 'beauty' and 'truth' of the 'universally' agreed-upon 'great tradition') and to the borders that conventionally divide fiction from non-fictional forms. They both try to offer reasons to rethink the notion of 'definitive' inscriptions of identity, especially the ex-centric, 'minoritarian' identity: Big Bear, Riel . . . women! In general, both feminisms and postmodernism 'situate' themselves and the literature they study in historical, social, and cultural (as well as literary) contexts, challenging conventions that are presumed to be literary 'universals', but can in fact be shown to embody the values of a very particular group of people—of a certain class, race, gender, and sexual orientation.

But this contestation is operating not just on the level of theory: women writers too have done much to challenge systems that 'totalize'—that unify with an eye to power and control, with an eye to obliterating traces of difference. They too have worked to replace 'universal' 'Truth' with particular truths. The techniques they have chosen make their work overlap with what I have been calling the postmodern: in their challenges to form, as well as in their ideological critique, these are postmodern writers—but they are also feminist writers, and the difference of agenda must be respected.

Two of the major 'universals' contested by both postmodernism and feminism are the notions of authority (in its various forms) and originality. One of the most common means of contesting used by writers of both persuasions is intertextuality in general, and parody in particular. Parody, in a sense, is a use and abuse of convention. By definition it is not fully original: it is borrowed or stolen—and only then altered. Like all forms of intertextual borrowing, it is ostentatiously not a single, unique utterance of an original genius. Herein lies the implicit critique of those liberal humanist 'universals'. If anything, intertextuality and parody signal a kind of textual collectivity, as well as a textual history: they deliberately recall other texts. They undercut the notion that authorial authority rests on a single meaning, fixed in the past, by materially reminding us of the process of re-interpretation that we call the act of reading. To re-present or re-narrate (parodically or otherwise) is always to re-conceptu-alize the possibilities of meaning: *Beautiful Losers* desacralizes the authority of the male, French, Jesuit inscription of the identity of the female, Indian saint Catherine Tekakwitha, by means of rather irreverent parody. And as I mentioned in Chapter 1, writers as different as Robert Kroetsch and Audrey Thomas translate or trans-code male narrative patterns (like the quest) into significantly different female forms, thereby demystifying their presumed 'universal' attributes and re-en-gendering them.

In much postmodern fiction it is the conventions of narrative in particular that get rethought, especially the so-called 'trans-parency' of stories and story-telling, whether in novels or in history-writing. As Marjorie Perloff has put it, postmodern story 'is no longer the full-fledged *mythos* of Aristotle . . . but a point of reference, a way of alluding, a source . . . of parody. To tell a story is to find a way— sometimes the only way—of *knowing* one's world.'[3] While my focus in this chapter will be on novelistic intertextuality and parody, a few things must be clarified. First, these are in no way the only means at the disposal of writers to de-form and challenge literary 'universals'.[4] Second, novels are clearly not the only generic form in which they work their challenges.[5] Third, parody in particular can exist on other levels than that of genre. Any coded form of communication or behaviour can be parodied. For instance, in *Lives of Girls and Women* Alice Munro parodies our cultural codes regarding the loss of female virginity (the need for the show of blood) through Del's provocative allegorical lie about the tom cat and the bird told to mother: it both calls attention to and explains the presence of (her) blood on the flowers by the house. Or, to offer one further example, many feminist novels parody certain theoretical notions: those of Nicole Brossard and Louky Bersianik take on the Lacanian psychoanalytic theories about the feminization of the child's relation to the parents.[6]

Parody—or intertextuality in general—plays an important role in much women's fiction today, as it seeks a feminine literary space while still acknowledging (however grudgingly) the power of the (male/'universal') space in which it cannot avoid, to some extent, operating. This enforced complicity does not diminish the impact of its protest, but it does set up the conditions within which it will exist. The representations of women in so-called 'universal' conventions are still being contested. In Smaro Kamboureli's terms:

> Whether [women writers] adhere to a radical or non-radical feminist ideology, or whether they choose forms and structures that conform to the literary tradition or depart from it, they all take exception to the anemic double of the feminine body that male language and mythology have constructed. They do so by deconstructing the culture that has hosted them as parasites.[7]

Parody is one way of deconstructing that male-dominated culture; its simultaneous use and abuse of conventions that have been deemed 'universal' works to reveal the hidden gender encoding.

This kind of parody has been powerfully deployed in Québécois as well as English-Canadian feminist fiction. For example, Louky Bersianik's *L'Euguélionne* parodies the Bible in form (chapter and verse; parable; sermon) in such a way as to emphasize its inversion of the patriarchal content that links the Word to a male God. By parodically inflating the language of male power—from that of Adam to that of St Siegfried [Freud] and St Jacques Linquant [Lacan]—it deflates those pretensions to 'universality'. In *Le Picque-nique sur l'Acropole: Cahiers d'Ancyl* she takes on Plato's *Symposium* as a symbol of male Greek culture and its lasting authority. Again she uses parody of structure and form of argument in order to offer a feminist inversion of our (very male) Hellenic inheritance.[8]

As an ironic form of intertextuality, parody is today one of the most popular feminist 'modalities' or what Nancy Miller calls ways of 'marking what has already been said, of making a common text one's own'.[9] It is one of the ways of investigating the position of women *within* the tradition, as a way of discovering possible positions *outside* that tradition.[10] Like all forms of intertextual reference to other texts, parody is as compromised as it is potentially revolutionary: it always acknowledges the power of that which it parodies, even as it challenges it.[11] And this is, of course, what makes it such an attractive mode for postmodernism's paradoxically complicitous critique.

While these theoretical issues are important to note, it is even more interesting to see them in operation in the fiction. Audrey Thomas's novel *Intertidal Life* offers a good example of the self-conscious parodic 'problematizing' of both the novel form and its relation to questions of gender. It is a powerful study of writing and its relation to sexual difference, and extended intertextuality is one of its major means of articulating how textual meaning and sexual identity are fixed through and by literary representations of women. It illustrates well the impossibility of separating the social and the sexual from the literary when dealing with the writing—and lives—of women.

Intertidal Life is a novel about friendship and also about marriage: about its rituals, its expectations, and its disappointments. This is a serious investigation of the difference between *love* (affection and respect over time) that the protagonist, Alice Hoyle, believes in—because of and in spite of experience—and the *passion* of the moment (the glamour, intensity, and romance that her husband, Peter, desired). This is the emotion that the novel links to the clichéd world of Harlequin romances that Alice and her young daughter occasionally read while living on their small, edenic BC island. In the background, as part of the social critique of the novel, is an entire period—the sixties and seventies—with its hippies and drugs, its gentleness, meditation, and peace that mask what Alice sees as a need for authority (gurus) and considerable secret aggression and pain.[12] Alice finds she has little patience for the Kahlil Gibran-quoting, inarticulate, humourless, and narcissistic 'takers' who have not learned how to give: 'They did not care to change the world or make it better. . . . It was as though they had had the moral equivalent of a stroke.'[13] This 'flabbiness of spirit' is as much what offends her as her (now ex-) husband's attraction to a freer, 'alternate' life-style—though, of course, the two are not unrelated. Alice thinks it is a major trivialization of life and love to want to revert to being a child, to playing at being Peter Pan and the Lost Boys. As both writer and mother, creatrix and nurturer, Alice finds she is offended by this sort of passive rejection of both creativity and responsibility: 'Somebody's got to be the parent' (p. 183). The social and the sexual cannot be separated.

Intertidal Life is a novel about women and woman, but only and also in the same way that Joyce's *A Portrait of the Artist as a Young Man* is about men and man, not about the 'universal' artist. This is specifically a portrait of the artist as mother, of woman as creatrix. Thomas suggests that, for biological and social reasons, women have had a different relationship to creation and to being an artist than men have. Alice wonders: 'Can you imagine a man thinking, well, once I get married I can think about being a composer or a painter or whatever! Once I find the right woman' (p. 179). We are told that women create under the auspices of the moon, not the moon as 'Chaste Diana' (p. 195), but rather as that which determines her bodily rhythms as surely as it does the rhythms of the tides: 'Men are related to the sun. The sun never changes his shape. Sisters of the moon we are, shape shifters but oh so predictable in our shifting. We hold the waters of the world in our nets' (p. 206).

In this novel 'intertidal life' refers, then, to female life. Alice and her daughter, spending the summer on their island, plan to study 'seaweeds and intertidal creatures' (p. 12), but, through memory, it is the specifically female creatures of that isolating island[14] that take up their attention. Following her separation from her husband, Alice had noted that she had failed to learn the necessary intertidal lesson of the limpet—who knows how to hang on. She had failed to hang on to her husband, 'formerly Peter the Rock', to hang on 'for dear life or limpet life' (p. 60). But there is good reason for this. In this novel, as in Susan Swan's *The Biggest Modern Woman of the World*, women are constantly associated with water, with the sea, but also with tears, cups of tea, menstrual blood, and the waters that break at birth. In British Columbia, Alice's particular geographical locality, water has also provided the body that men have used as a means of exploring, of getting somewhere, of finding a land to conquer. The epigraphs of the three sections of the novel are from the book Alice is reading: *A Spanish Voyage to Vancouver*. These two seemingly very different associations with water (female and male) are not unrelated, however. In imagery reminiscent of that of Margaret Atwood's poem 'Death of a Young Son by Drowning' in *The Journals of Susanna Moodie*, Alice sees that '[b]abies drop out of us from our most secret places, through the channels the fathers have charted and laid claim to. Rivers of pain and blood' (p. 205). The imperialistic male exploration theme is also linked to that of creation, for Alice feels that the early ages of maritime discovery, which inspired the seventeenth-century language of John Donne (the language of maps, new lands, compasses, and so on), are now finding their twentieth-century equivalent—and hence, perhaps, the reason for the maritime imagery in her own (and Thomas's) writing about human relations: 'what's happening to men and women today is just as exciting and terrifying as the discovery that the earth was round, not flat' (p. 171). Clearly the impact of feminist (consciousness-raising) critique is seen by Thomas to be one of major cultural proportions, both 'exciting and terrifying'.

It is also the case, though, that the ages of exploration were indeed ages of imperialism, and Alice argues that it is only women who can put a stop to the modern age of male imperialism, for it is women who have willingly consented to their own conquering: 'Women have *let* men define them, taken their *names* even, with marriage, just like a conquered or newly settled region, *British* Columbia . . . *New* France' (p. 171). Could women themselves ever become the explorers, the namers, though? She acknowledges the difficulties: 'Would we take our children with us, on these voyages of discovery? . . . Would our lovers wait faithfully for us until we returned?' (p. 70). Whether real or metaphorical, the voyages of women could never be like those of men: 'one went on a true quest alone. . . . One didn't bring along three kids, a lame dog and a spiteful cat' (p. 141). Anchored down at times by her own inertia as much as by responsibility, Alice accepts her different fate. And the epigraph to the final section of the novel can be read to suggest a victory of the female moon and the powers of her waters, the 'intertidal life' force: 'We put out our oars,' write the male explorers, 'endeavouring with them to counteract the current, but alas the efforts of the sailors were in vain' (p. 245).

Thomas, however, confronts the problems and contradictions of womanhood today head on. The 'Moon-ladies' of the novel are all shown to revolve around the male sun, Peter (pp. 218, 239). We see 'the moon only shining by reflection' (p. 274). Nevertheless, it is women and the friendship of women that offer ways for Alice to deal with this and to survive the 'great tidal wave . . . of hatred' (p. 75) that engulfed her when Peter left her. Through her daughters and her female friends on the island Alice learns about herself and about women in general. She ruthlessly investigates the articulations of female stereotypes in our culture: its clichés that she finds even herself mouthing without thinking (p. 33), its popular songs (pp. 108-9), its magazine images (p. 101), its religion (pp. 52, 134), its education (p. 98), its laws (p. 157), and its family structures (pp. 81-2, 210), structures that women as mothers actually help to enforce. And Alice also refuses—although herself a writer—to spare our literature (both serious and popular) from this rigorous examination (p. 103). The Harlequin romances that she and her daughter read, with their stereotyped and stereotyping male and female roles (pp. 14, 16, 260-1), are certainly presented as more guilty (or perhaps just more overtly guilty) of conditioning their readers' expectations of life and love. Alice consoles herself with the fact that her daughter is also reading *Madame Bovary*, a novel she quite rightly considers a good antidote to the Harlequin romances, for it is indeed the tale of a woman whose reading of analogous romances brings about her death. Emma Bovary read as a realist—believing that the events of those books were 'out there' in life, waiting for her. And she was wrong. What interests Alice is women's willingness to accept such roles. She tries to understand the part that women themselves play in their subjection to patriarchy's myths of romance. She mercilessly studies her own and other women's needs to define themselves in terms of their men, and also their shared yearning to seek stability, security, and guidance from men, rather than from themselves. The radical critique of women's subjectivity or sense of self, here, is the equal of any poststructuralist-feminist theoretical one available today.[15]

Thomas's postmodernism and her feminism overlap in the novel's metafictive suggestion that it is because Alice is a writer that she can articulate both her emotions and this kind of analysis. This characterization device and the narrative form of a frame and an interrupted journal are the two main structural tools by which Thomas builds her critique. With them she can help the reader put together the fragments of the puzzle she calls 'Alice Hoyle: 1,000 Interlocking Pieces' (p. 158). But in this postmodern fiction, just as she can articulate her emotions and her investigation of the role of women in society, Alice can also write about writing. *Intertidal Life* is a reworking of the traditional male *Künstlerroman* form through both feminist refocusing and postmodern metafiction. Its 'journal' part presents us with the (representation of the) material product of her writing (including the scribbles she tells us she draws to avoid writing [p. 61]), along with a commentary on the fact of her writing, and specifically on the problems of being both a writer and a mother, or more generally, both a writer and a woman, a woman who is expected by society—including other women—to put other people before her work (pp. 21, 68). Consequently, Alice's attitude to her writing is a clearly ambivalent one. Writing is both important if 'lonely work . . . trying to see' (p. 62) and the form that women use when they want to lay blame: her mother writes such letters (p. 62) and the guilt induced in Selene by her mother's letters causes asthma attacks.

But we must not forget that writing is also what women can turn to in order to try 'to see' or to understand. As writer Alice is a postmodern female Adam, a namer. And names are of obvious significance in the novel, both in their symbolic echoing and in their relation to things. At one point Alice composes a list of 'Household Words' made up of the names of people who indeed did give their names to 'things': it begins with 'M. Guillotin' and ends with 'Mr Hoyle' (pp. 146-7). Later, this last term is explained: as Mrs Hoyle Alice too is a thing, a 'household word' (p. 172), a fate she once accepted with pleasure. Her husband changes in the novel from 'Peter the Rock' to 'Peter Pan' (p. 225) as he peters out (p. 134). He is also 'Peter Peter pumpkin eater / Had a wife and couldn't keep her' (p. 70). Alice is the Alice of Wonderland (pp. 98, 123, 280) who has trouble making sense of the new male-less world into which she has fallen.

It is clear that women writers today—like feminist critics— do not deal just with the themes of the social and psychological nature of the feminine. Both the writers and the critics are concerned with formal issues too, in particular with issues about language that have come to be associated with what I have been referring to here as 'poststructuralist' theory. This label seems to have stuck and is accurate insofar as the theory was made possible by the structuralist rethinking of language inaugurated by Ferdinand de Saussure, and yet went beyond the structuralist limitation of restricting linguistic concerns to the system of language alone, ignoring social and ideological, as well as individual, contexts. In this novel too Alice is a writer and so is obsessed with language and also with its contexts. It is a family joke, in fact (p. 111), that she always has her dictionary in hand, searching etymologies and meanings. These appear in the novel in at least three different forms.

Sometimes they are given simply in their factual bareness as dictionary entries, and yet their textual context characteristically provides a certain narrative irony. For example, in bed, missing and desiring her absent husband, Alice offers us: '*Pudendum*, n. (usu. in pl. *-da*) / Privy parts—. (L. *pudere*, to be ashamed.)' (p. 80). There are other instances, however, that provide more of a commentary on a word and its derivations, either for the benefit of Alice herself or for others, such as: 'Stoned. Such an interesting word. As compared to "sloshed" or "smashed" or "pissed", for example. A hard word, "stoned". Who had thought it up? From astonish, probably, so it must have been a professor unless a happy accident' (p. 135). Most often, though, puns, verbal play or personal word associations are made part of the normal fabric of Alice's language, with no additional comment: 'I could hear the "end" in "friend", I could see the "rust" in "trust"' (p. 30).

It is this verbal side of Alice that is a sign of what she herself perceives as her true intellectual strength: 'Alice's mind was the heavyweight champion of the world in the disguise of the Scorpio Housewife. Washing the dishes, she let her mind off the leash, let it run and snuffle. . . . Let it bring back prizes. Images, single words. The occasional complete paragraph' (p. 226). However, this verbal facility is only part of the definition of Alice as creatrix. The other is perhaps less intellectual and more visceral. Writing in this novel (as in some of Atwood's, as we shall see in the next chapter) is explicitly connected with pregnancy and birth. Alice makes this clear when she tells a female friend: 'When I have to leave something as big as that [her novel] it's like trying to interrupt a pregnancy and then take it up again three months later. I'm always scared the little creature will have died' (p. 107).[16] Moon-like, she cannot reject pregnancy and motherhood, as can and does Stella, the star (with parodic echoes of Tennessee Williams' Stella) (p. 58). But Stella rejects fertility at the price of creativity. There is also a short fragment that suggests an abortion (p. 189), an act that has caused a 'sea change of a most terrible sort' (p. 190) in Alice. This fragment is followed directly by her explanation of why she had to kill her cat's kittens. We learn too that in the 'real' world, '[a]fter the Immaculate Conception', comes 'the maculate delivery' (p. 52).

In other words, these female functions—pregnancy, giving birth, mothering—are inevitably ambivalent functions for the female as artist. A matter of worry (p. 9) and of skill (p. 82), motherhood is both the consequence and the reward of creation. It is both the source of and the threat to Alice's sense of self. 'Who can see the "other" in mother?' (p. 136), she asks. She feels that this is the cause of the loss of her boy-husband's love (pp. 154, 205-6), not only because of his immaturity and Oedipal problems, but because her mother- and novelist-roles took up most of her energies. She confesses, 'Artists are never "always there" and mothers generally put children before husbands' (p. 161). But Thomas is not one to skirt the contradictions, however painful: while motherhood brings with it pain and responsibility, it also wields power (pp. 180-1, 205), and can give strength (p. 243).

Despite the constant theme (albeit ambivalent) of creation and creativity, death also haunts the novel. Nevertheless, there is none of that obsessive association of sex and death with creativity that we have seen in the recent work of some Canadian male novelists: Kroetsch's *Alibi*, Wiebe's *My Lovely Enemy*, or Blaise's *Lusts*. Death does frame this novel, though—both figuratively (the death of the marriage) and literally (as Alice awaits and fears her possible death in surgery). From the very start, the island on which Alice lives is tainted with death through the early mention of the suicide of the lighthouse-keeper's wife (p. 6). But from this point on, readers soon become aware that it is a very *literary* kind of death that we meet in this novel.

All of the death references are directly related to some literary work or figure. The (self-) drowned Virginia Woolf is perhaps the most present of all. Alice consciously contemplates that suicide (p. 243), and Woolf's novels are also very much in the background: *The Waves*, with its central but absent male figure, and *To the Lighthouse*, with its two women—the artist, Lily, and the mother and wife, Mrs Ramsay—here rolled into one. There are other literary echoes of death here as well, and not all are from the writing of women:[17] Alice calls the west the 'land of the dead' (p. 230), thereby recalling for us her own earlier reference to Joyce's story 'The Dead' (p. 119). (Nora, the woman of Joyce's life, however, has—thanks to her evocative surname—an even more symbolic function in the intertidal life of women: 'N. Barnacle, God's holy name for us all' [p. 263].) The other echoes of death evoked through intertextual references are just as self-evident. While contemplating the comforting notion of being buried in (and thus nourishing) her beloved garden, Alice cites T.S. Eliot's *The Waste Land*: 'that corpse you buried in your garden / has it begun to sprout' (p. 258).

Not surprisingly, perhaps, in a feminist Canadian novel, the source of *Intertidal Life*'s most extended set of echoes is Margaret Atwood's *Life Before Man*, with its similar symbolic time setting of Hallowe'en (and All Souls' Day) and with all the verbal play, both in general and in particular. For instance, Atwood's Elizabeth, also a mother of daughters, plays on the word '*Mummy*': 'A dried corpse in a gilded cage. *Mum*, silent. *Mama*, short for mammary gland.' This is very close to Alice's own extended play on the meanings and forms of mother and mummy (p. 136). Certain scenes appear to be echoed directly: while in the bath, Elizabeth reads a child's riddle book that contains a saying about an hourglass, a saying that she relates to her sister's death by drowning and to her own possible demise. In Thomas's novel Alice too cites a riddle in her daughter's book: 'Q. What does a Baby Ghost call his parents?' The reply is 'Dead and Mummy' (p. 240). On a more general level, both are novels about marriage disintegration, human relations, and how women cope with solitude and parental responsibility. In addition, the opting of Atwood's Lesje (said to be a variation on the name Alice) for creative birth, instead of a life lived in the past of either fantasy or museum relics, finds its echo in Thomas's novel, for 'intertidal life' is indeed, in a very real sense, 'life before man' and also life after man.

In other words, this is a highly 'literary' or metafictional novel, and not only because its protagonist is a writer. Its very verbal fabric is made up from the texts of the past. To give other examples: it seems that George Bowering's *Burning Water*, with its metafictive concern for writing and exploring (and for the historical George Vancouver), is always in the background, if only ironically at times; Malcolm Lowry too is directly cited (p. 213). But it is not just references to British Columbia that point to the specifically Canadian literary context. For instance, the trunk label 'NOT WANTED ON VOYAGE' (p. 277) may well be an accidental nod to Timothy Findley's novel of that name, but the references both to the biblical Book of Daniel's 'MENE, MENE, TEKEL, UPHARSIN' (p. 118) and to the Duke and

Duchess of Windsor (p. 157) do suggest (through additional shared themes of judgement, abdication of responsibility, and divorce) a connection with Findley's *Famous Last Words*, yet another Canadian novel about the writer as witness.

There are many more direct references in this novel to other works of literature. Some of these are to books *about* women (*Justine* [pp. 172, 242], *Women in Love* [pp. 198], and the repeated line from Tolstoy [e.g., p. 276] to the effect that happy women have no histories) or by women (Radclyffe Hall's *Well of Loneliness* [p. 168] and Woolf's *A Room of One's Own* [p. 238]). It is noteworthy that Alice always writes on the kitchen table, for she never does get that desired 'room of her own'. Other intertextual echoes are similarly directly related to the novel's central themes. The most obvious configuration of echoes centres around the figure of the drowning woman: the adulteress of myth (p. 5), 'Drowned Ophelia horizontal underneath' (p. 273), Virginia Woolf (p. 243). As in *The Waste Land*, water is an ambivalent image here: it is both the (female) source of life (intertidal too) and purification, and also the cause of death. Fittingly, Alice sees herself at the end of the novel as a version of Ophelia, being wheeled into the operating room, a 'horizontal woman' (p. 280).

And the ending of the novel is similarly ambivalent. The positive reading of the epigraph to the last section that I offered earlier could also be inverted and seen as a negative, as a surrender to the currents of danger and death: 'We put out our oars, endeavouring with them to counteract the current, but alas the efforts of the sailors were in vain' (p. 245). Although her garden has flourished after years of care, and although her daughters flourish as well (one is, after all, called Flora), Alice does not feel that her life is in order as she faces her surgery. We are left to ask if the novel about creation and birth ends, in fact, with death. Certainly the echoes of *To the Lighthouse* are ominous: Flora and Peter in the rowboat suggest Woolf's James and Mr Ramsay finally rowing to the lighthouse— *after* the death of Mrs Ramsay. But we should probably also recall that the final words of Woolf's novel are those of the female artist-figure, as indeed they are here. Lily Briscoe, like Audrey Thomas and Virginia Woolf, finishes her work of art as the novel that we are reading ends, and she does so with the words 'I have had my vision'. So too have we.

This kind of extensive intertextual recalling of other literary texts—especially those by and about women—works to undercut those humanist 'universal' notions of originality and uniqueness. In novels like *Intertidal Life* community (literary and social) and an interest in open process are made to replace individualism and the concern for closed, finished products. To use Edward Said's terms to describe intertextuality, writing today is no longer to be seen as a single and unique inscribing. That image of writing gives way now to one of parallel script.[18] Another example of this same kind of acknowledgement of a community of discourses that would radically condition any notion of originality is to be found in Susan Swan's more overtly parodic novel about an actual Canadian giantess, *The Biggest Modern Woman of the World*. Here there are clear and obvious references within the text to famous literary giants—from Rabelais's Gargantua and Pantagruel to Swift's Gulliver. Even the political allegory of the novel is intertextually derived, this time from Haliburton's Sam Slick tales. But here, in a very postmodern conjunction, national differences and politics cannot be separated from sexual differences and politics. As a Canadian Anna Swan writes to her mother after her marriage to an American:

> I feel I am acting out America's relationship to the Canadas. Martin is the imperial ogre while I play the role of genteel mate who believes that if everyone is well-mannered, we can inhabit a peaceable kingdom. That is the national dream of the Canadas, isn't it? A civilized garden where lions lie down with doves. I did not see the difference until I married Martin. We possess no fantasies of conquest and domination. Indeed, to be from the Canadas is to feel as women feel—cut off from the base of power.[19]

This historically real giantess manages to become a paradoxically ex-centric Everywoman figure, and it is the parodic intertexts that make this possible. Anna's power over nature, for example, is manifest early in her life and in the novel: 'The month of my birth, Poppa's little plot burst forth with mammoth love-apples, squash as big as wagon wheels, zucchinis as long and as fat as men's thighs, and potatoes the size of faces' (p. 9). This power over growth and fertility is sadly ironic, for neither of Anna's children survives its birthing. The intertextual reference here is to García Márquez's Petra Cotes, the lover of Aureliano Segundo in *One Hundred Years of Solitude*. Though their union too remains childless, nature responds to their passion and lust for life, food, and each other: Petra Cotes's animals multiply at an amazing rate.

Yet another scene recalls, perhaps, Richardson's *Pamela*, not to say Fielding's parody of it in *Shamela*. On her honeymoon Anna writes: 'I sit writing in my diary before the dressing table. . . . Martin moves closer and insinuates his frame between myself and the lamplight' (p. 208). She goes on: 'In the glow from the wall candle, I can see Martin's face moving closer to mine. . . . I look up; I will speak to Martin whose black hair is lit like a dark halo around a planet. . . . My lips part slowly: I will speak against the blue light from his eye pouring into my interior.' The naked man, the sexual titillation, her act of continuing to describe the scene *as she writes* as well as experiences it, all these parodically recall Fielding's already parodic fun with both Pamela's modesty and her continuous writing.

There is another important intertexual echo in this novel, and to another Canadian work: Atwood's *The Edible Woman*. There, as the protagonist becomes engaged to be married, the narration's point of view changes from first- to third-person as a way of signalling her loss of voice and of sense of self. Similarly, Anna Swan contracts laryngitis at the very moment that Martin announces their engagement. She then has to turn to writing to communicate.[20] Her loss of voice continues through to the marriage ceremony itself, though no one but herself seems to notice. Anna bitterly notes in parentheses: '(Perhaps the wedding ceremony is designed for women like me who are too shocked to comment on the upheaval of their lives)' (p. 204).

This sort of intertextual echoing has several functions, one of which, as we have seen, is to contest the post-romantic notion of uniqueness or originality and single meaning. At times it can also operate more directly in terms of parody—marking the ironic difference at the very heart of intertextual repetition. Of course, forms of parody today can vary in intended response from the angrily mocking[21] to the playful and even the respectful. But in all cases, because of its ironic double-voicing, parody allows women novelists an alternative to silent rejection of male 'universals': they can address their culture directly, without risking co-option by its values. Parody can also be a weapon against marginalization: it literally works to incorporate that upon which it ironically comments. It can be simultaneously both inside and outside the dominant discourses whose critique it embodies. But in that respect it is very postmodernly paradoxical: both complicitous and contesting.

Marian Engel, to offer a concrete example, presents an ironic parody of the picaresque novel form in her novel *Lunatic Villas*. The traditional male rogue figure, travelling—footloose and fancy-free—on the road, is parodically inverted here to become the woman into whose house and life various rogues enter. Like Thomas's female explorer, this woman cannot, in fact, live 'on the road', however much she might yearn for such freedom, since she cannot ever escape her children and her financial responsibilities. But the most self-conscious and extended parody of the pícaro as male adventurer is in Aritha Van Herk's feminist playing with the same conventions in her postmodern version of the western in *No Fixed Address: An Amorous Journey*.[22]

This book is the novelistic expansion of an earlier essay she wrote urging women to cast off passivity, to reject being 'fixed as mothers/saints/whores, muses all'.[23] The essay, 'Women Writers and the Prairie: Spies in an Indifferent Landscape', opens with: 'Face it. The west is male. Masculine. Manly. Virile.' As landscape the west is horizontal, straight; it is not curved. Or is it? Since the 'impact of landscape on artist or artist on landscape is unavoidable' (p. 15), as a women writer she actually begins to see undulations in the prairie: 'We can get into it, enter this world, because it belongs to us' (p. 18). But, she adds, this must be done stealthily, in disguise: 'Keep low, stay down' (p. 19). Women enter in disguise, but in the flesh: 'We are beginning to dot this landscape but we can't be seen. Refusing to be silhouettes, we enter the fiction of the prairies' (p. 19), following in the footsteps of the foremothers—Nellie McClung, Martha Ostenso, Margaret Laurence, Sharon Pollock, Betty Lambert, Sharon Riis. Van Herk, however, uses parody and satire rather more than these other writers have in order to define a female position in this male world.

One reason may be that there is an important postmodern and male intertext to both her essay and her novel: Robert Kroetsch's 'The Fear of Women in Prairie Fiction: *An Erotics of Space*'.[24] In this essay Kroetsch designates external space as male, internal as female. It is the latter that men fear, for women 'contain the space' and 'speak the silence' (p. 49). He sets up the basic 'grammatical pair' of the story-line of prairie fiction:

house/horse—or female/male, or stasis/motion. Women stay *in* houses; men move *on* horses. In *No Fixed Address* Van Herk offers an alternative to Kroetsch's dialectic resolution of horse/house as the 'whore's house' in her image of the 1959 black Mercedes driven by her heroine—she lives *in* it and also moves along the roads of the west. Kroetsch argues that the prairie novel's obsession with travel is an evasion of the sexual, a substitute: travel is 'the true intercourse' (p. 53). Van Herk's heroine manages to use travel not to evade, but to provoke the sexual. For this is the female version not only of the male rogue picaro, but of the travelling salesman—the cliché of dirty jokes. With the unlikely name of Arachne Manteia, her picaresque rogue travels to the small towns of Alberta and Saskatchewan selling ladies' underwear!

By giving her protagonist this name, of course, Van Herk prepares her readers for parodic possibilities from the start. Manteia suggests the predatory female mantis, and there are moments when Arachne is with her 'road jockeys' that confirm this association. But it is obviously her first name that is the most loaded. In the Greek myth, you will recall, Arachne was the mortal woman who challenged Athena to a trial of skill in weaving. In Van Herk's version Arachne and Thena are friends and their trials of skill come in their metafictive weaving of tales.[25] In the myth Arachne is punished for her presumption (and this is one way of reading the ending of this novel too), and hangs herself. She is then turned into a spider, thereby giving her name to the *arachnid*. In *No Fixed Address* this naming process is reversed: it is the spider that gives Arachne her name. The appropriately named Gabriel announces the name (if not the fact) of the child about to be born. He points to a spider on the window. It is injured but 'that did not hinder her design or ambition' (p. 82). He names it (arachnid) and then adds prophetically and parodically, 'Spiders are rogues.' Simultaneously Arachne's pregnant mother tries to ignore 'the elbows and knees of her kicking baby' (p. 83)—the rogue-to-be, Arachne. Later the maps and roads that the grown Arachne will love so much are constantly referred to in the novel as 'spidery' webs. And, I might add, her lover, Thomas Telfer, who makes the maps, recalls in his name the famous Scottish civil engineer and road builder Thomas Telford.

Names alone, then, set up an intertextual frame of reference.

In addition, there are at least three levels of generic parody operating in this novel. The first is the women's travel tale, of which Canada boasts a long history. But this woman does not explore the west because her spouse went there; she travels alone. She is no outsider, even if she is from BC, so there is none of the (often unconscious) ethnocentric bias that comes from looking at the Canadian west from outside. She is also not a wealthy adventurer; travelling is her job. In other words, Arachne's travels both echo and parodically invert the tradition of women's travels—and the writing about them. Here there is a deliberate adoption of a kind of protest against the freedom from social convention allowed to *male* questers: the sexual mores of Arachne-on-the-road resemble the stereotype of male erotic adventure, not female.

The second level of generic parody is that of the western, linked together with the 'novel of the land'. Arachne and her Mercedes can be interpreted as a parody of the cowboy and his horse as much as of Don Quijote and Rocinante. Her relation to the land she travels is not that of the male tradition of mastering and controlling nature, perhaps most obviously because the male tradition had usually seen the land as gendered female.[26] Maps in this novel, unlike those in Hodgins' *The Invention of the World* and Atwood's *The Journals of Susanna Moodie*, are more ambivalent than negative images: they may be human impositions on the patterns of nature, but they also enable travel—for women as well as men.

But the major parody that structures this novel is that of the picaresque genre and the picaro as hero. There did exist, in the original Renaissance Spanish tradition, a female *pícara*, a non-heroic, nonidealized female protagonist. In works like *La pícara Justina*, the male conventions were altered essentially for social reasons: things male heroes did were forbidden to women (leaving home to seek their fortune on the road; joining the army, etc.). Traditionally, in the pícaro's tale, women played limited and traditional roles: wife, lover, mistress, mother. As one critic puts it:

> The male protagonist plays out a drama of tensions between freedom and entrapment, responsibility and determinism, high aspirations and sordid accommodations. It is difficult to see how a pícara could have faced similar tensions without exposing the

unexposable, the traditionally venerated roles of womanhood, wife and mother.[27]

It took a feminist and postmodern world to allow that exposition, and Arachne Manteia is one possible articulation of it. When her sexually liberated behaviour is translated back into seventeenth-century terms, it is revealingly presented as prostitution. The pícara's life was totally determined by her gender: 'Endowed by her sex with one commercially valuable resource denied to her male counterpart, it is obvious that the unfortunate girl early must have become involved in some degree of prostitution.'[28] The pícara was granted a certain earthy pleasure in her sexual activities, but the final lesson was usually that her deplorable moral condition was the result of social helplessness, not promiscuity. Arachne, however, just enjoys sex. Though devoted to Thomas, her 'Apocryphal lover', while living at home, on the road she seeks out 'undemanding men'—the 'road jockeys' who to her are 'just bodies, you could put a paper bag over their heads' (p. 33). The male sexist cliché here underlines Van Herk's feminist inversion of both seventeenth-century and contemporary conventions. Arachne is almost aggressively sexual: 'I get this itch' (p. 174).

It is less the relatively minor figure of the female pícara[29] that Van Herk takes on here than the dominant male pícaro. The opening of a scholarly work on this topic ironically points to her major focus of attack: 'In considering the pícaro as both human being and literary genre, one must describe not only what *he* was, but also what *he* was not.'[30] Although the author does not intend it, his use of the gender-marked pronoun says it all, in a way: the first thing 'he' is not is a woman. The history of the picaresque genre from Renaissance Spain through eighteenth-century England, France, and Germany is generally agreed upon, as is its definition, and in all cases it involves a *hero*. A good summary of the conventions of the form (which shows what Van Herk had to work with to open up formerly unheard-of feminine possibilities) is that of Richard Bjornson:

> [The story] involves a rootless, unattached individual who must secure his own survival and psychological well-being in a society which openly espouses traditional ideals, while actually sanctioning the most dehumanizing modes of behavior. Characterized by an ambiguous or non-existent link with his father, this outsider

(or 'half-outsider') inherits no place which can be considered a home, no trade by means of which he can sustain himself, and no social position to provide him with well-defined relationships to other people. Prematurely made responsible for his own welfare, he usually undergoes a rude awakening (or initiation) which shocks him into an awareness of what he must do in order to survive. Because he lacks the strength and absolute integrity to impose his will upon a hostile world, he adapts himself to diverse situations by serving different masters, inventing clever ruses, or wearing a variety of masks during a peripatetic life of alternating good and evil fortune.[31]

If you change the 'he' into 'she', you almost have the plot of *No Fixed Address*, but that change is crucial, and the literary, social and ideological reverberations echo beyond the novel's covers.

The fact that this is a picaresque novel is overtly signalled from the start. The first two-page section of the novel ends with: 'No art, no novel, no catalogue of infamy has considered the effect of underwear on the lives of *petty rogues*' (p. 10, emphasis mine). And thus begins the story of Arachne, the travelling underwear saleswoman who refuses to wear underwear. To be on the road has been legitimized into a job, but, like the male pícaro, Arachne 'travels light' (p. 13). She too has a history of petty crime (theft, etc.) and ambiguous origins. In fact, she knows who her parents are, but for a long time refuses to believe it: 'She isn't convinced that she has a mother' (p. 38) and finds her links to that woman 'tenuous and unproven.' She was an unwanted child, who often ran away, and grew up without any hovering parental presence. Solitary, she grows up tough because, like the pícaro, she had to, in order to survive. There are times she wishes she were a man, especially when she becomes a bus driver. But Arachne loves to drive, to move, for it convinces her that 'her life is not static and fuzzy' (p. 68); it gives her the 'illusion that she is going somewhere, getting away' (p. 68).

Sharing what we now call working-class origins with the male pícaro, Arachne grows up 'concerned with survival and protection', obsessed with her 'hunger: to be fed, clothed, loved, to possess this thing or that' (p. 76). She feels like an imposter in the 'respectable world' of Thomas's family where people talk of 'relationship, lifestyle, recreation, career, situation' instead of using her more familiar words: 'shacked up, life, fun, job, mess'

(p. 119). Like the pícaro, Arachne wears many masks, but her 'natural inclination to dissemble' (p. 141) is, we are told, not that of an actress, but of a criminal or double agent. On one level Arachne is a straightforward female version of the traditionally male pícaro: 'she knew, the only way to get anything was to go after it herself' (p. 177). But there are parodic inversions too: she always comes home to her 'salvation'—Thomas, his house, his maps; her travels are her job and she is very successful. The traditional pícaro may need the stability of the social order against which to play off his disruptive tendencies, but Arachne is a little more implicated in that social order. However, at the point in the narrative when she literally is on the run (from the police), the comic picaresque tone changes to a darker, more menacing one. While she does glory in her 'nostalgia for disorder and unwholesomeness, the satisfaction of a tattered life with no obligations or rewards', she also meets a male rogue (Dougall McKay) who tricks her out of her (tricked) money. Her revenge upon him signals perhaps the death of the picaresque in the novel. The tale ends ambiguously: the Arachne we read of may be alive or dead, 'real' or the fantasy of the narrating researcher, who announces, 'She has been back to Vancouver and died there, one of her lives certainly over' (p. 301). In the end, the narrator follows Arachne's trail of panties to beyond where the mapped road ends in northwestern Canada: 'Her life has become movement without end' (p. 304). Perhaps women cannot quite live the pícaro's life, even today. Or can they?

This ending raises questions about the form of picaresque narration as well as its characteristic protagonist. The picaresque has been defined as 'a fictional work that contains a narrative structure in which the protagonist, who is usually the narrator, passes through a variety of social milieus that, together with the cumulative (rather than in-depth) treatment of those experiences, provides an opportunity for social and philosophical criticism, as well as for psychological portraits'.[32] It is easy to see that, with the third-person narrating figure following Arachne's trail and clearly identifying with her quarry at the end, the narrative of No Fixed Address is a variant on this structure.[33]

By this definition the picaresque, in fact, has much in common with the postmodern. The socio-economic and politico-historical contexts are central to both. The poverty of the conventional pícaro is matched here by Arachne's situation. Her working-class origins are underlined as a major cause of her vulnerability and her toughness. Her encounter with the concert pianist puts a new edge on her dissatisfaction. She asks herself: 'Ambition? To better herself, to culture herself? What good would it do? She only knows that she has stepped perilously close to another knowledge. And that is dangerous' (p. 74). She thinks in terms of gender-defined roles because in her experience it is men who embody this world she both envies and rejects. She thinks she can never become 'middle-class, respectable, a wife, a mother, a keeper of clean tea towels and hot casseroles' (p. 77) and she is right. True to herself, she never does ('With her inclinations? With her background?'), though she does compromise to some extent. To ur-middle-class Thomas, however, this is her attraction: she is 'wild and natural', 'one of those who keep their skin as substitute for fur' (p. 101). It takes Arachne a long time to trust his love for a woman who speaks ungrammatically, who 'does not mind dirt under her fingernails' and who 'does not feel that deodorant is necessary every day' (p. 98). Thomas, of course, also inverts gender conventions: he is cook, cleaner, and literally home-maker. But she responds to his parents' world (which she calls 'the aristocracy') as would a true pícaro, for it makes her feel like 'a swarthy peasant without stockings or shoes, dressed in cast-offs, unable to manage the simplest tools, unwashed, illiterate, unsocialized' (p. 131).

Arachne as female pícaro is also very much the postmodern ex-centric: the solitary, neglected child who gathers around her all the other 'misfits and discards': 'fat and squeaky, cross-eyed and retarded' (p. 191). She consistently takes jobs that are not traditional for her sex: as a bus driver or a travelling salesperson. Her behaviour—sexual and social—breaks the rules of society's game. That game's sexism and classism define ex-centricity here. So too does ageism: her friend Josef's ninety years have made him an ex-centric in both his family and his society. His ethnic background as a Serb, first in Europe and then in Canada, is offered as analogous to the 'bitter displacement' (p. 228) Arachne feels as a working-class woman.

There are also connections on the level of literary history between the postmodern and the picaresque. The latter has been seen as a realist reaction against a false—that is, idealized— literature: chivalric romance, epic, pastoral. The postmodern is, in many ways, a critical response to that realist reaction.[34] And many of its parodic, satiric, or just generally ironic impulses derive from this need to respond to what has come to be the dominant definition of the novel as a literary form: realism. Of course, there are philosophical and ideological interrelations between the postmodern and the picaresque too. If, as Robert Alter argues, the picaresque that was born in the Renaissance shares its period's 'characteristic expression of a vigorously active individualism in a rugged, competitive world',[35] then the postmodern is what parodically challenges such notions of individualism and its relation to the rugged, competitive world of late-capitalist society: this postmodern pícaro has a job and is good at it!

The use and abuse of conventions, the complicity and the critique, that is signalled by irony in postmodernist texts has its parallel in the picaresque 'middle ground' between 'the confidence of faith and the skepticism of irony'.[36] In fact, the picaresque's embodiment of paradoxes like this makes it a form that is inherently attractive to postmodernism: the pícaro has been called the image of both human solitude in the world and human solidarity with the world. 'He' is said to rely only on himself and yet is parasitic and, at times, generous to others. 'He' contests the social system, refusing to let it pin him down, yet accepts willingly a position of subservience within it.[37] All of this can also be applied to the female postmodern protagonist of *No Fixed Address*.

In formal, structural terms, this novel also follows and yet ironizes many of the conventions of the picaresque narrative.[38] The self-reflexivity of *Don Quijote* is reflected in the italicized sections called 'Notebook on a Missing Person'. But it is also embedded in the novel in the form of *mises en abyme* or structural metaphors.[39] The novel opens with one of these: the notion of the hidden but supporting reality that shapes the body—of woman and of fiction. The underwear Arachne sells is directly related to the shape of women's bodies: 'the final appearance of the outer costume was inevitably controlled by a supporting apparatus beneath' (p. 9). The novel's 'supporting apparatus' that controls its shape and 'final appearance' consists of all those intertexts, from myth to the picaresque. Like that of the novel, the shape of woman has changed over the years, altering with fashion that is determined according to 'a standard inevitably decided by men' (p. 9). Just as postmodernism and feminism have revealed the maleness of 'universal' standards of both literary conventions and norms of representation, so this novel takes on the clothing conventions of the female body.

This body forms the link to another major structuring metaphor in the novel. Thomas is a cartographer who, when he makes love to Arachne, is said to map her body as he does the land (p. 199) and whose very presence gives her 'an ultimate map' home (p. 173). Looking down on the land from a balloon, Arachne 'thinks of travelling, spidering her own map over the intricate roads of her world' (p. 223). It is a commonplace of metafiction to use maps that record roads as images of linear narrative. Here Van Herk both exploits this double linearity and subverts it. The constant, epic, linear listing of the towns (e.g. 'Acme, Carbon, Twining, Linden, Stalwell, Sunnyslope and Allingham' [p. 106]) through which Arachne travels (and which the realist reader can find on the map) is interrupted constantly by either desire or memory, as sexual episodes or flashbacks to her childhood break up the narrative line. Even maps provoke these temporal/spatial breaks: the old maps that Thomas collects appeal to her because they 'could lead you into the past so easily, lead you through history to another frame of time' (p. 117)— as indeed occurs at the end of the novel.

Thomas's maps also are what teach Arachne that freedom is on the road, quite literally. He maps the roads; she drives them. His is the product; hers is the process. He says to her: 'I put it all on paper. Think of me next time you use a road map' (p. 92). Like the writer, the cartographer turns process into product, but with few of the negative connotations we shall find in Atwood's work: here maps are 'images that trace out hope, mapping an act of faith, a way of saying, I have been here, someone will follow, so I must leave a guide' (p. 118). Novels and maps are guides. Like the writer, the cartographer makes possible the renewal of process: reading is the analogue of travelling. The language of the novel makes the metafictive level overt: 'He is the author of those maps but he has never known their ultimate affirmation, the consummation of the pact between traveler and traveled. He only draws them' (p. 164). The reader's surrogate in the novel is, in some ways, Thena, to whom Arachne tells all—'Every adventuress requires a teller of her tale' (p. 146), but also a listener: 'For what is a traveler without a confidante? It is impossible to fictionalize a life without someone to oversee the journey' (p. 154). Readers are overseers and confidantes; reading is vicarious adventure. In Robert Kroetsch's terms, 'geography is also part of text in a strange way and I think geography is not fixed, it's changing— every journey across it or through it is another reading in a way.'[40] We read both maps and books, after all.

This novel is postmodern in form not only because of its *mises en abyme*, however. The narrative address, stressing as it does from the first its *énonciation*, in a manner rare in the third-person convention, is typically postmodern. The first of the sections labelled 'Notebook on a missing person' opens the novel with: '*You* discover in the course of your research that the fashionable woman's shape has always been a state of constant change. *We* have come to be what we are after years of changes in cut and color' (p. 9, emphasis mine). The self-referring second-person address here also, inevitably, is inclusive: readers are implicated too, by grammar if nothing else. The first-person plural 'we' furthers that inclusion and en-genders it female: 'we' women have come to be what we are. . . . The narrator continues this collusion with her readers, often at Arachne's expense: 'She does not think of [her Mercedes] as a post-Hitler car, as a car built in Stuttgart—she has never heard of Stuttgart—' (p. 48). Several other times in the novel (pp. 51, 70), the narrator makes this kind of remark to us as readers, underlining Arachne's limitations. As narrator she also allows us to see events from several points of view: the stubborn stand-off between Josef and Arachne at the graveyard is presented through both sets of eyes.

This explicitly fictionalizing narrator comes up against realist conventions, however. The narrator suggests that Arachne is 'real' and that in researching her 'real story' she must find eye-witnesses: 'You try to get the next part of Arachne's adventures from Thena. . . . At first she's reluctant to talk. . . . But you are persistent' (p. 237) and convince her that 'you are the keeper of history'. Believing Arachne to be dead (as reported in the newspaper), the narrator is shocked to find that Thena thinks she is still alive: 'The story's not over yet' (p. 240)—and indeed, sixty pages of the story still remain for us to read! The 'you' of the final section of the novel, as the narrator identifies with (and follows the trail of) Arachne, becomes the most inclusive pronoun possible: it includes the narrator, the reader, and the protagonist.

Postmodern fiction often aims, as does feminist fiction, at a particular audience. Ishmael Reed's *The Terrible Twos* offers a black narrator addressing a male, white, middle-class reader— thereby making explicit the particularities that have been generalized into 'universals'. Daphne Marlatt's *Touch to My Tongue* overtly excludes the male and perhaps even the heterosexual female reader. This kind of particular address foregrounds and at the same time debunks the humanist notion of art's 'universal' accessibility to the 'common reader'. Postmodernist fiction is not really any more democratic or accessible than earlier modernist fiction;[41] it is just as contrived, manipulative—élitist, if you like— but it acknowledges this in its self-situating limitations of address.

The picaresque is by no means the only form of feminist or postmodernist challenge to male 'universal' conventions and their ideological implications. An interesting domestication of the traditionally male wilderness novel occurs in Canadian women writers' work in the form of the cabin or cottage novel:[42] *Abra, Bear, Surfacing, The Diviners, Intertidal Life*. Susanna Moodie's experience in the bush is one of the major literary forebears of the lives of these women characters as they cope with the wilderness that is both outside and inside them—that both of physical nature and of their human/sexual nature as women and, often, creatrix-figures as well.

In the next chapter we shall see that parody can also be used to subvert élitist or high-brow concepts of what constitutes 'serious' literature, sometimes with an eye to revitalization by contact with the energy of popular art forms.[43] Timothy Findley's *The Telling of Lies* uses and abuses the traditional mystery novel form, and Margaret Atwood's parodic incorporation into *Lady Oracle* of the structures and conventions of both the 'costume gothic', or popular romance, and modernist hermetic verse can also be seen to work to democratize the class-inspired hierarchies of an earlier time.[44] In this case, as in *No Fixed Address*, parody becomes the formal mode of voicing a social and cultural critique of the destinies of women: as authors, as characters (in the narratives of life and art), and as readers.

These ultimately political strategies do not appear only on the level of form, of course. In terms of content, many thematic lacunae in our literary experience are now being filled. Thanks to the work of Alice Munro, Gail Scott, Margaret Laurence, Sylvia Fraser, and others, we are finally learning what it feels like, for instance, to be *female* and growing up in repressive small-town Canada. The traditional *Bildungsroman* takes on different forms and emphases when its subject is female. In novels like *Lives of Girls and Women, The Diviners,* and *Pandora* we can see examples of what feminist critics have described as major reworkings of the 'universals' of the (male) novel of development: 'Novels that depict female apprenticeship and awakening not only alter the developmental process, but also frequently change its position in the text. The tensions that shape female development may lead to a disjunction between a surface plot, which affirms social conventions, and a submerged plot, which encodes rebellion.'[45]

In other words, while critical feminisms have been pushing contemporary literary theory in directions it could not and would not have taken, so fiction by postmodern women writers in Canada, as elsewhere, has actually wrought major changes on the novel genre, on its traditional forms as well as its themes. Through intertextuality and parody they have particularized and situated the 'universals' of liberal humanism, not by rejection of (male) literary and cultural history, but by foregrounding its power and dominance in and by ironic challenges to its universalist pretensions. These 'shape shifters' have managed to do this as well without suffering from what one of Susan Swan's Canadian giants called 'emblem fatigue': 'an affliction peculiar to giants [and women, we might add], who are always having to shoulder giant expectations from normal folk' (p. 139).

Notes

[1] For a study of the problems of native and ethnic women, see section II ('Writing Against Double Colonization') in *In the Feminine: Women and Words/Les Femmes et les mots* (Conference Proceedings 1983), ed. Ann Dybikowski, Victoria Freeman, Daphne Marlatt, Barbara Pulling, Betsy Warland (Edmonton: Longspoon Press, 1983), pp. 53-74.

[2] Maria Campbell, *Halfbreed* (Halifax: Goodread Biographies, 1973), p. 2.

[3] Marjorie Perloff, *The Dance of the Intellect: Studies in the Poetry of the Pound Tradition* (Cambridge: Cambridge University Press, 1985), p. 161. Perloff's focus is American postmodern narrative poetry, but her point

is valid not only for the Canadian long poem, but for much Canadian postmodern prose fiction.

4 See Smaro Kamboureli, 'Dialogue with the Other: The Use of Myth in Canadian Women's Poetry' (in *In the Feminine*, pp. 105-9), on how women poets deform and demythologize myths and stereotypes of the feminine that act as 'paradigmatic models for reality' through a variety of deconstructive and dialogic strategies—of which parody is one.

5 For example, from the same volume, on poetry see Daphne Marlatt's 'musing with mothertongue', pp. 171-4; on short fiction see Gail Scott's 'Shaping a Vehicle for Her Use: Women and the Short Story', pp. 184-92; on drama see Pol Pelletier's 'Myth and Women's Theatre', pp. 110-13 and Solange Collin, 'An Alternative to the Traditional Theatre in Québec', pp. 219-23.

6 See Carolyn Hlus, 'Writing Womanly: Theory and Practice', in *A Mazing Space: Writing Canadian / Women Writing* (Edmonton: Longspoon/NeWest Press, 1986), pp. 295-7.

7 Smaro Kamboureli, 'The Body as Audience and Performance in the Writing of Alice Munro', in *A Mazing Space*, pp. 31-2.

8 See Jennifer Waelti-Walters, 'When Caryatids Move: Bersianik's View of Culture', in *A Mazing Space*, pp. 299-302; and, in the same volume, both Shirley Neuman's 'Importing Difference', p. 396 and Janet M. Paterson's 'A Poetics of Transformation: Yolande Villemaire's *La Vie en prose*', pp. 315-23.

9 Nancy K. Miller, 'Emphasis Added: Plots and Plausibilities in Women's Fiction', *PMLA* 96, 1 (1981), p. 38.

10 In Donna Bennett's terms (in 'Naming the Way Home', in *A Mazing Space*, p. 242): a 'feminine logic of structuring' might 'eliminate boundaries between such categories as form and content, or signified and signifier, without destroying the categories themselves. In other words, feminine writing would not be restricted by pre-existing concepts such as 'genres' and 'conventions', but would be able to absorb these concepts and transform, redefine or replace them.' Parody is one way to do this, but it also acknowledges, even as it challenges, the power of boundaries, of genres and conventions.

11 See Linda Hutcheon, *A Theory of Parody: The Teachings of Twentieth-Century Art Forms* (London and New York: Methuen, 1985).

12 For a fictional account of the sexism that was also part of the radical left politics of the sixties, see Gail Scott's *Heroine* (Toronto: Coach House Press, 1987).

13 Audrey Thomas, *Intertidal Life* (Toronto: Stoddart, 1984), p. 97. All further references will appear in parentheses in the text.

14 Another novel that links an island and women in terms of female collectivity and harmony with nature is Nicole Brossard's *Picture Theory* (Montréal: Nouvelle Optique, 1982).

[15] See, for example, Jane Gallop, *The Daughter's Seduction: Feminism and Psychoanalysis* (Ithaca: Cornell University Press, 1982); Kaja Silverman, *The Subject of Semiotics* (New York: Oxford University Press, 1983); Teresa de Lauretis, *Alice Doesn't: Feminism, Semiotics, Cinema* (Bloomington: Indiana University Press, 1984).

[16] Through creative birthing, Alice also turns out to be connected to her cat, Tabby, by more than an overt reference to the Cheshire Cat (p. 123). Appropriately, they are linked in the text itself by the sexual play on the word 'pussy' (p. 32). Similarly, both are always associated with their offspring: Alice walks 'mother-catlike' (p. 119) to her room at night. It is as both novelist and mother that Alice knows the pains and pleasures of birth. Like Tabby, she has had her children alone (pp. 13, 250-2); so too she must write alone.

[17] In Québécois feminist writing it has been argued that the major sources of parodic intertextuality are specifically the texts of women writers. See Louise Dupré, 'From Experimentation to Experience: Québécois Modernity in the Feminine', in *A Mazing Space*, p. 357: 'The awareness of their collective alienation is making women writers feel the desire for a language common to all women. A meaningful intertextuality of dedications, quotations and references is emerging by means of which women writers name, greet, stimulate, re-read and interpret one another. They are inspiring one another and seeking to establish a kinship which History will be unable to forget.'

[18] Edward Said, *The World, the Text, and the Critic* (Cambridge, Mass.: Harvard University Press, 1983), p. 139.

[19] Susan Swan, *The Biggest Modern Woman of the World* (Toronto: Lester & Orpen Dennys, 1983), pp. 273-4. All further references will appear in parentheses in the text.

[20] Another way of reading this reversal is that, as she enters a male realm of control, she must give up a female mode of expression (oral) for a male one (written). See Chapter 3 above.

[21] A good example of the angry extreme would be Betty Lambert's *Crossings*, which Aritha Van Herk describes as being written in a style 'that refuses to be elevated or dignified' and is 'an ultimate violation of the epic of male'. See her 'Double Crossings: Booking the Lover', in *A Mazing Space*, p. 277.

[22] Aritha Van Herk, *No Fixed Address: An Amorous Journey* (Toronto: McClelland and Stewart, 1986). All further references will appear in parentheses in the text.

[23] 'Women Writers and the Prairie: Spies in an Indifferent Landscape', *Kunapipi* 6, 2 (1984), p. 18. All further references will appear in parentheses in the text.

[24] In *Open Letter* 5th series, no. 4 (1983), *Robert Kroetsch: Essays*, pp. 47-55. All page references will appear in parentheses in the text.

25 Nancy Miller has, in fact, called women's writing 'arachnologies' in her talk 'Arachnologies: The Woman, the Text, and the Critic', University of Toronto, 20 March 1985.

26 See Annette Kolodny, *The Lay of the Land: Metaphor as Experience and History in American Life and Letters* (Chapel Hill: University of North Carolina Press, 1975).

27 Peter N. Dunn, 'The Picara: The Rogue Female', in *Upstarts, Wanderers or Swindlers: Anatomy of the Picaro*, eds. Gustavo Pellon and Julio Rodriguez-Luis (Amsterdam: Rodopi, 1986), pp. 245-6.

28 Frederick Monteser, *The Picaresque Element in Western Literature* (Alabama: University of Alabama Press, 1975), p. 4.

29 In 'Picaros and Priestesses: Repentant Rogues', *Humanities Association of Canada Newsletter*, 3, 1 (1984), Van Herk says the pícara never interested her: Moll Flanders and Fanny Hill always seemed 'incomplete and repentant, as well as being at the mercy of their very femaleness' (16). Her models for her completed and unrepentant rogue are more Mother Courage or Justine (16) or Kroetsch's Hazard Lepage (14).

30 Monteser, p. vii, emphasis mine.

31 Richard Bjornson, *The Picaresque Hero in European Fiction* (Madison: University of Wisconsin Press, 1977), p. 6.

32 Gustavo Pellon and Julio Rodriguez-Luis in their introduction to *Upstarts, Wanderers or Swindlers*, pp. 8-9.

33 In 'Picaros and Priestesses' Van Herk writes of her attraction to Huck Finn's 'lighting out for the territory at the end' (p. 14) and of the traditional ambiguity of the rogue's act of repentance at the end of his tale. She says there can be no story after repentance because authority is legitimated. Therefore we must assume the rogue to be unrepentant and the story must go on and on (p. 17), as it theoretically does here.

34 See Alison Lee, 'Realism Doesn't . . . ', Ph.D. dissertation, McMaster University, 1988.

35 Robert Alter, *Rogue's Progress: Studies in the Picaresque Novel* (Cambridge, Mass.: Harvard University Press, 1964), p. 79.

36 Ibid., p. 4.

37 Ibid., pp. 10-15.

38 Although there are many specific echoes of individual picaresque novels (such as *Don Quijote, Lazarillo de Tormes*, and the English tales of the pícaro/a, such as Smollett's Rodrick Random and Defoe's Moll Flanders), I shall limit myself here to more general generic parody.

39 Van Herk herself suggests that the picaresque in general may be a metafictive *mise en abyme* in 'Picaros and Priestesses': 'Like the picaro, the modern artist is both isolated from and imprisoned within society. She longs for an excuse to behave badly, to indulge her libido' (16).

The artist, then, is in a picaresque position, but 'cannot play the part' or rejoice in her rogueries. All she can do is become a 'priestess of bad behavior', proselytizing the picaresque condition (17).

[40] In Shirley Neuman and Robert Wilson, *Labyrinths of Voice: Conversations with Robert Kroetsch* (Edmonton: NeWest Press, 1982), p. 8.

[41] This is John Barth's argument in 'The Literature of Replenishment: Postmodernist Fiction', *Atlantic* January 1980, pp. 65-71.

[42] Heather Murray calls this the 'pseudo-wilderness' location that ironizes the continuum between city and wilderness. See her 'Women in the Wilderness', in *A Mazing Space*, p. 75.

[43] Such, of course, was Bakhtin's notion of the function of parody and 'popular-festive' folk forms in the medieval carnival, as we have seen in Chapter 2. See his *Rabelais and his World*, trans. Hélène Iswolsky (Cambridge, Mass.: MIT Press, 1968).

[44] See Raymond Williams, *Culture and Society* (New York: Doubleday, 1960), pp. 124-7; and Stuart Hall and Paddy Whannel, *The Popular Arts* (Boston: Beacon Press, 1964), p. 39.

[45] Elizabeth Abel, Marianne Hirsch, and Elizabeth Langland, *The Voyage In: Fictions of Female Development* (Hanover, NH: University Press of New Hampshire, 1983), p. 12.

Chapter 7

Process, Product, and Politics:
The Postmodernism of Margaret Atwood

We have seen that one of the major recurring motifs in Canadian postmodern fiction is the paradox of concern for dynamic process (reading, writing) being unavoidably articulated in the form of a static product (the thing read and written): examples can be found in the work of Cohen, Wiebe, Findley, Blaise, Ondaatje, Hodgins, and especially the women writers, such as Thomas, Van Herk, and Munro.[1] Atwood's fiction (and poetry, for that matter) is not only not the exception, but in some ways the epitome of this postmodern contradiction.[2] It is its ironic metafictional awareness of this paradox that distinguishes Atwood's postmodernism from any more familiar romantic concern for the creative imagination. Her novels are thematically and formally obsessed with the tension between art as kinetic process (its writing and, again, its reading) and the final result—'Art'—as inevitably a fixed and final product. And this tension remains unresolved. There is no dialectic or even real dichotomy, just postmodern paradox.[3] As I suggested in the last chapter and in Chapter 1 as well, Atwood's work is postmodern in yet other ways: for instance, in its use and abuse of traditional (male) literary conventions, including novelistic realism. Also, as someone 'formed' in the sixties Atwood is at ease with the political dimension of postmodernism, and always has been.[4] In the early seventies she was best known, perhaps, for her Canadian nationalism; then for her feminism. Of course, the two issues are not wholly distinct for Atwood: like Susan Swan, she herself has frequently compared the powerless status of Canada to that of women.

Yet often, in Atwood's public statements about her art, it is her formalism that is even more noticeable than her politics: 'What people fail to understand about poetry and novels and criticism is that they are hypothetical, and they are patterns of words and ideas.'[5] The traces of her academic literary training with Northrop Frye are visible here, but what has increasingly become evident in her work is her direct involvement with the cause of Amnesty International: her gender and national politics have been joined to a strong concern for human rights. Yet the metafictional interest in the unresolved paradox of art's definition in terms of the contradictions of fixity/flux or product/process is consistently the metaphoric ground in which this political dimension is rooted. Writing and ideology cannot be separated, no matter how formalist or self-conscious the writing. For Atwood, issues of power pervade both the product and the process of creation. Her dualities are always 'violent dualities':[6] the active creating of art is made possible only by and in the deadly fixing of life. Or, as she writes in *Power Politics*: 'Please die I said / so I can write about it.'[7] In her poetry, art-as-product is associated—as is love, significantly— with closed circle games (which include, but also exclude), with photographs, maps, roads, and fences, or with the acts of naming, labelling, and knowing. A negative view of culture is confronted by a positive one of nature; the sterile black and white of print stand judged by the fecund green of the natural world. Superficial and cold, mirrors and ice are opposed to images of flowing water or places deep underground; Christian sacrifice is measured against Amerindian redemption.[8] And all of this thematization of the opposition between product and process, as we also saw in earlier chapters, is doubly ironic: first, the binary opposition's very structure means that the one side needs the other for its very definition and can therefore never escape complicity; and, second, these contradictions (which thematically tend to give more value to process) are still self-consciously played out within the confines of the black and white of the printed product. Atwood's art cannot escape these ironies any more than can that of Wiebe or Findley. But this does not necessarily mean that her 'gorgon touch'[9] prevails; rather, it suggests that the *paradox* always remains. To look at it from the other direction, we may bring the text to life as we read, echoing therein the act of creation of the author, but the text itself still consists of static and dead black marks on a white page.

The fact that, like Kogawa, Cohen, Musgrave, and Ondaatje, Atwood is also a poet is important, and not only because, as George Woodcock puts it, she brings 'the poetic resources of metaphor and fantasy' to fiction.[10] Her short and powerful lyric poems have always continued to be written alongside her longer narrative pieces—almost as a kind of allegory of the tension between product and process that persists in her work. By this I mean that narrative could be seen as, by nature, a more kinetic and temporal form than the lyric; self-conscious metafictive narrative that foregrounds the act of writing and reading is even more potentially open to considerations of process. But even then, of course, the irony is that once again we come to understand that process only through the printed product. The other advantage of narrative as a form of investigation for a political writer like Atwood is that, while poetry is often seen as the place (in her own words) where 'language is renewed . . . where precision takes place',[11] the novel has traditionally been seen as a more powerful and appropriate vehicle for social and ideological critique, either in its positing of common assumptions between reader and writer or in its didactic desire to create that commonality. But if the novel is written as metafiction, this addition introduces a new tension between the outward-directed didactic/mimetic motivation and the more inward-directed self-reflexivity. For instance, Atwood's first novel, *The Edible Woman*, may on the surface look like straightforward realist fiction,[12] but its feminist and anti-consumerist politics actually find their particular expression through the articulation of postmodern contradictions in metafictional themes and forms that we usually associate with more narcissistic, formalist impulses in fiction.

In fact, however, this tension is precisely what drives the novel's plot and structure. When her friend, Duncan, informs the protagonist, Marian, that hunger is more basic than love,[13] not only is he echoing Schiller's view that the entire conduct of the world is controlled by these twin appetites, but he is also setting up the poles of a paradox that orders the entire novel, a novel about the many and various forms (and dangers) of consuming. George Woodcock has seen this as a theme of 'emotional cannibalism',[14] conflating the two terms of the opposition of appetites into one memorable phrase. But the text itself retains the separation of the two, and indeed it even emphasizes (within each of them) the contradictions underlying both—between process and product, or, in the most general formulation possible, between life and art. As was the case in Thomas's

Intertidal Life, the processes of birth and natural death play their physical, material, organic roles here too (the fecund—but metaphorically vegetating—Clara is also a member of a burial society), but they quickly also take on figurative (specifically creative) associations: the graduate English student Fish (at dinner, of course) expounds on the need for a new cataclysm, for the birth of the 'goddess of birth and growth and death', the new Venus 'big-bellied, teeming with life, potential, about to give birth to a new world in all its plenitude, a new Venus rising from the sea' (p. 200). The ironic version of this damp Venus will prove to be Ainsley soaked in Len's baptismal beer. Fish will, understandably, 'adopt' her, 'patting her belly tenderly . . . his voice heavy with symbolic meaning' (p. 241). Hunger and love.

Process—be it in the form of literary creation or of natural cycles—is not, however, always presented in positive terms, and when it is not it is usually a signal of Marian's unreliability as what Henry James called a narrative 'centre of consciousness': images of drowning, dissolving, drifting into a natural realm are viewed as negative at first, that is, from Marian's limited, unreliable point of view. Such loss of individuality as is implied in these images of merging with process is therefore perceived as dangerous to her personal sense of herself (and her self). This loss of a firm hold on identity because of some sort of mingling with the human or natural environment is at first interpreted by Marian as a threat. At an office party she fears submersion in a (rather intertextually loaded) 'thick sargasso-sea of femininity': 'she was one of them, her body the same, identical, merged with that other flesh' (p. 167). In a panic, she flees to the cold outside. Later, preparing for her fiancé Peter's party, she sits in the bath, 'afraid that she was dissolving, coming apart layer by layer' (p. 218). Again, she quickly gets out of the tub, feeling 'safer' on the cold tile floor. She then further attempts to control at least her bodily definition—with a girdle and a tight dress. Since this part of the novel is told in the third person, as a kind of narrative signal that Marian's sense of self has been alienated, the reader is likely to become suspicious of her fear of warm, dynamic process and her longing to be cold, fixed, and firm. We come to see all of this as a necessary prelude to the salutary splitting of the restrictive seams of the symbolic target-red dress that Peter had liked so much, but that Marian correctly sensed to be alien from the start. Like many feminist theorists too, Atwood is challenging male definitions of selfhood as applied to women. She destabilizes or de-centres the 'normal' notions of subjectivity—female subjectivity: becoming defines being.[15]

For women selfhood has often been seen as defined primarily through relationships. Here, however, Atwood renders 'being in love' a most problematic state, for it becomes the focus of all the possession motifs of the novel. Marriage is presented as owning, as entrapment, even as consuming: Marian walks 'slowly down the aisle, keeping pace with the gentle music' (p. 172), but the aisle is not the expected one of a church, but rather that of a supermarket. Atwood is careful not just to make all of this into a dastardly patriarchal plot; as in Thomas's fiction, women here are shown to will and create their own traps too, their own illusions in love. Since loving as possessing is specifically *mental*, an act of mind, and also directly involves power, then love is the opposite of bodily hunger, just as product is the opposite of process, or as natural death is shown to be the opposite of the death of animals killed by conquering hunters. Peter-the-hunter is, not surprisingly, Peter-the-photographer too: in English, once again, we shoot with both guns and cameras.

Images of the coldness of unnatural death and stasis are associated, perhaps surprisingly at first, with love and marriage. Images of dynamic warmth have totally other associations—initially, as we just saw, threatening ones. Again, from her restricted and restricting perspective Marian first thinks that cold is preferable to heat; it keeps her 'self' whole, together—like the girdle. But to be whole in this novel is also to be fixed, static, isolated—an object, like Ainsley's doll that Marian cannot help identifying with, or like Marian herself, made up and dressed in that red dress for Peter's party: Peter, the Rock of the society that feels safer when it owns things, including loved ones. The final image of the edible cake woman is explicitly the most consumable object image of the novel. It is also the figurative coming together of the hunger and love poles. Marian must bake the cake herself (heat, action), but it must be chilled before being *iced* and consumed. The punning play on 'icing' here recalls a recurring motif in Atwood's verse that links the stasis of ice to that of art, a connection amusingly spoofed in the Canadian 'con-create art' (squashed frozen animals) in *Lady Oracle*. Atwood's self-consciousness of herself as an artist who unavoidably transforms process into product is also made clear in her fascination with such processes as those of water turning to ice, of living beings becoming fossils. The tensions of the mind/body or love/hunger polarity that structures *The Edible Woman* are tensions that duplicate those of the postmodern contradictions between the written product and the act of writing that can be found in all of Atwood's work.

In other words, it is not just her fiction that is postmodernly paradoxical. Like Ondaatje's *The Collected Works of Billy the Kid*, Atwood's *The Journals of Susanna Moodie* offers a poetic version of historiographic metafiction, and, not surprisingly, very similar postmodernist concerns reappear. In this narrative collection of lyrics centred around the life of the nineteenth-century Canadian pioneer woman of letters, the dynamic process vs. static product paradox is worked out in terms of both history and language. Upon her arrival in Canada the Englishwoman feels like 'a word / in a foreign language';[16] her understanding of her new country is made difficult by what she sees as her 'damaged / knowing of the language' (p. 15). In poems like 'Paths and Thingscapes' she openly acknowledges that nature has its own codes and signals, which we must all learn, for these are *not* of our making. But in these poems, as in *The Edible Woman*, nature is not just that which is external to us: the land Moodie finally accepts turns out to be the tomb of the fruit of her own womb. The moving poem 'Death of a Young Son by Drowning' ends with 'I planted him in this country / like a flag' (p. 31). The acceptance of death as part of the process of nature and life ('planted'), however much the culture resists this acceptance ('like a flag'), helps Moodie face the paradox of having two unreconciled and irreconcilable voices: her English illusions and her Canadian experience, what she ought to have felt and what she did in fact feel.

These are the contraries explored by Atwood's poems. But, as in so many other Canadian long narrative poems (such as Stephen Scobie's *McAlmon's Chinese Opera* or Daphne Marlatt's *How Hug a Stone*), language is both the vehicle of exploration and the site of combat; its limitations and powers become metafictional obsessions, and never more so than in the poems about the paradoxical interplay of life/art, process/product. But language also has the illusionist's ability to signal process even within its products: witness the present-participle title of *Sur-*

facing. It is this that distinguishes Atwood's unnamed narrator's particular journey from those other mythic journeys into nature (and the self) that also focus on the paradoxes of death and rebirth, past and present, nature and society. This trip into nature, into the literal and symbolic landscape of the island, is the voyage of a woman and an artist; it is her attempt to find her self (moral and psychological), her past (personal and gendered), and her identity (private and national). But, as Robert Lecker has noted, this is also a parody of the 'search for identity' novel, largely because of the final ambiguity of the protagonist's position.[17] I think I would add a good dose of irony to that notion of final ambiguity. Both Atwood's feminist and postmodernist impulses work to question the very nature of selfhood as it is defined in our culture: that is, as coherent, unified, rational. Since, as I suggested in the last chapter, women (along with madmen and fools) have traditionally been denied access to this definition of self (and have been offered in its stead the realm of 'feminine intuition'), perhaps irony becomes the only mode available for a female protagonist who realizes that the unified self her culture has taught her to desire may be inappropriate for her as a woman. And maybe the human subject of the male gender too is more radically split or fragmented than our humanist notions of it might allow us to think? Feminism and psychoanalysis have pushed the postmodern questioning of subjectivity in these directions . . . and, of course, so have novels like this one.

Also a parody of the traditional ghost tale, *Surfacing* tells of a coming to terms with the haunting, separated parts of the narrator's self—in this case, including her aborted child and her family—after surfacing from a dive (a symbolic as well as real descent under water) and from a revealing and personally apocalyptic vision. Our all too familiar separation of mind and body, intellect and emotion, is challenged (but never erased) in the protagonist's realization of the symbolic significance of her parents' marriage, a union that brought together (without ever denying the separateness of) her mother (traditionally viewed as the instinctive, intuitive force—whose legacy to her daughter is a picture of a child in the womb) and her father (the man of reason, the photographer/scientist). Like the destructive 'American' hunters who turn out to be Canadian and also like her friends' nasty play at movie-making, her father's attempt to photograph—to fix life—has ironically led to death (physical and spiritual) and to defeat by the forces of nature. To immerse oneself in nature is also, Atwood suggests, to accept the natural within: the surfaced and possibly pregnant narrator finally accepts that there might be a foetus inside her 'undergoing its watery changes'.[18] Now the protagonist-artist can opt for the creation of life, but only after she has learned the lessons of natural process.

In replying to the critics of this novel, Atwood insisted that *Surfacing* was not a feminist/ecological treatise (as American reviewers believed); nor was it a nationalistic manifesto (as Canadians seemed to think). It was quite simply a story. But for Atwood, stories, however self-consciously stories (that is, fictional and written in words), can rarely be separated from politics, even if only in the sense that she is aware that she writes within a society where political ideas exist—and are lived out, filtered through peoples' minds, visible in their behaviour. This is as true of nationalist as it is of sexual politics. But we should recall that Susanna Moodie and the narrator of *Surfacing* are both artist-figures, as are the protagonists of *Coming Through Slaughter, Intertidal Life, Famous Last Words,* and so many other Canadian postmodern novels. In *Lady Oracle* Atwood further and more explicitly explores the artist as both the instigator of the creative process and, indeed, as a product of her own art. Here parody and self-parody meet in a feminist exploration of the art/life paradoxes in the context of the notion of female subjectivity. Unlike men, who in our Western culture are said to have a firm sense of a single, coherent, rational identity (or to think that such a sense of self is possible and desirable), Atwood's women seem to possess subjectivities that are much less easily defined in traditional terms, that are more fragmented and even multiple.

The protagonist of *Lady Oracle*, however, parodies even this postmodern tendency: the unnamed narrator of *Surfacing* becomes the multi-named narrator of *Lady Oracle*. She is the once fat, prosaic Joan Delacourt, who by age nineteen weighed 245 pounds; she is also the now thin Joan Foster, who, after a fling with a Polish count (who himself writes nurse stories under the pen-name of Mavis Quilp), marries a dull Canadian political activist (!), and then proceeds to an affair with the 'Royal Porcupine', an artist whose 'con-create art', as we have just seen, consists of frozen squashed animals—a wicked parody of Atwood's own Canadian animal victim theme in *Survival*. But this protagonist is also both Joan Foster, author (via automatic writing) of a book of poems also called *Lady Oracle*, and Louisa K. Delacourt, successful writer of popular costume gothic novels (not unlike Canada's own Harlequin Romances). The self-parodic element is strong here: Atwood's own obsession with themes of metamorphosis in her art[19] becomes both the young, fat Joan's early desire in ballet class to be cast as a butterfly, and the later spiritualist's equally entomologically significant promise that 'we will emerge with beautiful wings; we will be butterflies'.[20] That dive into the clear northern lake and the vision that allows rebirth in *Surfacing* here become a fake drowning in Lake Ontario and an escape from a blackmailer by hiding in Italy. *The Edible Woman*'s theme of rejection of food here becomes an overindulgence in it, a use of eating as a means of defiance and escape. Even the satiric barbs of the novel are often self-directed. Joan becomes a cultural idol, a darling of the media, largely because her poetry makes men, including her own husband, feel threatened. The name of one of Atwood's publishers, House of Anansi, returns to part of its etymological root and becomes the ironically named Black Widow Press. Readers were not slow to pick up on these references, but their too literal, realist reading provoked Atwood to write a letter to *Saturday Night* in 1977 to explain that the Royal Porcupine was a fictional character, not a real person.

This incident is telling, not only with regard to readers' habits, but for what it says about Atwood's texts' relation to the still dominant—realist—form of fiction. While she parodically abuses its conventions, she also milks them for all they are worth. This is that postmodern paradox of complicity and critique that I mentioned in Chapter 1, and it is parody that engages it. Here this engagement is particularly complex in structure. The plot of *Lady Oracle* both mirrors and contains that which it consistently parodies: the forms of popular art. In Atwood's view '"[p]opular" art is a collection of rigid patterns; "sophisticated" art varies the patterns. But popular art is natural for serious art in the way that dreams are.'[21] In Joan's favourite movie—a movie about the choice between love and art—'The Red Shoes' is the name both of the film and of a ballet within the film. So too *Lady Oracle* is the name of Atwood's parodic novel and also Joan's parodic book of modernist hermetic verse within it. Similarly, the novel Atwood writes parallels her heroine's (a.k.a. Louisa K. Delacourt's) *Stalked by Love*. The gothic maze of the latter becomes the objective correlative for the plot structure of the former. Even plot details are ironically paralleled: adultery with *Otterly* is not so very different (in fact or in name) from adultery with the Royal *Porcupine*.

However, *Lady Oracle* contains as well as parallels the costume gothic, and the two plots and even styles actually begin to converge, as Joan's life begins to sound more and more like her art, that is, like her heroine's life in the romance *Stalked by Love*. (The reverse also occurs: she wants more and more to make her ideal gothic characters sweat and burp.) As the narrative progresses, Joan's life comes to seem as sinister and complicated as the world of her creation, and her paranoia and desire for escape drive her to her pseudo-suicide—a trashy, melodramatic fiction, stagily convenient and perhaps morally reprehensible. But the reader can be pardoned for wondering if she has really accepted the implications of her narcissistic drowning and ironic rebirth, for the story we read is that told to the stalking reporter who finds her in Italy. She does claim to have learned her lesson and will give up writing costume gothics about an unreal past. However, perhaps she is not giving up escapist literature altogether: she says she will take up science fiction instead. Of course, the entire story is also told to us by the Joan who—like Emma Bovary—prefers escape into fictional versions of life (that is, art) to any acceptance of the limitations of living in the reality of it. How much of the narrated tale of this novel is meant to be read as Joan's fabrication, as her new fantasy?[22]

The aesthetic and ideological issue of the contrast between mundane (yet threatening) reality and exotic (but escapist) fantasy appears in much of Atwood's work. So too does the notion of art as safely fixing (as well as elaborating fantastically upon) both that banality and that danger. But there is yet another dominant metaphor for the process/product paradox in Atwood's work that I have not stressed so far, but that takes on increasing significance in her more recent work: the image of the process of birthing a child (the product). The title of one of the stories of *Dancing Girls* is 'Giving Birth', and although (as the narrator duly notes) no one ever talks of 'giving death', both are natural acts of the human body, as both *The Edible Woman* and *Surfacing* explore. But it is pregnancy and birth that constitute the important images of the creative process for Atwood as woman, a process that the human mind, through its (male?) need to articulate and understand, falsifies and reifies into a thing, a product, as the English verbs *to give* (birth) and *to deliver* suggest. But, as we have already seen in the work of Audrey Thomas, there is a particularly feminine version of those postmodern metafictional paradoxes inherent in this notion of birthing as process: it is specifically the mother birthing a child who is the analogue of the artist (and reader) giving life to a world of words.

Especially in Atwood's later work, alongside this image of birthing we find the notion of the dynamic structure of narrative itself self-consciously becoming the other dominant paradigm for holding process and product in an unresolved but productive tension: 'A language is not words only, / it is the stories / that are told in it.'[23] Yet on the surface a novel like *Life Before Man* formally appears to be a move away from the metafictional self-reflexivity of *Lady Oracle* towards a new engagement with realism. But this change is only an apparent one; what in fact happens is that the interest in the creative power (and danger) of imagination merely changes places or contexts: from now on in Atwood's fiction, it is not just artists, writers, or even graduate English students to whom creation is important. The context now becomes overtly that of life, as well as art; or rather that of life and/as art. Like many of Atwood's women characters, Lesje here turns to a (learnèd but child-like) fantasy world both to compensate for and to offer escape from life. But we shall see that this is a world that is left behind at the end of the novel, as life and creativity—in the form of her unborn child—assert themselves. The earlier pattern of images of stasis (ice, photographs) is replaced, or rather augmented, here by a series of associations centred on the Royal Ontario Museum as the receptacle of natural history: fossils and bones of once alive beasts, now reduced to fixed skeletal models, catalogued and labelled, safe from the disorder of real life. It is no wonder that Lesje finds a pregnant paleontologist a contradiction in terms.[24]

One critic has argued that this novel represents a new stage in Atwood's development: it is her first attempt at social and domestic realism unmediated by satire, comedy, or symbolism.[25] While this is true to some extent, at least on one level *Life Before Man* can also be read as being very much a part of that same self-conscious postmodern preoccupation both with stasis—and the ideological (as well as artistic) control that is implied in the creating of it—and also with the forces within society that at once fight and are defeated by this human (male?) rage for order. Yet on the surface it is indeed the classic realist tale of marriage (Nate and Elizabeth) and adultery (Nate and Lesje; Elizabeth and Chris).

The novel's world is a familiar one, one that teaches women and men that safety and security lie in order, in control. Elizabeth's greatest fear is to be out of control, that is, to find herself dependent on others. The high price (in moral and emotional terms) that she must pay for her confining self-sufficiency is evident, both for herself and for Chris, her lover, whose literally fatal attraction to her was based on the fact that she had 'what he wanted, power over a certain part of the world' (p. 161) and over himself. Product, artifice, coldness, enclosure: these images are once again related to power and control as negatives. Lesje is also caught in this same circle game, but for her its particular metaphoric space is the labelling, the controlling, rational ordering of science that offers safety from the contingencies of life. Lacking Elizabeth's socialized power and control, Lesje turns to her cataloguing work and her science-inspired fantasies in order to create a world she can control. It is only at the end of the novel, when fantasy ceases to work as evasion and when she thinks that her job at the museum is threatened by her pregnancy, that the unknown, natural order can assert itself. As Atwood writes in *You Are Happy*, 'this body is not reversible'.[26] The mind, as in the earlier novels too, sometimes has to be forced to listen to the body's order.

Atwood's choice of symbolic narrative locale for this novel does not come as a surprise to readers of earlier poems such as 'A Night in the Royal Ontario Museum' (in *The Animals in That Country*). Here the natural-history museum is seen as a place to collect and label, a 'crazed man-made / stone brain', 'the mind's / deadend'. Here lost life forms are fixed and dead. It is a 'bone- / yard' where, as Lesje knows, entire 'chunks of time lie ... golden and frozen' (p. 308). But it is also safe compared to life outside, especially for the insecure and tentative Lesje. It is only at the end, when she can symbolically walk through the Gallery of Vertebrate Evolution in the wrong direction and sit there contemplating the foetus growing inside her, that Lesje fully perceives the fictional nature of the labels and of the historical facts she has always turned to, both for solid support and for material for her wish-fulfilling fantasies. Just before this, Lesje has the urge to cry out to those who want (as she did) definitions and facts from history and science: *'The Mesozoic isn't real. It's only a word for a place you can't go to any more because it isn't there. It's called the Mesozoic because we call it that'* (p. 290, italics hers). Thanks to Lesje's 'sea-change', the artificial and the dead can be connected once again to the natural and the living.[27] The past and the present are brought together, but not merged; the tension between them continues. A pregnant paleontologist remains an oxymoron.

The ROM also functions as the focus of a theme introduced in another earlier poem, 'Elegy for the Giant Tortoises'. The tortoises there are historically heading for extinction and museums, for a fate as 'relics of what we have destroyed'. Even if there were not a scene in the novel in which Lesje catalogues the remains of giant tortoises (p. 182), the title *Life Before Man* would suggest this theme of historical extinction. There is an obvious and thematically important play on words here: life before man as the species, and before man as the sex. The fact that the novel takes place in the present, in a 'life after dinosaurs', suggests that there could easily be a life 'after man' in both the feminist and the ecological senses. Like 'man', dinosaurs 'didn't intend to become extinct; as far as they knew they would live forever' (p. 290).

That humanity shares this hubris (what Freud called the death instinct) is clear: dead bodies litter this novel. Some of the dead are long in the past and therefore cannot really be remembered: Nate's father who died in the war and Lesje's Aunt Rachel, a victim of the concentration camps. But people in this world play out an ironic version of the giant tortoise role as 'relics of what we have destroyed' too, because, with the exception of Elizabeth's aunt's cancer, it is *self*-destruction that dominates. The novel opens a few weeks after Chris's bloody suicide. The effect of this upon his rejecting lover, Elizabeth, is to stir up painful memories of the deaths of her mother and sister. Every other female character in the novel contemplates or threatens suicide: Elizabeth (p. 301), Lesje (p. 293), Martha (p. 110). Even Nate's mother entered into her charity work and her campaigning against political injustice as an alternative to suicide (p. 287), deciding to change, rather than exit from, a kind of world she knew she did not want to live in. Even the temporal setting of the novel underlines the death/stasis motif: the first part ends on Hallowe'en, the eve of All Saints' Day, and the next section opens on Remembrance Day. Still obsessed with memories of Chris's suicide, Elizabeth takes personally the words of the poem 'In Flanders' Fields' ('If ye break faith with us who die / We shall not sleep' [p. 57]) and feels their moral pressure. For Lesje, too, the ROM is a kind of cemetery of the past, where even the model of the paleontologist in a display case seems to look like a corpse. The planetarium next door, which Elizabeth visits, is a graveyard of the future, of cosmic disasters, of black holes. But, as in all of Atwood's fiction, death and its associations of stasis are played off against life and process. At the end of the narrative, in anger and out of the 'fear of being nothing', Lesje thinks of suicide, momentarily identifying with Chris (p. 293), but instead she throws out her birth-control pills and opts for life, albeit a rather vengeful one.

This, then, is a novel that begins after a suicide and ends before a birth. Out of revenge, threatened death, anger, and failing relationships can come the promise, at least, of new life. Creation can and does assert itself, but this time not in specifically artistic form. There is no Joan Foster in this novel. Nate does make rocking horses and other toys, but he sees these at first as regressions and, by the end, only as museum pieces of his past. Chris had built taxidermic animal models at the Museum.[28] But any artistic pretensions in their work would appear to be undercut by the parodic presence of a girl at a party who announces that she makes plastic models of Holstein cows for breeders and dealers but hopes to get into 'painted portraits of individual cows, for which she could get more money' (p. 108). Atwood had embedded a similar parody in *The Edible Woman* in the Lawrentian Fish's praise of birth: 'the very process of artistic creation was itself an imitation of Nature, of the thing in nature that was most important to the survival of Mankind' (p. 198). Because he sees the artist as 'pregnant with his [*sic*] work', his taking on of Ainsley and her forthcoming child is credible: graduate students and academics have a role to play in the care and nurturing of the creative.

In that first novel this important notion of creativity is an explicit theme, discussed overtly by the characters, almost as it would be in an essay. In *Life Before Man* it is, instead, integrated into the narrative structure itself, with the result that, as in Audrey Thomas's fiction, women in general (and not just artists in particular) are shown to have a different relation to creativity than men: pregnancy and birthing are the domain of the female of the species. Despite this less metafictive thematizing of the creative process, *Life Before Man* is not a straightforward realist novel: that process/product tension is still to be found in what is, in essence, a postmodern interest in the creative potential (and danger) of fantasy. All of Atwood's heroines are highly imaginative; their creative processes, however extreme or comic, also in a sense mirror that of the novelist herself, which in turn mirrors our own as readers. Atwood once said of her fiction that in large part the characters create the world they inhabit, and that she thinks we all do that to some extent, or at least do a lot of rearranging. Fantasy as a process is as much a part of life as it is of art. But fantasy does not simply mean escape, as each novel makes clear in its own way. With creation always comes responsibility. The ideological implications of the power to create are not lost on any of Atwood's protagonists; nor are the consequences of retreating into a fantasy world to escape the 'real' and its dangers. Like the narrator of both *Surfacing* and *Bodily Harm*, Lesje in *Life Before Man* finally renounces at once the passivity that permits victimization and also the evasion offered by fantasy, and opts for life and responsibility. The creative act of her pregnancy becomes a metaphor for the novelist's act of creation, that is, an act of moral responsibility for the creation of life. But the responsibility is also—in a more extended sense—a political one, and this is what Atwood's subsequent work has investigated even more explicitly.

In the poems of *True Stories* the postmodern paradox of complicity and critique that we have been seeing is given voice in the poet's anguish over the ineffectual nature of art's power in the political world, anguish that makes her doubt the worth of her words: 'How can I justify / this gentle poem then in the face of sheer / horror?'[29] The poet, the manipulator of words, is in some senses condemned (like the novelist) to be an observer, the passive witness of the 'true story' who nevertheless must still try to come to terms with her artistic responsibility in the face of the suffering of others: 'She is dying for the sake of the word. / It is her body, silent / and fingerless, writing this poem' (p. 67). In Canada it may be safe today to write with impunity; 'elsewhere' it takes real courage to write (p. 71). Atwood's involvement with Amnesty International has clearly sharpened and focused her political interests: 'The facts of this world seen clearly / are seen through tears' (p. 69).

I would disagree completely with B.W. Powe's view[30] that Atwood 'discovers' political commitment only in the novel *Bodily Harm*. Her feminism and her Canadian nationalism are very closely related political concerns with which she has consistently been engaged, and to ignore these is more revealing of the critic than of the novelist. Powe feels that she 'plays safe' with her 'vaguely leftist' politics of 'anti-colonialism, anti-dictatorship, anti-violence, and anti-censorship'. The real source of irritation here, however, is made evident in the critic's claim that she 'avoids taking the risks of exploring and revaluating human nature and human values'. Both the feminist and the postmodern contexts in which Atwood works have suggested that the real tasks to be undertaken within a liberal humanist culture are those of exploding, not exploring, the myths of 'human' nature and 'human' values. Such 'universals' have been revealed as anything but universal: generic 'Man' has been exposed as male, middle-class, and white—to put it bluntly.[31] Exposing the tendency to ignore gender, class and race is where the real risks lie today, according to many feminists, Marxists, poststructuralists, postcolonial theorists . . . and novelists.

In *Bodily Harm* themes of violation (physical, psychological, and ideological) provide the focus for Atwood's particular challenge to the male-'universal', and sexual politics are shown to have their direct analogue in national politics once again. It is men who wield the surgeon's knives, men who dismiss (by pornographic misogyny), men who rape, and also men who, on many levels, both repress and revolt (equally oppressively). Women are among their victims; but so too are men, for they victimize themselves. Frank Davey presents the process/product paradox articulated here as one of chaos/order that is specifically gender-defined: that is, female/male. But he also sees that the tension between the contradicting poles not only is never resolved, but can never be resolved: 'Male order may constitute a travesty of female chaos and its gestural language, but only a wary appropriation of that order enables a speaking of either.'[32] The postmodern paradox remains. So too do gender differences, of course.

While *Bodily Harm* is a novel more overtly about human rights and politics than the others, her previous political concerns persist. For example, the theme of the subtle interconnections between bonding and bondage here takes on new power. Women's need to bond with others is counterpointed to our society's tendency to label and limit women through its cultural clichés of femininity. Atwood also explores many of these same clichés in her collection of short stories *Bluebeard's Egg*, clichés such as the cult of the slender, delicately female form. Typically, however, it is as much women's complicity in their own victimization as men's victimizing that is the focus of attention. This particular collection, though, also includes very formally self-reflexive stories that again articulate the process/product paradox that pervades Atwood's work, though this time it is rooted again in the realm of art. For example, in 'Unearthing Suite' the narrator's house is said to contain both a clean, rigidly ordered room and a messy room full of paper. But, and here is Atwood's explicit, metafictional restatement of her commitment to creative process, it is the writing room that is the one ruled by images of flux and organic life.

Of all of her more overtly postmodernist works, perhaps the most deliberately provocative are certain parts of *Murder in the Dark: Short Fictions and Prose Poems*. The title piece, for example, is an extended play on remarks Atwood once made on a very postmodern distinction—that between the 'thing written' and the thing being written (and read): 'It is my contention that the process of reading is part of the process of writing, the necessary completion without which writing can hardly be said to exist.'[33] Reading, like writing, is a 'process which moves in time and through time'. 'Murder in the Dark' is presented as a mystery game with either the writer as murderer, reader as detective, book as victim, or with the critic as detective, reader as victim, book as total *mise en scène*. She plays here on 'plot' (the plot to kill and the plot of narrative) and on the fact that the truly inventive author is, in a sense, always a plotting (and Cretan) liar: 'by the rules of the game, I always lie. Now: do you believe me?'[34]

The parodic self-reflexivity of *Lady Oracle* reappears here in the parable 'Simmering', and, as is the case in that novel, it is not to be separated from the politics of Atwood's feminism. Here the male/female relation in the kitchen is ironically inverted: men take over cooking, quit their jobs (and so wives have to go to work), form exclusive clubs and secret societies centred around food. In the face of this exclusion, women begin to have 'kitchen envy': 'If Nature had meant women to cook, it was said, God would have made carving knives round with holes in them' (p. 32). This parodic history is handed down in manuscript form from woman to woman, copied out or memorized. The narrator knows it is subversive of her to write of this, but she wants to urge a change for women: she wants them to be allowed access to food again and to 'the ritual which now embodies the deepest religious convictions of our society: the transformation of the consecrated flour into the holy bread' (p. 33).

As we have seen in Chapter 6, parodic play like this is an ironic mode congenial to many women writers: it is a way to avoid the silence of renunciation of male forms while not being totally compromised by them. In a number of the pieces in *Murder in the Dark* auto-representational play and parody mingle to contest, in an even more explicit and direct fashion, the literary conventions that male writers have made into 'universals':

> Men's novels are about men. Women's novels are about men too but from a different point of view. You can have a men's novel with no women in it except possibly the landlady or the horse, but you can't have a women's novel with no men in it. Sometimes men put women in men's novels but they leave out some of the parts: the heads, for instance, or the hands. Women's novels leave out parts of the men as well. Sometimes it's the stretch between the belly button and the knees, sometimes it's the sense of humour. It's hard to have a sense of humour in a cloak, in a high wind, on a moor.
>
> Women do not usually write novels of the type favoured by men but men are known to write novels of the type favoured by women. Some people find this odd. (p. 34)

In other pieces she takes on male-structured endings ('Happy Endings'), plots and readers' powers of imagination ('Bread'), and the dangers and lures of Mallarmé's blank page ('The Page'). Highly metafictional, these short works are also, however, for the most part political. In the prose poem 'Iconography' woman 'arranged' by man is warned: 'Watch yourself. That's what the mirrors are for, this story is a mirror story which rhymes with horror story, but not quite. We fall into these rhymes as if into safe hands' (p. 52).

The book ends with an ambiguous note to its readers, telling us not to resist our 'third eye'—the visionary one: 'After that there are no more instructions because there is no more choice. You see. You see' (p. 62). Readers of Atwood's novels do, of course, see (literally and figuratively), and we are rarely allowed to lapse into passivity or literary consumerism. We are constantly being made aware of the fictive nature of the world we create through our reading, and of the fact that our participation in that act involves us willy-nilly in the process of creation that we share with the author. And here is the core of Atwood's postmodernism: with that participation comes responsibility—political, moral; public, personal.

In my introductory chapter, in discussing *The Handmaid's Tale*, I argued that politics and metafictive parody meet in a nightmarish projection of both history and its modes of narration. The oral/written paradox (as examined in Chapter 3) appears in the frame tale, and here it is once again the female who is associated with the oral, the male with the written. Yet the novelist in this case is female, and readers (of either gender) know this, even as they realize the association set up in the novel. This simultaneous mixture of involvement and distance makes this perhaps Atwood's most postmodern novel to date.

Self-conscious about the fact that this is a dystopia created out of words (feminist rhetoric, consumerist advertising, literalist fundamentalist ranting), it offers us a world carried to an extreme. Horrifyingly, it gives us a vision of the implications of current ideological trends. Here men still rule; women still collude. It would not be hard to read this novel in terms of the catastrophic extreme of the imposition of a certain kind of female order: women are respected above all for their mothering function; women burn pornography and punish deviation from the norm. To escape the slavery of men, though, there exists an Underground Femaleroad (p. 258). As the 'Historical Notes' at the end suggest, Gilead may be patriarchal in form, but in content much is matriarchal. An overtly political fable, *The Handmaid's Tale* foregrounds its female producer, but here Atwood attempts to offer us both process and product, life and art. The narrator self-consciously tries to tell her story (a true one, but also, she realizes, inevitably ordered, constructed, fictionalized), just as she had tried to get pregnant (in order to retain her position in her society as one of the rare fertile women). The travails of creativity are both narrative and physical; both involve issues of power and danger. Atwood herself once said that 'fiction is the guardian of the moral and ethical sense of the community'.[35] And, even more explicitly, in an address to Amnesty International she stated her view of the producer of art-products: 'The writer . . . retains three attributes that power-mad regimes cannot tolerate: a human imagination, in the many forms it may take; the power to communicate; and hope.'[36] *The Handmaid's Tale* is her fictional rendering of these three attributes in the face of a literal (and literary) 'power-mad' regime.

In all of Atwood's fiction formalist concerns (such as parody and metafictive self-reflexivity) are never separate from political ones, and this is largely because of the very postmodern paradox that ties them together: in her own (and my) constantly repeated terms, this is the paradox of art as both product and process, as both artifact and part of life. The complex relationship between these elements is not one of simple opposition so much as fruitful confrontation: 'this paper / world which is the real world / also.'[37] That 'also' is the marker of the postmodern contradiction. Although she once described Victim Position Number 4 (in *Survival*) as that in which humans recognize that they are 'part of the process' of nature, sexuality, life, and therefore 'free to move within space',[38] it is always as artist—as artificer, as maker of product—that she paradoxically becomes part of that process. She does not (and I would say, cannot) try to 'overcome dichotomies creatively'.[39] She needs them; her art derives its power and meaning from those very postmodern contradictions.

Notes

1 Lorna Irvine has pointed out the obsession in Munro's fiction with flux and process in 'Changing Is the Word I Want', in *Probable Fictions: Alice Munro's Narrative Acts*, ed. Louis K. MacKendrick (Downsview, Ont.: ECW Press, 1983), p. 99.

2 That Atwood is now considered 'mainstream' by most critics marks a major advance in postmodernism, though it is rarely seen in this way. Some place her in the very centre of a Canadian tradition (e.g., Sandra Djwa, 'The Where of Here: Margaret Atwood and a Canadian Tradition', in *The Art of Margaret Atwood: Essays in Criticism*, eds. Arnold E. and Cathy N. Davidson [Toronto: Anansi, 1981], pp. 15-34); others see her as merely fashionable in her interest in process or becoming (B.W. Powe, '"How to Act": An Essay on Margaret Atwood', in his *A Climate Charged* [Oakville, Ont.: Mosaic Press, 1984], p. 143: '[Atwood

writes] from the heart of darkness, inside the flux. She is the author of sophisticated self-help books, a writer working in what could be called the Nausea-Romance School').

3 This is not unlike the idea of overlapping antagonistic fields (subject/ object or earth/world) in Dennis Lee's *Savage Fields: An Essay in Literature and Cosmology* (Toronto: Anansi, 1977).

4 See Sherrill E. Grace, 'Articulating the "Space Between": Atwood's Untold Stories and Fresh Beginnings', in *Margaret Atwood: Language, Text, and System*, ed. Sherrill E. Grace and Lorraine Weir (Vancouver: University of British Columbia Press, 1983), pp. 1-3.

5 Interview with Linda Sandler, *Malahat Review* 41 (Jan. 1977), p. 19.

6 In Sherrill Grace's *Violent Duality: A Study of Margaret Atwood* (Montreal: Véhicule Press, 1980), a dialectic is implied. Grace sees the contradictions as only apparent, but I would argue that they are very real, and that they create a permanent unresolved tension.

7 *Power Politics* (Toronto: Anansi, 1971), p. 10.

8 See Marie-Françoise Guédon, '*Surfacing*: Amerindian Themes and Shamanism', in *Margaret Atwood: Language, Text, and System*, pp. 91-112 and, in the same volume, Lorraine Weir, 'Atwood in a Landscape', pp. 143-53.

9 See Frank Davey, 'Atwood's Gorgon Touch', *Studies in Canadian Literature* 2 (1977), pp. 146-63.

10 George Woodcock, 'Poetry', *Literary History of Canada*, ed. Carl F. Klinck, 2nd ed. (Toronto and Buffalo: University of Toronto Press, 1976), III, p. 294.

11 Interview with Alan Twigg in *For Openers: Conversations with 24 Canadian Writers* (Madiera Pl., BC: Harbour, 1981), p. 227.

12 It has also been seen as Frygian romance. See Catherine McLay, 'The Dark Voyage: *The Edible Woman* as Romance', in *The Art of Margaret Atwood*, pp. 123-38.

13 *The Edible Woman* (Toronto: McClelland and Stewart, 1969), p. 61. All further references will appear in parentheses in the text.

14 George Woodcock, 'The Symbolic Cannibals', *Canadian Literature* 42 (1969), pp. 98-100.

15 B.W. Powe's verbal violence against her decentring of the idea of self is an interesting (defensive-sounding) response. See *A Climate Charged*, p. 146.

16 *The Journals of Susanna Moodie* (Toronto: Oxford University Press, 1970), p. 11. All further references will appear in parentheses in the text.

17 Robert Lecker, 'Janus Through the Looking Glass: Atwood's First Three Novels', in *The Art of Margaret Atwood*, p. 178.

18 *Surfacing* (Toronto: McClelland and Stewart, 1972), p. 222.

19 See Frank Davey, *Margaret Atwood: A Feminist Poetics* (Vancouver: Talonbooks, 1984), pp. 120-1.

[20] *Lady Oracle* (Toronto: McClelland and Stewart, 1976), p. 107. All further references will appear in parentheses in the text.

[21] Interview with Sandler, p. 10.

[22] On the interpretive difficulties faced by readers of *Lady Oracle*, see Susan MacLean, '*Lady Oracle*: The Art of Reality and the Reality of Art', *Journal of Canadian Fiction* 28-9 (1980), pp. 179-97.

[23] *Two-Headed Poems* (Toronto: Oxford University Press, 1978), p. 25.

[24] *Life Before Man* (Toronto: McClelland and Stewart, 1979), p. 308. All further references will appear in parentheses in the text.

[25] Sherrill Grace, *Violent Duality*, p. 135.

[26] *You Are Happy* (Toronto: Oxford University Press, 1974), p. 69, italics hers.

[27] See Cathy N. and Arnold E. Davidson, 'Prospects and Retrospect in *Life Before Man*', in their *The Art of Margaret Atwood*, p. 221, italics theirs: ' . . . the museum by design *commemorates* what has died, is dying, is doomed to extinction. The dead, the defunct, the never-living artifact are all linked to the living and even to the as yet unborn.'

[28] Another way to look at this job is as that of restoring the appearance of life to dead bodies. See Frank Davey, *Margaret Atwood: A Feminist Poetics*, p. 88.

[29] *True Stories* (Toronto: Oxford University Press, 1981), p. 34. All further references will appear in parentheses in the text.

[30] In *A Climate Charged*, p. 149.

[31] See, for example, Catherine Belsey, *Critical Practice* (London and New York: Methuen, 1980), and almost any work of feminist theory or criticism.

[32] *Margaret Atwood: A Feminist Poetics*, p. 56.

[33] *In Second Words: Selected Critical Prose* (Toronto: Anansi, 1981), p. 345. The citation that follows immediately here is from p. 344.

[34] *Murder in the Dark: Short Fictions and Prose Poems* (Toronto: Coach House Press, 1983), p. 30. All further references will appear in parentheses in the text.

[35] *Second Words*, p. 346.

[36] Ibid., p. 397.

[37] *Interlunar* (Toronto: Oxford University Press, 1984), p. 79.

[38] *Survival* (Toronto: Anansi, 1972), p. 63.

[39] Sherrill Grace, 'Articulating the "Space Between"', pp. 5, 13.

Chapter 8

Seeing Double: Concluding with Kroetsch

As Douglas Barbour once noted about Robert Kroetsch, there are 'few Canadian writers who pay such *conscious* attention to what they are about'.[1] Consciously postmodernist, the work of this writer makes an appropriately inappropriate ending to this study—that is, I hope that its constant paradoxical combatting of the inevitability of closure will act as the analogue for this final chapter's attempt to both tie up and unloose notions of the Canadian postmodern.

In many ways it is probably redundant to call Robert Kroetsch a postmodernist; he is Mr Canadian Postmodern. As the previous seven chapters should have made clear, by that I mean more than what Robert Wilson meant when he agreed to label Kroetsch postmodernist 'insofar as it implies a purposeful playfulness and an uncompromising refusal to accept literary conventions as givens'.[2] While this is an accurate definition, it does not really go far enough, as I will argue. Kroetsch has been important to Canadian letters both as a writer and as a critic. In his novels and poetry he has radically problematized the notions of creativity and commentary: his creative characters are always as ambiguously creative (think of Hazard Lepage, Jeremy Sadness, William Dawe, Dorf), as are his ordering interpreters (Demeter Proudfoot, Mark Madham, Anna Dawe, Karen Strike). In his critical essays Kroetsch deliberately subverts academic convention: they are wilfully fragmentary, discontinuous, asystematic, incomplete—and provocative because of this. Frank Davey has linked what he sees as Kroetsch's radical suspicion of 'the existence independent of the temporal embodiment of idea, archetype, essence, or Platonic form'[3] to Kroetsch's philosophical roots in Heidegger, Wittgenstein, Husserl, Jaspers, Merleau-Ponty, and especially Derrida. The literary roots of Kroetsch's theory are clearly from formalist, structuralist, and poststructuralist work, including that of Kristeva, Todorov, and Bakhtin. The reason I stress Kroetsch's essays here is that the notions explored in them cannot be separated from those offered in his fiction. As postmodern, Kroetsch's work combines the theoretical and the creative, though with none of the heavy didacticism of a John Berger or even a John Fowles. The reason may well lie in his view of the critical act: he sees it as 'an extension of the text' that 'liberates the text into its own potential'.[4]

This merging of the theoretical and the literary is obviously not the only characteristic of postmodernism to be found in Kroetsch's work. Using the structure of this study for purposes of summary, we could say that, like Leonard Cohen, Kroetsch is the master of paradoxes, of opposites that do not merge dialectically, of doubles that stay double. We have already seen, in Chapter 3, how Kroetsch addresses the written/oral problematic of the postmodern scribe in *What the Crow Said*. We could add to this the tape-recording play in *Gone Indian* or his constant preoccupation with the tall tale. As Kroetsch has said, 'I'm still tempted by oral models where the story in the act of retelling is always responsive to individuals, to the place, to invention.'[5] Always aware of the context and 'situation' (what I earlier called the *énonciation*) of the text, all of Kroetsch's novels play off the tension between the oral and the written.[6]

Like the novels of Wiebe, Bowering, and Findley discussed in Chapter 4, Kroetsch's fiction confronts the written as fixed and fixing, in both literature and history. In questioning the existence of single historical Truth, Kroetsch problematizes both historical knowledge and historical narrative. His work plays on the borders and the boundaries of genre, as does Ondaatje's (Chapter 5), challenging the kind of distinctions we make all too readily, usually without thinking: between fiction and non-fiction, between fragment and totality, between the general and the particular. Kroetsch has acknowledged the impact of contemporary feminism on the questioning of so-called 'universals' that are, in fact, based on 'male supremacy', such as the quest narrative (L, p. 34). *Badlands* is his parodic response to this challenge.

While Kroetsch is not a feminist writer, he shares many of the concerns of those who are: especially the need to challenge unexamined humanist notions such as centred identity, coherent subjectivity, and aesthetic originality. He offers instead decentred multiplicity, split selves, and double-voiced parody. He shares Atwood's and Thomas's metafictive obsessions with dynamic process, despite both the lure and the danger of static product. In short, Kroetsch is at the paradoxical centre of the decentred phenomenon called postmodernism: as novelist, poet, critic, teacher, mentor, and clown. It is fitting that he should bring these essays to a close, then, though any last word given him is never his last.

As that last sentence suggests, Kroetsch, the master of double-talking paradox, drives his critics into paradoxical formulations. His work sets up co-ordinates we recognize from realist fiction, then proceeds to dismantle them. This is what forces commentators into statements about Kroetsch's 'desire to give form while breaking it, to incorporate myth while undermining it, to tell the 'truth' while labeling it absurd, to provide structure while blatantly truncating it'.[7] These are the words of Robert Lecker, who joins Peter Thomas, Rosemary Sullivan, and others[8] in seeing Kroetsch's work as caught in fundamental tensions characteristic of a border or boundary (or fence-sitting?) Canadian situation. In Kroetsch's own terms, 'Canada is a peculiar kind of borderland, and a borderland is often a place where things are really happening.'[9] In Lecker's terms, 'Kroetsch aggressively pursues . . . ambivalence because ambivalence is the hallmark of the borderman's art' (p. 20). Ambivalence, in this and in the Bakhtinian sense, is another word for postmodern paradox: the refusal to pick sides, the desire to be on both sides of any border, deriving energy from the continual crossing.

The border between art and life, words and the world, that we saw in the work of Ondaatje, Blaise, Atwood, Thomas, and so many others looms large in Kroetsch's fiction. In terms of characterization it appears in the constant interplay between characters with an ordering, controlling research (or documentary) orientation and those who represent a disorderly, explosively chaotic subversion of human notions of ordering and recording. In terms of form those contraries appear in the tensions between structure and randomness, between the closure and continuity of linear narrative and openness and discontinuity, between the conventions of realism and the play of parody. Lecker, for instance, sees each novel in terms of paradoxes: *But We Are Exiles* pits inherited vs. invented form, mimetic vs. expressive theories of art; *The Words of My Roaring* puts the paradoxes in terms of beginnings and ends, west and east, myth and history; in *The Studhorse Man* the doubles are different but related—myth and invention, teller and tale, permanence and impermanence; *Gone Indian* offers authority and control in the face of subversion and contingency, Eros in the face of Thanatos; the oppositions of *What the Crow Said* are between silence and story, the documented and the imagined; and in *Alibi* they are between the hidden and the revealed, the male and the female. As Lecker sums up his extended analysis, 'Kroetsch is fascinated by the space between polarities, inhabits that space, and writes from the viewpoint of one who is repeatedly seduced by the two poles he tries to embrace' (p. 148). This double seduction is never resolved in any ecstatic union of poles, however. The tensions remain unresolved.

The critics can be forgiven their obsession with Kroetsch's paradoxes and doublings: after all, Kroetsch's own writing is self-consciously obsessed with them as well. In very postmodern terms, he has described himself as playing 'on the edge of convention' (L, p. 50), as bending the rules: 'I am both using a set of conventions and subverting them: you have to hear that double thing' (L, p. 176). And you do. Kroetsch found in the theories of the Russian critic we met in Chapter 2—Mikhail Bakhtin—an echo of his own views about the unresolved paradoxes of art. In his book-length interview with Shirley Neuman and Robert Wilson, *Labyrinths of Voice*, Kroetsch discusses Bakhtin's theory of carnival laughter as asserting and denying, as a burying and reviving force (L, p. 35). The moments of carnival are anti-repressive, subversive of the dominant order, yet are only temporary, and we might add, are also authorized by the dominant order, as we saw in Chapter 2. There lies the full paradox.

It is not surprising that parody would be attractive to Kroetsch as a textual strategy: I would argue that it too, like the carnival, is a form of authorized transgression that is paradoxically both an inscribing and a subverting of what it inscribes.[10] The effect of Kroetsch's work has been rightly described as relying on 'the shock to our sensibilities that would not work without our attachment to realist conventions and a literary tradition implying continuity'.[11] Parody and intertextuality are ways of both asserting and challenging that continuity, both for readers (who must perceive the text's doubleness) and for the author. In Kroetsch's words: 'in a very real sense we make books out of books. The paradox and the terror is always that: the need to invent out of the already invented.'[12]

Kroetsch is not content merely to theorize about parody and the intertextual activity of both reader and writer. In *The Studhorse Man* Demeter Proudfoot's ostensible reason for writing is to record the life of Hazard Lepage. But the conventions of biography are as much parodied as followed, as much abused as used: metafictively self-conscious, Demeter presents us with the spectacle of the biographer fictionalizing as well as recording. He does not hesitate to fill in gaps in memory or received facts. He offers his dedication at the end, not the start. We are never given a full account of Hazard's life. Some chapters are lost, others left unfinished. Logic and continuity are self-consciously undermined. Any notions we might have of the presumed objectivity of the biographer crumble beneath the weight of Demeter's judgements: he revels in his subjectivity. He may collect documents and research materials, but the place in which he writes, with his newspaper clippings, his file cards, and his books around him, undercuts his scholarly pretensions: he sits in a dry bathtub. This parodic play presupposes readers' knowledge of the conventions of biography and works to invert our expectations.

As I mentioned earlier, feminism has influenced Kroetsch's view of the so-called 'universality' both of certain narrative conventions and, more importantly, of certain modes of behaviour and thought by showing them to be, in fact, gender-based and gender-biased. His use of parody to contest both is, however, a little different from the use we saw women writers making of this strategy, in Chapter 6. It is more ambivalent, more postmodern, perhaps. Kroetsch strongly installs the male will to knowledge and control (as embodied in quest narrative, for instance), even as he subverts and conditions it. In *Badlands* he self-consciously uses a female narration in a male story—with double effect. He seems to want to both render homage to and yet seriously criticize the narrative quests of Odysseus, Orpheus, the knight errant, Conrad's Marlow.[13]

Much of the parody in Kroetsch's fiction is parody of classical myth, either of individual figures (of Icarus and of Zeus and Danae in *What the Crow Said*, of Narcissus in *The Words of My Roaring*) or of the Homeric and Virgilian epic notion of the quest.

For years now critics have been working out the parodic interrelations between the *Odyssey* and *The Studhorse Man*,[14] *Badlands*,[15] and *Alibi*.[16] These parodies of the familiar and seemingly 'universal' do not so much destroy myth as de-myth-ify and demystify it into stories, fictions. These, in turn, are less 'universal' than recognizable and reusable, and the difference is crucial. They can be used and abused. Much of the mythic material is presented ambivalently: water, for instance, is symbolic of both death and rebirth in all of Kroetsch's work (as in Atwood's and Thomas's). While on the surface this resembles, as we have seen before, T.S. Eliot's modernist ambivalence about water in *The Waste Land*, Kroetsch's is more an ambivalence-as-mutual-undercutting, with no balancing of opposites, just underlining of duality.

In Kroetsch's work there is a always a postmodern tension between the implied 'universals' of mythic story and the 'anecdotal texture, narrativity' (L, p. 92) of fiction. The interchange here is what deconstructs myth and allows a way out of the 'entrapping' tendency of myth to want to explain everything one way. For Kroetsch the response is to 'retell it' and retell it differently (L, p. 96). The appeal of myth to modernism, if I may generalize a little recklessly, was in its promise not only of 'universality' but of coherence and lasting meaning. As Kroetsch puts it, 'the Postmodernist is more tempted by those momentary insights that spring up here and there' (L, p. 112). Anecdote counteracts the organizing principles of myth in his fiction, as in that of other postmodern writers. There is a paradoxical desire to show the temptation of the 'single' vision as seen in mythic 'universality', sameness, and system and yet to contest it by 'the allure of multiplicity' (L, p. 117)—parody, fragmentation, decentring. For Kroetsch Babel is a positive story because it recounts the breaking up of that originary single collectivity that allowed the multiple to flourish: 'making everything into *one*' (L, p. 118) at the expense of historical, cultural, and linguistic diversity is a negative in the eyes of the postmodern.

Kroetsch's parodies are not all mythic, however. Besides the conventions of biography, *The Studhorse Man* takes on everything from Nabokov's *Pale Fire* to Tennyson's 'The Lady of Shalott' (the mistakenly female-named Demeter, sitting in his bathtub, watches the world as reflected in a mirror). The broader conventions of the western genre are also parodied: Hazard and Poseidon both represent and misrepresent the traditional relationship between cowboy and horse. In *Gone Indian* the ending of the western is parodied:[17] Jeremy and Bea ride off into the sunset, but they are 'seeking NOTHING'. As we shall see later, *Alibi* similarly takes on and takes off on the conventions of the murder mystery.

As is frequent in postmodern fiction, ridicule or laughter are not the only aims of its parody. A kind of reverential or at least deferential signalling of complicity with the texts of the past (even if different from them in significant ways) is clear in Kroetsch's many echoes of Conrad—think of all those characters who leap—and of Gabriel García Márquez.[18] Intertextuality provides a certain 'allusiveness' and a feeling of 'multiple voices',[19] combined with a constant sense of irony. The Derridean 'fabric of traces' (L, p. 10) is the theoretical notion operating here to contest the idea of art as singular, original, or originary; in the novels themselves parody is its form. As Kroetsch puts it: 'I started off working at the parody level which is where you want to tell a story but you can't believe that there is only one assertable meaning in that story. You're left taking parody very seriously. Of course for many twentieth century writers parody has been a fundamental method for proceeding' (L, p. 89). To retell a story, parodically or straight, is always to interpret it, to undo its single and 'universal' meaning.

Myth and other stories are not the only forms of narrative that tend to suggest single meaning through totalizing narrative. Here again, by totalizing I mean unifying with an eye to power. History too for Kroetsch is potentially a form of 'coercive' narrative because 'it begins from meaning instead of discovering meanings along the way' (L, p. 133). Like Wiebe, he tends to associate Canadian history of the west (as it is written) with the machinations of the 'Eastern establishment' (L, p. 135). Even within Canada, history does not record the 'universal', eternally repeatable; it has none of the transhistorical stability of myth. By definition it is specific and temporally singular and unique. Just as Kroetsch's novels subvert, through the use of the inherent mendaciousness of the tall-tale tradition, the notion of mimetic truth-telling, so too they reveal historical Truth to be, in fact, shifty, relative, unstable. The archaeological search of William Dawe in *Badlands* is both for dinosaur bones and for a way in which to 'cite or fashion or plumb or receive or accomplish or postulate or pretend the absolute truth that would give him the necessary lie'.[20]

As Margaret Laurence once told Kroetsch, 'You are not writing an historical novel in any sense of the word, but what you are doing is seeing that the past in a sense is always present and the present is always the future.'[21] History often impinges on Kroetsch's fiction, but these novels are rarely what could be called historiographic metafictions. World War One is recalled in *The Words of My Roaring, The Studhorse Man,* and *Badlands*; the Acadian dispersal and Riel both figure peripherally in *The Studhorse Man* as well. That novel quite literally backgrounds, rather than foregrounds, history: think of the symbolic wallpaper of lions and fleurs-de-lis in Hazard's house, the statue of Queen Victoria, P. Cockburn's life-size wax figures of famous historical personages and types in the provincial museum. All of these backgrounded images share one thing: they are all static and lifeless—historical immortality, by definition, demands death first.

Kroetsch's ambivalence about history stems, he claims, from his realization of the fact that the 'authorized history, the given definition of history, was betraying us on those prairies'.[22] Like Wiebe's, his response has been to fill in the absences, the elisions of official eastern history. Kroetsch claims that for the prairie writer the archaeological model of Michel Foucault is a more apt one than the traditional notion of history. It could take into account more easily the 'particulars of place': the 'newspaper files, place names, shoe boxes full of old photographs, tall tales, diaries, journals, tipi rings, weather reports, business ledgers, voting records—even the wrong-headed histories written by eastern historians become, rather than narratives of the past, archaeological deposits.'[23]

Unlike Wiebe, however, Kroetsch embodies this view most materially—almost literally—*not* in his fiction, but in his poetry. The original 1977 edition of his *Seed Catalogue* takes an original 1917 seed catalogue from Glenbow and prints the first poems of the book on faint reproductions of its pages. This is Kroetsch's response to the material and textual history of the prairies that is usually ignored by the official historians of the east. As Kroetsch wrote in 'The Continuing Poem', the seed catalogue 'is a shared book in our society',[24] a book as common and important as those of the academic canon. In the poems fictionalizing meets history, both personal and public, in ways that make *The Seed Catalogue* a poetic form of historiographic metafiction.

Similarly, at the front of the 1975 Applegarth Follies edition of *The Ledger* there is a map with a circle around Kieffer, with a reproduction of a hand-written note: 'Yes, that's the *place*. RK.' This contextualizing and personalizing signing is omitted in the later reprinting, but its presence is a postmodern signal of the meeting of the past and the present. *The Ledger* also reproduces a page of a ledger that had been in Kroetsch's father's possession, the record of the family accounts when they settled in Bruce County, Ontario. This book becomes a record of family accounts in more than the financial sense, however. The poems retain the form of columns, even reproducing parts of the original ledger's text, but there is a subversion of the implied notion of 'balancing' the accounts: dualities, binaries remain separated by the space on the page, held in tension.

Like historiographic metafiction, this is both a document and a creation, a record and an invention. The long poem, in particular, interests Kroetsch as a mode of investigating the deposits of the past in those archaeological (rather than traditionally historical) terms: 'archaeology supplants history; an archaeology that challenges the authenticity of history [as a continuous narrative] by saying that there can be no joined story, only abrupt guesswork, juxtaposition, flashes of insight.'[25] This description may explain, perhaps, his use of poetry to explore this particular postmodern challenge to history. The tyranny of narrative, however subverted and undermined, is still the tyranny of 'joined story'. The scepticism Kroetsch reveals about the Truth of History is one he shares, though, with those historiographic metafictionists studied in Chapter 4. What Kroetsch adds to their suspicions about single, authoritative knowledge of the past is the fact that he thinks this is a particularly Canadian phenomenon: 'We are intrigued by it, by our past, and all sceptical about it.'[26] In Kroetsch's work the colonial history of Canada is often played out in the microcosm of familial history, as father figures are both acknowledged and defeated.

We have seen that the problematic nature of the act of writing about the historical past—from its traces, its documents, its archival evidence—is a preoccupation of both historiographic metafiction and current historical theory. In Kroetsch's fiction this concern reappears in the form of the problems of interpretation vs. fictionalization that hound his characters: that hound Anna Dawe working from her father's field notes; Madham transcribing and commenting on Jeremy's tapes; Demeter recording and writing the biography of Hazard Lepage; Liebhaber composing and typesetting the daily past of Big Indian in his newspaper. The document, in Kroetsch's words, is 'another telling . . . that invites a further telling because of what it leaves out' (L, p. 187).

The documents with which his characters must deal are specifically verbal documents, and as such they seem to create a certain anxiety 'about language being separate from reality or being its own reality' (L, p. 50). The entire question of reference, of the relation of word to world (and more generally, of art to life), is a central one for postmodernism, as I have been trying to show. Kroetsch's choice of poetry as his major medium to examine the history/fiction or past/present dualities may reveal a desire to sidestep rather than combat the teleology and closure of narrative: novelistic stories have to end, however ambiguously, however openly. Atwood uses narrative to fight the static completeness of the lyric poem, thematizing process over product in her fiction.[27] While Kroetsch does as well (in his novels), he also does the reverse (in his poetry). Clearly, while the interests of postmodernists are shared, their formal modes of dealing with them can differ. Nevertheless, Kroetsch's *Field Notes*, with its two subtitles—'1-8 / a continuing poem' and 'The Collected Poetry of Robert Kroetsch'—suggests that, for him as much as for Atwood, the wilful incompletion of process can be used to confront the inevitability of finished product, in poetry as in prose.

In *The Sad Phoenician* the answer to the question 'what do you do in life?' is offered in terms of pure process: 'I ing.' In the novels process often has to come to terms with product in material ways. At the end of *Badlands* Anna Dawe must throw away her father's field notes, as Anna Yellowbird does her set of photographs. The 'ing' (writing and photographing), as we saw in Chapter 3, may be process, but the written and the photographed are products, tied to the illusion of a direct mimetic link to the 'real' world.[28] Michael Sinnott, the photographer who sees the past dying and thus in need of capturing and freezing in his photos, is not totally unrelated to William Dawe's paleontological desire to recover the past, but Dawe rejects this link, arguing that while he recovers the past, Sinnott reduces it. Yet both acts, like Anna's narrating, are potentially modes of control that are paradoxically also modes of preservation and revivification.

Liebhaber, in *What the Crow Said*, is both journalist and typesetter, and in both capacities he fixes the process of experience into products: narrative reportage and newspaper type. His crisis is over this very double act. In *Alibi*, as we shall see shortly, the metaphor for the process/product confrontation changes once again. This time it is collecting: like historians, documentary filmmakers are also collectors, cataloguers of history's traces in the present. But, like the writing of history, the making of films is a process as well. The protagonist too collects, but he does not keep the products: they belong to his employer. Though he writes, it is Karen Strike, the filmmaker, who edits and orders his process into the product we read.

In the last two chapters we have seen that in the work of women writers the act of writing is often connected to specifically female processes such as pregnancy or mothering and to the notion of creation as birthing in physical as well as artistic terms. In Kroetsch's work it is less this than the erotic energy of sexual desire itself that becomes like writing: potential acts of creation, unpredictable, exciting (L, p. 100).[29] This is what can break through the neat balance of binary oppositions (such as female/male) that threaten stasis.[30] Rejecting equilibrium in the name of tension, Kroetsch offers a male gender-defined version of the procreative urge. The difference between the view offered in *Life Before Man* or *Intertidal Life* and that in any of Kroetsch's novels is one between the metaphors of woman as pregnant and nurturing and of man as sexually potent and desiring.[31] But given all those dead bodies that litter Kroetsch's novels—even the funniest ones—Eros and Thanatos, in Freud's terms, both play their role in Kroetsch's metaphoric space of creation.

If any novelist's perspective on the process of creating is gender-determined, so too is any critic's, perhaps. I have noticed that male critics seem to associate notions of stasis, closure, and death with women,[32] while female critics see the women also as symbols of life forces.[33] True to my gender-perspective, let me add that while there are indeed images connecting women to enclosure in Kroetsch's novels, these are often the images offered by a male narrator and reflect more upon his individual (limited) view of women than upon the text's view as a whole. Bea and Jill, in *Gone Indian*, may indeed be named the ominous 'Sunderman', but two things must be noted: first of all, it is Bea's *husband*'s name, and second, within a postmodern perspective, the notion of 'sundering man' may well be a positive, in the sense of both a breaking-up of male hegemony and a contesting of the notion of single, coherent subjectivity. While there are clearly men in the novels who represent the energy of disruptive challenge, they are often matched by *men* who represent the stasis of coercive ordering: Hazard has his Demeter; Jeremy has his Madham. In *Alibi* the gender distinctions get more subtle and the androgyne even makes its appearance, as we shall see. Kroetsch has always, though, worked to show how male and female roles are fictions, in the sense that they are creations of cultural constraints.

As we have noted in other chapters, the process that brings the product to life is that of reading, another 'ing'. The constant emphasis on the act of wri*ting* in Kroetsch's work marks another of his ways of attempting to combat the stasis of product: 'the having written excludes the reader.'[34] Writer and reader relate within a context that includes not just the text, but social, historical, cultural, and even political determinations.[35] The image Kroetsch most often uses for this relationship is again one from archaeology: the writer 'unearths' something that the reader 'has the task of fitting into whatever scheme he wants to fit into' (L, p. 14). This highly active role granted to the reader both demands effort and offers considerable freedom: 'I work a reader pretty hard, I guess, in that I want him to enter into the process with me' (cited in L, p. 57).

Kroetsch himself sees *What the Crow Said* as the novel that embodies his own (writer's) struggle 'with the temptation of meaning' and, he adds, 'it's the reader's struggle too' (L, p. 15). Often we are given reader-surrogates within the novel itself (often parodic ones, mind you): Demeter, Madham, Anna Dawe. As readers, then, we are both players and spectators, trapped within the text and yet free to interpret, especially when the text itself is fragmentary, untotalized, open: 'the reader has to run the risks, be culpable, face temptations, face the tests—the conventions that used to apply to the hero in the text, apply instead to the reader' (L, p. 175).

While *What the Crow Said* is Kroetsch's most fragmented, deliberately incomplete, thus most open and suggestive novel, it is in his accompanying book, *The Crow Journals*, that the fragment takes on its full potential. Called 'a not-quite-a-book book', it is Kroetsch's (ordered) version of a heap of his (dated) notes collected in a shoe box. Anything seemingly haphazard here is counteracted, of course, by those ordering dates. Paradoxes are unavoidably self-evident in the idea of a (whole, physically unified) book made up of fragments, whose explicit challenge to beginnings and endings takes the form of a dated progression. Kroetsch's constant desire to combat ordering impulses can be seen in the entry, for instance, where he reacts against the act of editing (for the journal *Boundary 2*): 'it becomes so goddamned *orderly*' that he wants to add pictures of crashing planes (and he does) to combat 'a humanism that coerces'.[36] His credo here is: 'the risk of creation involves the risk of destruction.'

The opposite or complement of the contingent individual fragment is perhaps the collection, as *Alibi* explores. Robert Wilson sees the collection as a powerful image of the 'arbitrariness of human systems'—anything can be collected, in any way—which suggests 'the shifting unreliability of all human attempts [including language and thought] to confer identity and substantiality' upon the world.[37] Nevertheless, the postmodern paradoxes remain: we watch the process of collecting; the products collected are of considerably less interest. This is, of course, one way to tease readers, to play with us. But we are never allowed to forget who is teasing, who is telling the tale (tall or otherwise) that we are reading: Anna Dawe follows her father's trail, Demeter sits in his bath, the Canadian Madham writes from the United States.

The full *énonciation* of these novels is foregrounded in such a way that readers are made aware that the process of reading the text is a dialogue with the writer, the characters, the words of the text, and the entire cultural context in which the reading and writing both take place. Kroetsch is aware that we are taught to read or interpret by ordering, by unifying (by violence, if necessary) parts of the text. His novels attempt to combat this taught (and learned) impulse in the name of process: incompleteness, not wholeness, is valued. Like the archaeologist, we 'may have only shards' (L, p. 10), but that is more exciting and provocative than finding something whole: 'why tell it all?' As a postmodernist Kroetsch has a radical suspicion of systems of thought that totalize experience. Multiplicity, fragmentation, incompleteness, and discontinuity are preferable, even if they are effective only when their opposites are posited as the dominant forces: single vision, unity, completeness, and continuity.

This does not apply only to narrative form. The radical challenges to the humanist notion of the self as coherent, unified, and stable by contemporary psychoanalysis and philosophy have left their mark on Kroetsch's theoretically self-conscious work. He too wants to combat 'the preposterous notion of self' (L, p. 6) in the name of the subject as 'a kind of fragment, a shifting pattern' (L, p. 7). He attacks Freud and Jung for their dated concepts of the self, for their 'confidence in a locatable center or explanation' (L, p. 107), a notion that echoes the conception of character in nineteenth-century realist fiction. While he argues for the recognition of the inevitability of the split within any self, he is characteristically postmodern in feeling uneasy both about the split and about any possible union that would deny it (L, p. 173). As he puts it: 'we are victims of a story that tells us to be heroes' (L, p. 179). But neither we nor his protagonists can be heroes any longer, so we tell stories, either to apologize for our failure or to construct ourselves as heroic. Consistent with his valuing of process, Kroetsch denies that the sense of self is ever a completed thing, a product; it is amorphous and ever changing. Like us, then, the character in a novel must be shown to be the 'consequence of many stories' (L, p. 189). Intertextual echoes replace personal self-narration, but the denial of a depth-model for both the psyche and novelistic characterization is a firm one here. No deep, single, stable, autonomous identity is available to us, except as an acknowledged human fiction—comforting, but illusory.

In the novels this conviction takes shape in the presentation of characters: Demeter as biographer identifying to the point of confusion with his subject; Jeremy Sadness being mistaken for Roger Dorck and thus enabled, in a sense, to live out his boyhood fantasy of being like Grey Owl. In *What the Crow Said* characters defy most obviously, perhaps, the novelistic tradition

of coherent and continuous identity. The psychological motivation of realist fiction is both installed and radically subverted
when characters can do things like remember the future. I think
Peter Thomas reads as a realist when he complains that Kroetsch
weakens the value of 'individual lives' in this novel, ignoring
'their existential weight in time'.[38] Kroetsch's point is that they
never had such individuality or weight: those notions are
conventions of both humanist ideology and realist fiction; they
are not eternal and 'universal' truths. And yet he can make that
assertion only because his texts presuppose our knowledge of
those conventions: the postmodern paradox. The split subject
in Kroetsch's work is usually a doubled subject: William William
Dorfendorf of *Alibi* is the most explicitly doubly named.[39] Or
the subject may be multiple. As Madham says in *Gone Indian*,
the northern prairies have great consequences for 'human
definition': 'the diffusion of personality into a complex of
possibilities rather than a concluded self.'[40] This is why Sunderman is not such a negative name after all.

In his theoretical statements Kroetsch relates this challenge
to the notion of self to the ultimate '*contra*-diction' of Canadian
writers: 'they uncreate themselves into existence.'[41] In an essay
called 'The Exploding Porcupine: Violence of Form in English-
Canadian Fiction' he expands on what he means by this
Canadian paradox. The exploding porcupine is, in general terms,
the image of the ego, the self, that must be 'violated from within'.
But in more specific terms it is '[t]he porcupine of English-
Canadian self-righteousness. . . . And boredom. And self-
congratulation. And timidity. And self-deception.'[42] He feels
strongly the need to combat any sense of self-satisfaction that
might come from creating a fiction of the wholeness of self, that
might resolve the inevitable splits and tensions. Part of the
reason for this we saw earlier in his delight in borders as places
of interaction, places where things can happen: on the margin,
off-centre, ex-centric.

Kroetsch seems to suggest, as do many other Canadian writers,
that Canada has a privileged place in postmodernism because
of its inherent ex-centricity: equally off-centre in relation to its
former imperial masters in Britain and to the more recent
imperial threat from America. The margins offer a paradoxical
site of both influence and freedom from influence. For Kroetsch
the British notion of a 'great tradition' (F.R. Leavis) is irrelevant,

even if still influential, in the judging of Canadian fiction. In the place of sure and fixed judgement, as he says, 'I am willing to let truth live from day to day as must the rest of us'.[43] Definitions of what constitutes Truth have never been stable, much less eternal and 'universal'; they have always changed drastically, depending on the place, time, gender, class, and race of the definer. This is one of the important acknowledgements of postmodernism. The protagonists of many Canadian novels today are those who do not fit the dominant definition of the centre: the heretic Giordano Bruno (in *Antichthon*), the giantess Anna Swan (in *The Biggest Modern Woman of the World*), the rebels Big Bear and Louis Riel (in *The Temptations of Big Bear* and *The Scorched-Wood People*), the silent, mad musician, Buddy Bolden (in *Coming Through Slaughter*), and the list could go on (and would include most of Kroetsch's characters). The ex-centric is a mirror of Canadian marginalization—but as more a privileged than a denigrated position. It both challenges the general notion of centre and, at the same time, undoes that particular idea of the possibility of a centred, coherent subjectivity.

Kroetsch certainly has an eye for the marginal and the ex-centric. Exiles, outsiders, outrageously eccentric, his characters incarnate this positionality. But another aspect of the problematizing of margin and centre is also very important to Kroetsch's fiction: that particular postmodern challenge to centring impulses that takes the form of a refiguring of the idea of the regional into the concept of the specific and the local (as opposed to the general and the universal). Kroetsch's work is rooted very firmly in the geographical, historical, and cultural world of Alberta.[44] Like so many other Canadian writers, he eschews the so-called 'universal' (which he sees as a construct that is, in fact, rather limited) and prefers the particular and the different, just as feminists and ethnic writers everywhere have also been doing.[45] Of course, to feel the need to contest the 'universal' in this way is also implicitly to acknowledge the power that concept still possesses in our culture: that too is the paradox of postmodernism.

Paradoxes haunt the writing of all the contemporary writers I have been examining in this study. Kroetsch's latest work has revealed an even stronger and more acute sense of the enormity of the contradictions with which the writer must deal. Robert Lecker has argued that lately Kroetsch's narrators must cope with their stories being 'about what [they] will never capture—absence, space, silence' (p. 97). But perhaps this is what all his novels have been about. And perhaps the most recent one is the culmination thus far of his postmodern concerns. That a book called *Alibi* should begin in the following way may not be surprising: 'Most men, I suppose, are secretly pleased to learn their wives have taken lovers: I am able now to confess I was.'[46] The 'confession' that follows, however, offers anything but the one we might expect from a conventional detective story 'alibi'. It has none of what Kroetsch called the murder mystery's 'promise of a wrap-up ending, a solution, an untangling, a resolution of mystery'.[47] As postmodern fiction this novel offers no solutions, resolutions, or untanglings.

Nevertheless, the form of the detective story is generally attractive to postmodern writers[48] for other reasons. As the investigation of the nature and existence of lies, the murder mystery is inherently a marker of metafictionality. In other words, it is a readily recognized way of signalling to readers the conventionality and fictionality of what they are reading. It is itself a most self-conscious genre: think of all those little ironies uttered by characters within Agatha Christie novels about how 'things like this only happen in detective stories—never in real life' (that is, in this book). But the other characteristic of the genre that makes it so apt for metafictional purposes is the importance it openly accords to the hermeneutic act of interpreting. Detective-story readers are the paradigm for all readers: they are detectives tracing clues. The author is both creator and murderer, according to this metaphor, which is obviously set up by a play on words: the plot of narrative and the plot to kill. As we saw in the last chapter, Atwood spoofs this in her metafictional parody 'Murder in the Dark'.

In *Alibi* many of the trappings of detective fiction are present: the lone hero, the dangerous sexy women, mysterious death. But there are also other conventions we cannot ignore, conventions more reminiscent of eighteenth- or nineteenth-century fiction: the first-person narrative based on journal notes and the intrusion of a third person in the often sarcastic chapter headings, such as '(Or, in which Dorf claims to have got laid)' (p. 10). But the subtle doubling of voicing that occurs through the ironic tension between heading and chapter becomes the formal analogue of the entire doubling structure of a novel whose protagonist, named after two grandfathers with the same name, is Billy Billy Dorfen (or, in full, William William Dorfendorf). His two daughters are named Jinn and Jan, suggesting both Ying and Yang and *Jules et Jim*, perhaps. Dorf is a man with two lives and two lovers; things happen to him in twos, even attempts on his life. 'It's a plotted world we live in,' he wryly observes. Typically postmodern, though, the novel's doubles stay separate. In Cohen's terms, 'all the polarities, things and their images', stay polarities.

Dorf's first life, as a husband, father, and museum curator, ends when he points a gun at his wife's lover and realizes that he could indeed pull the trigger. In his second life he rejects all human ties that cannot be dealt with 'in financial terms': he organizes his time around the whims of a reclusive Alberta oil millionaire, Jack Deemer, a man bent on collecting anything there is to be collected. As Deemer's agent Dorf has come to see his employer as 'an artist in his own right, a kind of looney sculptor intent on tacking together . . . all the loose pieces' of the world (p. 20), 'according to his own design, of course' (p. 47). Within the context of Kroetsch's other works such a view of the artist is both accurate and suspect. This ambivalence continues, as the novel progresses, because the collector becomes a discoverer figure, like Columbus, and a conqueror, like Philip II. And it is the collector's agent that makes these roles possible: 'The collection itself only confirms the discontinuity of this scattered world: it's my talk that puts it together' (p. 195), according to Dorf. Given Kroetsch's views about systems that totalize, that impose continuity with an eye to power, this statement cannot be taken as being fully affirmative.

The ambivalence of *Alibi*'s collecting is what marks it as different from that of Fowles's *The Collector*, for instance, where to collect is only to kill. Here collecting is still lethal, but it is also a heroic, if futile, attack on randomness (p. 58). Like the writing of history (another totalizing, coercing system for Kroetsch, as we have just seen), collecting is a way of coping with time past, 'a calling up of ghosts from a million ancestral pasts' (p. 74); it is a means of 'acting out reality' (p. 109). In all of these functions, collecting becomes for Dorf a metaphor for writing. (Karen Strike, the woman who gives Dorf his journal as a gift, adds the realization that writing is related in turn to subjectivity: 'You invent yourself, each time you sit down to make an entry' [p. 61]). When ordered to investigate and buy a collection of skeletons, Dorf makes the collecting/writing link overt: 'I couldn't leave the city to go to whatever Turkish port was home to that treasure. Just as I couldn't write in my journal' (p. 187).

Dorf's two lives are separated by his realization that he is capable of destruction, of killing someone. The presence of death looms over this novel, as it does over Kroetsch's other fiction. Like them, it is (postmodernly) paradoxically a bawdy, funny romp that is obsessed with death. Yet the deliberate intertextual echo of Joyce's 'The Dead' ('I drove through the falling snow. Snow was general on the eastern slope of the Rockies' [p. 11]) signals to the reader that this story will also be one about loving and living, as well as dying. Ambivalence is again the key to interpreting the dominant imagery of earth and water here: both are sources of life and death—mythically and in specific plot terms within the novel itself. Kroetsch's ambivalence unsettles, upsets, subverts all notions of possible answers to questions posed by contraries unresolved.

The story revolves around Dorf's search for a perfect spa for Deemer. From the bowels of the earth (the source of his oil money) Deemer appears to seek some fountain of youth through healing waters.[49] In the first spa he visits, Dorf meets Julie, Deemer's dangerous lady, who offers him both spa-style sex (underwater) and a simultaneous threat of death, should he ever find that perfect spa. Julie in particular but woman in general, as in all of Kroetsch's work, partakes of the same ambivalence as water and earth: she is both womb and tomb, the goddess of abundance and life (Dorf's sister is an egg producer) and the vengeful deity of death, who (presumably) is ultimately trapped in her own machinations. To enter the earth's caves in search of healing waters is unavoidably linked structurally in this text to being buried under an avalanche of solid, frozen, considerably less healthy, water—talk about process fixed into lethal product! And it is Julie who leads Dorf to both. Sex and death, desire and destruction: the familiar dualities of Kroetsch's fiction.

The underlying basic doubleness of the novel is also a very familiar one (though in more general terms) both for readers of *Beautiful Losers* and for Western readers in general—that of body and spirit: 'We dwell in the body, nowadays. With the world gone hank-end and haywire too, we live in the self's body. As if to cure the body's pain is to be cured. We are all St Augustines in this broken world; saints not of the soul but of the body, of the bloodstream and back' (pp. 113-4). It is as if Kroetsch, like Cohen, wanted to challenge what D.G. Jones once called 'Western idealism's Manichean dualism': 'life becomes a battle of opposites whose final goal is the total victory of mind over matter, the world of the flesh and the devil.'[50] Kroetsch's parodic inversion here contests and recontextualizes this 'universal' in particular twentieth-century terms, in the terms of the health- and fitness-obsessed North America of the 1980s. In order to gratify Deemer's desire for health to match his wealth, Dorf must search for curing waters from Alberta to Bath to Portugal and, finally, to Greece, the cradle of Western civilization, as the cliché would have it. Throughout his search the doubling and the paradoxes proliferate. Meeting her again at a spa in Portugal, Dorf becomes involved in a bizarre sex triangle with Julie and a dwarf doctor, Manuel de Medeiros. Not content with the Dorf/dwarf verbal doubling, Dorf repeatedly links Manny to his other woman friend, Karen Strike, who shares his blond hair and narrative connotations of voyeurism, sex, and danger.

But it is Julie who, after recounting another doubling (Deemer and Manny), introduces the title of the novel: 'We all live by our alibis, don't we, Dorf? . . . We were somewhere else when it happened. Or should have been. Or shouldn't have been' (p. 125). No doubt Kroetsch wants to recall the Latin meaning of 'alibi' as 'elsewhere'. Perhaps there is also an allusion to Thackeray's 'Women are not so easily cured by the alibi treatment', for Julie is not allowed either a cure or an alibi: her death, in an automobile accident over a cliff, ironically recalls her engineering of the attempt on Dorf's life (by an avalanche, as she watched from a cliff edge), but despite her plunge she is denied a return to the tomb/womb of the earth: the grave diggers in Calgary are on strike and she must remain in her coffin on top of a frozen ice rink.

The imagery involving sexual desire and woman in the novel is always doubled and ambivalent, even when related to the source of life. To Dorf 'omphalos' may be a 'mountain word' (p. 128), but it is clearly also another of those ubiquitous 'holes in the ground' of the mother/earth that bring forth both healing and death. All of these metaphors culminate in the 'smelly woman' in Greece and her mud cave. We are primed for both the scene's expected cultural centrality (and 'universality') and its subversion by parallels drawn to earlier parts of the novel (textual doubling, if you like): to Dorf Greece is reminiscent of the prairies at home; Philippi, near the mud cave, was also an important mining centre. Lining up with the other men to enter the mud cave, Dorf has his ('beautiful losers') vision of Everyman: 'We were a road-construction gang, ten threshing crews from the dirty thirties. We were the people who missed every bus on a wet and muddy street with a lot of traffic passing. We were a soup line. We were the ragtag survivors of Napoleon's visit to Moscow.' Then he adds: 'We were the bearers of human ache' (p. 164). But despite the generalizing impulse (and perhaps because of the echoes of Cohen's themes and ironically inflated rhetoric) Dorf remains unavoidably and unmistakably Dorf. Individual subjectivity and its paradoxical corollary—'universal' human essence, of which each individual is said to partake—are simultaneously subverted even as they are inscribed.

Realizing 'what work and disease and age will do for the human body' (p. 165), Dorf enters the cave and discovers the elemental conjunction of water and earth: mud. One figure in the mud draws 'an opening', a figure of female genitalia on his head, '[a]s if he'd figured a way to escape the world. Or enter it' (p. 166). This figure turns out to be the 'smelly woman'—that is, a hermaphrodite. In accepting all the dualities and ambivalences that constitute life, Dorf can then begin to construct himself anew, literally, out of mud. He breaks the rules of the spa: he exits naked but 'decently coated in mud' (p. 177), is reborn as part of nature, and then re-enters the cave to plunge into the mud, but this time during the women's hour. This rather obvious return to the womb results in another of Dorf's sexual experiences fraught with symbolic value, but this time the mud and the women offer love and life, not threats of death.

This is no final resolution of the ambivalences of the novel, however. At Julie's coffin Dorf finds a message about what will be Deemer's perfect spa, and its paradoxical name is not insignificant: Deadman Spring. Here Dorf works out his salvation. In a parodic inversion of Ulysses and the Cyclops, Dorf gives a nameless, one-eyed man one of his doubled names (Billy Billy), and his cure and curing seem to begin. Dorf must be led from his initial vision of life—'blood, semen, sweat, shit, hair, fingernails, toenails, piss, pus. The infinite dribble of excrement

that is life. Why go on? For the mixed pleasure of an orgasm?'
(p. 29)—to an acceptance of the body and its desires as also good
and natural. It is important that, up to now, what has been
associated with these same natural qualities is the act of writing:
Dorf tends his journal 'as a gardener tends his sprouts and his
blossoms' (p. 135). Writing remains the core of the novel, both
in theme and in form. Desire exists in word as well as deed:
'To be intimate. To intimate' (p. 136). He tries to explain to Julie
once that to touch is to talk: 'Intimacy is, finally, an intimacy
of telling' (p. 136). Hence the journal; hence the novel.

At Deadman Spring Dorf waits for Deemer (whom he has never
met or spoken to), a Godot figure earlier described as 'unap-
proachable', 'a conundrum', 'a mystery' (p. 94). Heralded by
Karen Strike and her fixing, objectifying documentary cameras
('Deemer sent me'), is Deemer too a doubled figure, a punningly
parodic re-Deemer? He arrives, enters the cave in a blinding
light (Karen's camera lighting) as a 'walking skeleton' (p. 224).
In the equally blinding darkness that follows, the cave in the
ground becomes inverted into the cosmic 'final black hole' in
which touching as telling takes on its full scope of meaning. There
is no overt threat of death or loving orgasm this time; the
ambivalence remains unresolved. No anonymous hands bring
pleasure, despite Dorf's naive trust that they will. Although he
finds he later has difficulty writing down—telling—what actually
occurred in the—touching—dark, we learn in the last journal
entries (said to be not yet ordered or novelized, not yet reworked
into narrative, structured and interpreted by hindsight) that he
was 'violated'. (The echo of the male rape scene in the dark baths
in Findley's *The Wars* is likely not accidental.)

Retreating afterwards away from the bowels of the earth to
a cabin on a cliff in the woods, Dorf composes the narrative we
have read. Instead of constructing a mud man, this time he makes
a word man. But the last pages are pure journal and as such
work to contest traditional novelistic closure: they provide no
neat, satisfying ordering or resolving, in short, no overtly
fictionalized end. The rewritten part of the story ends with a
memory of Julie's death as Dorf is 'violated', a memory and a
metaphor: her car plunging over the cliff 'like a period, on a blank
page' (p. 228). To leave one's mark, either on the landscape or
on the page, is to court death, as Kroetsch explored in *What the
Crow Said*. Writing fixes and kills, but it can also offer a means

to new life through the revivifying act of reading. Alone in nature, writing, Dorf can accept ambivalence, most succinctly symbolized by the salmon 'spawning and dying' (p. 233) in the creeks. His interest in the life of the young osprey learning how to fly is countered by his being accidentally (?) responsible for another death. The doubled cry of the osprey ('*Gwan-Gwan*') that ends the novel reasserts duality, and in so doing reasserts life—though always in the face of death. Plummeting to the earth on their first (and perhaps last and fateful) attempt to fly, the young birds find their wings and soar, tearing at last, in Dorf's words, 'the sadness from my heart'.

These final words of the novel may suggest some resolution, but it is paradoxically one that must come from acceptance of ambivalence. Quests in postmodern literature lead to questions, not answers. There are always excuses, alibis, elsewheres. The final great collectors, the final artists, are subverted even as they are inscribed: 'Death like love, is a great arranger. This collector, too, has a corrosive sense of style' (p. 196). The final duality we are left with is the postmodern novelist's constant obsession: that of art and life. As Kroetsch once put it, 'it would be an error not to perceive the differences between life and art, just as it would be an error not to see that they are they same' (L, p. 68).

Yet it is interesting that in 1974, when Kroetsch edited a special Canadian issue of *Boundary 2: A Journal of Postmodern Literature*, he included only poetry and criticism, not fiction. He argued in his introduction that 'Canadian literature evolved directly from Victorian into Postmodern'.[51] But in poetry the McGill group and others did give us some taste of modernism, just as Margaret Laurence and Sheila Watson did in fiction. And to argue this Victorian/Postmodern leap as a generalization is perhaps also dangerous, because it tends to underplay the strong *continuing* tradition of realist fiction in English-Canadian writing as well as the fact that Canadian postmodernist fiction presupposes the existence of dominant realist conventions in order to effect its parodic postmodern challenges. Kroetsch himself pointed to this when he said, 'Perhaps we are mimetic, nowadays, under erasure' (L, p. 201). That too is a paradox of the postmodern. Kroetsch once called the artist a 'sick healer' and a 'lying truth-teller',[52] and these are other formulations of the contradictions of postmodernism. And all are always unresolved paradoxes: 'possibilities not only co-exist but contradict', as Kroetsch insists.[53]

Robert Kroetsch is Mr Canadian Postmodern, if anyone is. His work, both critical and creative, stands among the most obvious challenges to canonical notions of a literature of certainty, comfort, stability, and security. Any attempts at totalizing systems of thought or expression are subverted, even at the moment of their installation. The tension between use and abuse is crucial: there is no resolution in either direction. The postmodern does not reject or exemplify, lament or celebrate, the results of our decentralized, post-industrial, communications-obsessed age.[54] It does both—and neither.

Like so many Canadian women writers, Kroetsch is a problematizer and questioner of our cultural givens. He does not deny their existence, but he challenges their authority. As he puts it, 'I guess I don't like to solve the problem' (L, p. 4). Solving the problem(s) would mean having answers, would mean stasis and product; the process of asking interests him more. One of the things he and all the other writers I have discussed in this study have done is help us stop talking about writing and the written text as fixed and dead products; we are urged to 'ing'— to see that reading and interpreting are processes in which we too participate as, equally, makers of our culture. That culture may be unavoidably part of what Fredric Jameson calls 'the cultural logic of late capitalism',[55] but it freely acknowledges its complicity as well as insisting, nevertheless, on its power to critique. There are no alibis here either.

Notes

[1] Douglas Barbour, Introduction to Robert Kroetsch, *The Crow Journals* (Edmonton: NeWest Press, 1980), p. 8.

[2] In 'Robert Kroetsch', in *Canadian Writers Since 1960, First Series; Dictionary of Literary Biography* vol. 53, ed. W.H. New (Detroit: Gale/Bruccoli Clark, 1986), p. 241.

[3] Frank Davey, Introduction to *Robert Kroetsch: Essays* (hereafter, *RK: E*), special issue of *Open Letter*, 5th series, no. 4 (1983), pp. 7-8.

[4] Kroetsch, 'Beyond Nationalism: A Prologue', *RK: E*, p. 83.

[5] Kroetsch, in Shirley Neuman and Robert R. Wilson, *Labyrinths of Voice: Conversations with Robert Kroetsch* (Edmonton: NeWest Press, 1982), p. 13. All further references will appear in parentheses in the text, preceded by L.

[6] One aspect of this tension not studied here, but of relevance, is the Native oral tradition, not only in Kroetsch's work, but in that of Native

women writers, where questions of paraliterary form and ethnocentric bias enter as well. See Barbara Godard, 'Voicing Difference: The Literary Production of Native Women', in *A Mazing Space: Writing Canadian/ Women Writing*, ed. Shirley Neuman and Smaro Kamboureli (Edmonton: Longspoon/NeWest Press, 1986), pp. 87-107.

[7] Robert Lecker, *Robert Kroetsch* (Boston: Twayne, 1986), p. 47. All further references will appear in parentheses in the text.

[8] Peter Thomas, *Robert Kroetsch*, Studies in Canadian Literature (Vancouver: Douglas & McIntyre, 1980) and Rosemary Sullivan, 'The Fascinating Place Between: The Fiction of Robert Kroetsch', *Mosaic* 11, 3 (1978), pp. 165-76.

[9] In Russell M. Brown, 'An Interview with Robert Kroetsch', *University of Windsor Review* 7, 2 (1972), p. 4.

[10] See Chapter 6 and Linda Hutcheon, *A Theory of Parody: The Teachings of Twentieth-Century Art Forms* (London and New York: Methuen, 1985).

[11] W.J. Keith, *Canadian Literature in English* (London and New York: Longman, 1985), p. 165.

[12] 'Contemporary Standards in the Canadian Novel', in *RK: E*, p. 42.

[13] See W.H. New, *Articulating West: Essays on Purpose and Form in Modern Canadian Literature* (Toronto: New Press, 1972), pp. 179-80 especially, on parody of the Greek epic as opposing the past dead order to the present lively chaos of Hazard's trek across the prairies. See too Christine Niero, 'Making Stories: Studies in Contemporary Canadian Metafiction' (Ph.D. dissertation, Queen's University, 1987), pp. 30-1, on parallels of structure and detail with the *Odyssey* and epic conventions.

[14] See Ann Mandel, 'Uninventing Structures: Cultural Criticism and the Novels of Robert Kroetsch', *Open Letter* 5th series, no. 8 (1978), p. 65, and Lecker, pp. 84-5.

[15] See Alberto Manguel, 'No Excuses', *Books in Canada* October 1983, pp. 20-2.

[16] As Peter Thomas argues, p. 80.

[17] Russell Brown also points out many other parodies here, including those of the work of Dante, Virgil, and of Indian and Norse myths. See his 'Robert Kroetsch' entry in the *Oxford Companion to Canadian Literature*, ed. William Toye (Toronto: Oxford University Press, 1983), p. 419.

[18] See, in *The Crow Journals* (Edmonton: NeWest Press, 1980), p. 19 (Kroetsch on the impact of García Márquez on story, characters, paragraphs, time, and place in his own writing) and p. 29 (Kroetsch on the use of the third-person narrator which combats realist conventions). See too Robert Rawdon Wilson, 'On the Boundary of the Magic and the Real: Notes on an Inter-American Fiction', *Compass* 6 (1979), pp. 37-53.

[19] These are Shirley Neuman and Robert Wilson's terms in *L*, p. xi.

[20] *Badlands* (Toronto: New Press, 1975), p. 239.

[21] In 'A Conversation with Margaret Laurence,' in *Creation*, ed. Robert Kroetsch (Toronto: New Press, 1970), p. 60.

[22] 'On Being an Alberta Writer,' in *RK: E*, p. 71.

[23] Ibid., p. 76.

[24] In *RK: E*, p. 82.

[25] 'For Play and Entrance: The Contemporary Canadian Long Poem', in *RK: E*, p. 93.

[26] In Robert Enright and Dennis Cooley, 'Uncovering Our Dream World: An Interview with Robert Kroetsch', *Arts Manitoba* 1, 1 (1977), p. 34. Ann Mandel links this to a specifically prairie view of history in her 'Uninventing Structures', pp. 68-9.

[27] See Linda Hutcheon, 'From Poetic to Narrative Structures: The Novels of Margaret Atwood', in *Margaret Atwood: Language, Text and System*, ed. Sherrill E. Grace and Lorraine Weir (Vancouver: University of British Columbia Press, 1983), pp. 17-31.

[28] For a related argument applying to Kroetsch's poetry, see Shirley Neuman, 'Figuring the Reader, Figuring the Self in *Field Notes*: Double or Noting', *Open Letter* 5th series, nos. 8-9 (1984), pp. 176-94. Here writing is presented as rereading and reading as a response to writing which subverts the authority of the written.

[29] See too Geoff Hancock, 'Interview' with Robert Kroetsch, *Books in Canada* October 1983, pp. 35-6.

[30] Kroetsch sees this as a particularly Canadian temptation, caught as we are between the binary oppositions of English/French, East/West, Ontario/Alberta (L, pp. 124-5).

[31] For a very interesting reading of desire in the metafictive terms of Roland Barthes's erotics of reading, see Lecker, pp. 106-22.

[32] For instance, Lecker, pp. 49 and 79.

[33] For instance, Aritha van Herk, 'Biocritical Essay' in *The Robert Kroetsch Papers: An Archival Inventory* (Calgary: University of Calgary Press, 1986), pp. xxviii-xxix, and Shirley Neuman in L, p. 168.

[34] In *RK: E*, p. 82.

[35] On the comparable importance of these political implications in the writing of Nicole Brossard and other writers who publish in *La Nouvelle Barre du Jour*, see Barbara Godard, 'Writing and Difference: Women Writers of Quebec and English-Canada' (in *In the Feminine: Women and Words/Les femmes et les mots (Conference Proceedings 1983)*, ed. Ann Dybikowski, Victoria Freeman, Daphne Marlatt, Barbara Pulling, Betsy Warland [Edmonton: Longspoon Press, 1983]), pp. 125-6; and, in the same volume, Gail Scott, 'Shaping a Vehicle for Her Use: Woman and the Short Story', p. 184.

[36] *The Crow Journals*, p. 15.

[37] Robert R. Wilson, 'Robert Kroetsch', p. 53.

38 Thomas, p. 113.

39 Names in Kroetsch's work often suggest an ironic departure from realist convention (and more of a link with the naming in satire): Hazard Lepage, Demeter Proudfoot, Roger Dorck, Bea Sunderman, Liebhaber. See W.F.H. Nicolaisen, 'Ordering the Chaos: Name Strategies in Robert Kroetsch's Novels,' *ECW*, 11 (1978), 55-65; and Sylvia Söderlind, 'Novel Territory: The Metamorphosis of Fiction in Canada and Quebec, 1965-1975,' chapter on *'Gone Indian*: The Novel as Rebus,' Ph. D. dissertation, University of Toronto, 1986, pp. 260-308.

40 *Gone Indian* (Toronto: New Press, 1973), p. 152.

41 'Unhiding the Hidden: Recent Canadian Fiction', *RK: E*, p. 21. See too 'Canada is a Poem' in the same volume, p. 35: 'Canada invents itself daily'.

42 In *RK: E*, p. 63.

43 'Contemporary Standards in the Canadian Novel', *RK: E*, p. 40.

44 Aritha van Herk, in 'Biocritical Essay', sees his 1960 travel book *Alberta* as the 'core' of his work (p. xviii).

45 See the preface to *A Mazing Space* by Shirley Neuman and Smaro Kamboureli, p. x: the women's texts used in the articles of this collection are 'not those of the literary histories with their binary model of center and margin. Center: Canadian (read anglophone) literature. Margin: Québécois literature. Centre: white, 'born-in-Canada' writers. Margin: native, colored, and immigrant writers. Center: fiction and poetry. Margin: letters, diaries, autobiographies, travel writing, oral history, performance poetry, theory. Nor are their texts those which nostalgically seek origins in two, or even many, solitudes. The long-established binary models have ceased to signify for women writers. Out of the margin they have made many centers.' See too the special issue of *Fireweed* (16 [1983]) on 'Women of Colour' and Claire Harris, 'Poets in Limbo', in *A Mazing Space*, pp. 115-25.

46 *Alibi* (Toronto: Stoddart, 1983), p. 7. All further references will appear in parentheses in the text.

47 'Beyond Nationalism: A Prologue', *RK: E*, p. 88.

48 See, for instance, Timothy Findley's *The Telling of Lies* (New York: Viking, 1986).

49 There are echoes here of Michael Hornyak's quest for the fountain of youth in *But We Are Exiles* and of the symbolic rebirths of *Gone Indian*.

50 D.G. Jones, 'In Search of America', *Boundary* 2 3, 1 (1974), p. 236. This issue was edited by Kroetsch.

51 *Boundary* 2 3, 1 (1974), p. 1.

52 'Contemporary Standards in the Canadian Novel,' *RK: E*, p. 45.

53 In Diane Bessai and Robert Kroetsch, 'Death is a Happy Ending: A Dialogue in Thirteen Parts', in *Figures in a Ground: Canadian Essays on Modern Literature Collected in Honor of Sheila Watson*, ed. Diane Bessai

and David Jackel (Saskatoon: Western Producer Prairie Press, 1978), p. 210.

54 Cf. Frank Davey, *From There to Here: A Guide to English-Canadian Literature Since 1960* (Erin, Ont.: Press Porcépic, 1974), pp. 20-1.

55 Fredric Jameson, 'Postmodernism, or The Cultural Logic of Late Capitalism', *New Left Review* 146 (1984), pp. 53-92.

Appendix:

The Novel (1972-1984)
from *The Literary History of Canada*, Vol. 4

To examine the Canadian novel[1] of a period that is already weighed down by a series of '-isms'—postmodernism, poststructuralism, feminism, not to mention nationalism and regionalism—is to discover, not the move towards consolidation that Laurie Ricou has found in the Canadian poetry of the 1970s and 1980s, but rather a set of challenges to existing traditions that literary criticism was not slow to label. Voices, previously muted, offered different ways in which to explore different experiences with language and life, and were recognized as 'other', as new and contesting voices. In addition, the fiction of these years came to us in a somewhat unsettled literary critical climate, one that revealed an increasing suspicion about the value and the authority of literary histories as creators of the so-called 'canon' of novelistic works.[2] This suspicion developed in the wake of some radical questioning of the presupposition that the importance and, indeed, meaning of literature rested only in how it expresses the individual genius of the author. This basically romantic view of art had been challenged by contemporary literary, philosophical, and psychoanalytic investigations into the notion of the coherence and continuity of the 'self'. In such a climate, this literary history of the Canadian novel from 1972 to 1984 can, for me, only be precisely that: a history of the *novels*, rather than of the *novelists*. The 'great tradition' of novelists has been dissolving; the supposedly universal culture and values in which it was based were found to be rooted in a particular place, time, class, and possibly, even sex. For these reasons, this chapter will outline not the progress of individual novelists over these years, but instead the changes in the form and focus of the novel as a genre. (Readers wishing to get a sense of particular writers' chronological development should refer to the works discussed in the Bibliography.)

Canadians became especially aware of the normative power of the literary canon over teachers, publishers, scholars, writers, and readers through the 1978 Calgary Conference's attempt to draw up a list of Canadian 'classics' (see Steele), thereby demonstrating the dangers of fixing (or fetishizing) fiction. What constitutes a 'classic' novel? Is it a matter of simple critical consensus, as some claim (e.g., Cude)? If so, who is to be involved in that consensus, and when is it to be arrived at? The history of the novel is especially full of examples of best-sellers becoming great unknowns in a few decades' time. It is true that the act of selecting novels for mention is itself, in appearance, an evaluative act. Nevertheless, since the very number of novels written in this period precluded reference to each one, the necessary selection was based on dominant modes of writing; examples used were those that illustrated best the formal and thematic characteristics being described. In other words, a literary history of the Canadian novel of this period that is itself being written during the 1980s must find some way to deal with theoretical questions like that of evaluation. Similarly, it must also face the issues raised by the contemporaneous radical reformulations of the structure, nature, and power of all historical models, for, increasingly, we have come to see that literary history—especially of the novel genre—can likely never be separated from other forms of history. The canon, whether formed deliberately or inadvertently, will always reflect the discourses out of which it derives: social, cultural, ideological.

In his chapter on fiction in Volume 3 of the *Literary History of Canada*, W.H. New wrote convincingly of the 'palpable effect' of the decade of the 1960s on Canadian writing. That effect continued to be felt because many of the novels of the 1970s and early 1980s were written by those 'formed' in those years, years of relative plenty that seemed to allow Canadian youth, in particular, the freedom to turn their attention to broader social concerns: ecology, peace, and women's rights. Significantly, that last volume of the *History*—unlike this one—also had an entire chapter devoted to 'Politics and Literature in the 1960s'. Although the late 1970s and early 1980s brought economic recession and a return to both conservative values and politics, the novels of the period continued to reflect the ideological climate of the 1960s in their broadly political orientation. There were not a great many novels about growing up amidst radical political confrontation and protest, though several novels studied the aftermath of the iconoclastic, anti-establishment counter-culture: Audrey Thomas's *Intertidal Life* (1984), John Gray's *Dazzled* (1984), and Victoria Brandon's *Mrs Job* (1979). More remarkable was the variety of kinds of fiction with a strong ideological *engagement*, which amplified the novel form's long tradition of moral and social commentary.[3]

The range of formal, tonal, and thematic possibilities within what we might call the novel of ideology was a vast one. For instance, *Obasan* (1981), by Joy Kogawa, was a personal and poetic evocation of the fate of Japanese Canadians, whose search for assimilation and economic security was met by evacuation and internment at the hands of the government of their own country during the last war. At the other end of the range of novelistic possibilities was Timothy Findley's *Famous Last Words* (1981), where the same kind of mixture of the fictional and the factual served as the background for a more general investigation into the relationship between fascism and aestheticism, between public history and private fantasy, in what purported to be the 'writing on the wall' for our century. While Margaret Atwood's *Bodily Harm* (1981) was specifically ideological in combating such things as political tyranny, other novels fought more local oppression—that more subtle, but no less ideological, repression in the name of bourgeois middle-class values. Many of these novels appeared, on one level, to be psychological studies, but the constant implied matching of the private with the public dimension suggested a broader perspective in which such fiction should be read: for instance, Janette Turner Hospital's *The Tiger in the Tiger Pit* (1983), with its focus on the puritanical ethics of a certain class and age, or the personal *and* public rebuilding after moral and physical devastation in Elizabeth Spencer's *The Salt Line* (1984). Some of the impetus to politicize the English-Canadian novel—in both form and content—likely came from the influence and example of Québécois revolutionaries and writers such as Hubert Aquin. The novelist *engagé* also appeared in the new cultural, or at least new media, roles that Canadian novelists adopted in these years. Not only did many of them actively participate in the 1981 Amnesty International's 'Writer and Human Rights' congress in Toronto, but many—like Margaret Atwood, Timothy Findley, and Rudy Wiebe—took upon themselves the responsibility of giving voice to the oppressed or of acting as the conscience of power. And the ethical sense of community became increasingly an international one.

The 1960s in Canada were also years marked by that heady Canadian nationalism (both cultural and economic) portrayed in Harry Boyle's *The Great Canadian Novel* (1972). The government, partly through the CBC and the Canada Council, partly through direct grants to publishers, launched a long campaign to create a literary community in Canada. And it more or less succeeded. One of the important manifestations of the existence of this community, as W.H. New explained in the last volume of this *History*, was the creation of many new presses to champion experimental or non-commercial novels: House of Anansi, Oberon, New Press, Coach House, ECW, Talonbooks, NeWest Press, and so on. Many of these flourished; some merely survived. Some went under (Virgo), and others rose in their place (fittingly, Groundhog Press). Some tried new innovative marketing techniques: Quadrant first sold only by subscription. All this activity outside of the 'establishment' culture made possible the existence of other than what are known as 'commercial' novels. Increasingly the larger publishing houses found that they had to play to the big book chains and clubs in order to survive in the face of a bleak economic climate and a more fragmented readership. Some presses, like McClelland and Stewart and Anansi, deliberately balanced their solid sellers with more daring (that is, less commercially viable) novels. The smaller presses often found that they just could not afford to print novels without government subsidies: fiction did not always pay for itself in the marketplace. However, more positive signs appeared in the book market as well. Three publishers introduced mass-market paperback series of 'Canadian classics' to be made available to the large number of Canadian literature courses in the schools and universities. The media paid considerable attention to new novelists who would normally get ignored, and in some provinces (Alberta, Manitoba) and in *Books in Canada*, there were annual contests and awards for the best first novel.

The steady increase in the number of 'popular' novels written, published, and purchased in Canada, marked another kind of continuity with the publishing changes begun in the 1960s. 'Popular' fiction generally means light entertainment, those works which tend to confirm, and rarely challenge, our beliefs. For this reason, however, they can often exemplify cultural patterns even more overtly or more stereotypically than more 'serious' fiction does. This kind of novel frequently relies on pre-formulated narrative structures and, for this reason, is often referred to by the collective title of genre or formula fiction. Canadian 'popular' novels came to be written according to every conceivable formula and on every imaginable topic—from gambling and sports to international spy intrigue, from general urban crime and courtroom drama to specific tales of nefarious deeds at the CBC or in the Canadian publishing industry, from heist stories to psychological thrillers, from domestic soap-opera to soft-core pornography, from fantasy and science fiction to the western and the detective story. These were set in locales ranging from the exotic to the familiar. Some of these novels clearly had a didactic message (such as those of the prolific Richard Rohmer), while others claimed only to tell a good tale (those of the equally prolific John Ballem). The growth of an indigenous Canadian 'popular' fiction industry reached its height in Harlequin Enterprises, which cornered a market both inside and outside Canada. The quality of this 'popular' fiction, needless to say, varied from novel to novel. Not all the detective stories were as entertaining both as mystery and as comedy as Howard Engel's Benny Cooperman series: *The Suicide Murders* (1980), *The Ransom Game* (1981), *Murder on Location* (1982), and *Murder Sees the Light* (1984).

Publishing affected the history of the novel in Canada in other important ways too. At a very basic level, publishers, in fact, controlled what novels got published in the first place. If there were certain clear trends in the novel, it might well be more because some publisher thought a market was developing for historical novels, for instance, than because more historical fiction was actually (statistically) being written. However, the Canadian novel was, on the whole, very fortunate in having, on the one hand, many fine publishers—both national and regional—who were deeply committed to the advancement of Canadian literature[4] and, on the other hand, governments who were willing to provide generous subsidies and even bail out floundering companies. Despite this good will, the future of Canadian fiction publishing by no means looked assured in the mid-1980s.

The 1960s also witnessed the so-called 'sexual revolution', and Leonard Cohen's early novel, *Beautiful Losers* (1966), was likely the archetype of that challenge to both sexual mores and novelistic form. With that challenge had come a questioning of sex and gender roles that has been a major force behind the continued development of the novel about women—written by both men and women. This heritage of the 1960s later promoted increased investigation of the consequences of what some novels (such as Jane Rule's *Contract with the World* [1980]) saw as a very Canadian refusal or reluctance to face sexuality (heterosexual or homosexual). The novels of Keith Maillard (*Two Strand River* [1976], *The Knife in My Hands* [1981], *Cutting Through* [1982]) studied male and female sexual identity and gender confusion.

These were among the once muted voices to be heard more loudly in Canadian fiction by the late 1970s. But they were not the only ones. This period also saw the coming of (writing) age of a generation of immigrants or children of immigrants, some writing in English, others in their native tongues. Their novels were frequently fictionalized autobiographies which either took the form of a generational saga or a *Bildungsroman*. They dealt with the problems faced by any newcomer to any society, problems both within the self and the family structure and also with the new world to be confronted. These works were, quite naturally, obsessed with social, psychological, and physical displacement; their tales were of struggle for survival and against alienation. One might well imagine the many tensions to be resolved before these writers could face—in print—their past, perhaps especially because that past involved a major cultural uprooting. Canadians have traditionally prided themselves on their multiculturalism, their ethnic 'mosaic' that allowed cultural diversity. But this liberal concept of a mosaic could turn into a tyrannical model as well: as the fiction revealed, it demanded that one retain one's ethnic roots *and* become a Canadian too (Jan Drabek's *Report on the Death of Rosenkavalier* [1977]). And arrival in liberal-thinking Canada did not always mean a total escape from racial prejudice. This ironic narrative pattern could be seen in novels such as Michael Cullen's *Goodnight, Sammy Wong* (1983) and Saros Cowasjee's *Goodbye to Elsa* (1974), and it was turned amusingly upside-down in the inverted missionary tale of Harold Sonny Ladoo's *Yesterdays* (1974). In general, it seemed to take a second generation of writers, often born in Canada, to explore (with some distance) both the immigrant pains of dislocation and the exhilarations of new possibilities. These novels continued, in this way, to be very Canadian investigations into the nature of national and cultural identity.

It was unfortunate, perhaps, for that process of identity-seeking that there continued to be little extended fiction actually written in the Inuit, Indian, or Métis communities, perhaps because of the strength of the oral tradition in these societies. Many white writers, however, attempted to take the mythology and history (both past and present) of the Native Peoples as their subject matter in their own search for their roots. The culture of the Inuit was the focus for James Houston's *Spirit Wrestler* (1980) and Harold Horwood's *White Eskimo* (1972). The ethical issues of the fate of both the Arctic and its people were the focus of a number of other novels, like Peter Such's *Riverrun* (1973). Other fiction focused more directly on the often disastrous interaction of native culture with that of the whites: W.O. Mitchell's *The Vanishing Point* (1973) and Rudy Wiebe's *The Temptations of Big Bear* (1973). In some novels there was a strong documentary quality dominating the presentation of Indian culture. Nan F. Solerno and Rosamond M. Vanderburgh's *Shaman's Daughter* (1981) was perhaps the extreme of this mode in its anthropological documentary style. In others, such as Wayland Drew's powerful *Wabeno Feast* (1973), this impulse was wedded to a concern for the ecological and sociological fate of the Native Peoples. When white and Indian worlds met in fiction of this period, they did so in any number of forms and tones: from the comic irony of James Polk's *The Passion of Loreen Bright Weasel* (1981) to the serious polemic embedded in David Williams' *The Burning Wood* (1975) and Matt Cohen's *Wooden Hunters* (1975). Although the second half of Susan Musgrave's *The Charcoal Burners* (1980) went in a surreal and horrifying direction, the first half certainly shared these concerns.

The Indian mythic figure of the trickster continued to prove attractive to the Canadian novel, which was searching, as always, for its own mythology. Alan Fry's *The Revenge of Annie Charlie* (1973) and Robert Kroetsch's *Gone Indian* (1973) both made interesting, if very different, uses of this figure. T.D. MacLulich (196) has noted that, in general, the Canadian use of Native characters in fiction differed from the American. According to this argument, American novels have tended to see in the meeting with the Indian a meeting with one's true self. Canadian novels, on the other hand, have related the Indian and the Inuit to the wilderness in which they live: both Native and nature have come to embody some eternal spiritual essence. This is an image of the Native who has managed integration with nature, who can live in harmony with natural forces in a way admired and sought after by whites. In short, these novels could still be seen as grappling with those topics that have dominated Canadian literature: identity and the relation of man to nature. The need to feel rooted in the land has often taken on primitivist or romantic associations through the process of identification that Terry Goldie has called 'indigenization', but equally often the message presented was an ideological one, as in the white historian hero's dealing with the Cree Maskepetoon in Rudy Wiebe's *My Lovely Enemy* (1983) or, again, in Kroetsch's more daringly parodic *Gone Indian* (1973).

This particular concern clearly takes us beyond the context of one decade, the 1960s, and into the more general continuum of literary history in Canada. Many novels in the 1970s and 1980s adhered to that strong sense both of place and of the potency of nature that resulted in the general labelling of Canadian fiction as regional. But it is a truism of the novel as a mimetic genre that it is set in a particular place and time. Given that, what novel would not be regional in some way? The density of realistic social and geographical detail in David Adams Richards' Faulknerian novels about the Maritimes have earned those works the label of regionalist. But what does this mean? In the sixties, Henry Kreisel argued that the landscape had a particularly important social and psychogical impact on the Western novel, where, to use Laurie Ricou's evocative phrase, vertical man met a horizontal world. But surely the very specifically rooted Manawaka novels of Margaret Laurence, like those of Richards, transcend geography—as do the novels of Joyce, Dickens, and Balzac. In the novel form, it is difficult to write about the individual without placing her in a geographical and social setting, and thus writing about an entire society, with its communal history and values. Novels as diverse as Wiebe's *The Scorched-Wood People* (1977) and David Williams' *The River Horsemen* (1981) revealed an interest in places and communities that had some spiritual anchor, some vision of the world that belonged particularly to them.

In all of these very universal 'regional' novels a double pull operated. On the one hand, there was the clear attraction to an almost National Film Board-like documentary realism. On the other hand, there was a pull toward the presentation of the local and the natural as symbolic or metaphoric. This could be seen as one way of domesticating or taming the unknown, but, on a more positive note, it could also be a way to articulate and give voice to a relationship with the land. Both impulses focused on the two obvious settings: the city and the country. The country here either meant the small town, or sometimes the family farm, or it could also mean the Canadian wilderness, where the attractions of a kind of modified mythic and romantic mode were never very far away, even in tales of survival like John Buell's *Playground* (1976), Thomas York's *Snowman* (1976), and Rudy Wiebe's *The Mad Trapper* (1980). According to Margaret Atwood's thesis in *Survival*, Canadians were seen in their literature as the victims of hostile natural forces. Alan Pritchard (36-7) has argued that, in novels from British Columbia at any rate, the pattern was reversed: it was the wild paradise that was victimized by Canadians and their American-inspired machine civilization. Perhaps, then, the typical Canadian model for a response to the wild was, in fact, a rather ambivalent one.

Certainly some novels suggested this ambivalence in (paradoxically) clear terms: in Marian Engel's *Bear* (1976), a citified and literary woman confronted nature and sexuality in the form of a bear, while the more destructive forces of that nature were faced—in the same bear form—by the equally literary hero of W.O. Mitchell's *Since Daisy Creek* (1984). Yet, from evocations of symbolic meaning to tales of the ecological, these novels all used the wilderness as both setting and subject, often more primitive than pastoral. Another version of this Canadian sense of place seemed to have been created specifically for and by women— novels that took place at a cottage or cabin, a domesticated home in the wilderness: Joan Barfoot's *Abra* (1978), Engel's *Bear* (1976) again, Atwood's *Surfacing* (1972), and even Margaret Laurence's *The Diviners* (1974). Obviously, it was Susanna Moodie's and Catharine Parr Traill's experiences in the bush that were the literary antecedents of the lives of these women as they coped with the 'wilderness' that was both outside and inside—both that of physical nature and that of their human and sexual identities as women and, often, as creatrix-figures as well.

During these years, however, the major locations in which to set novels (for realistic and symbolic purposes) were certainly the big city and the small town. There was Alice Munro's Jubilee, Robertson Davies' Deptford, Margaret Atwood's Griswold, Margaret Laurence's Manawaka, Matt Cohen's Salem, Graham Woods's Tamerack, and Jamie Brown's Shrewsbury. Occasionally these small towns were presented as idyllic places of rural felicity or as refuges from urban madness. But most frequently and most powerfully, the small town in Canadian fiction came to represent a limited and limiting society from which protagonists yearned to escape. Matt Cohen's communities in southeastern Ontario took on gothic proportions as human desire was transmuted into puritanical sin (*Flowers of Darkness* [1981] and even, to some extent, *The Sweet Second Summer of Kitty Malone* [1979]). The intellectual, psychological, and emotional confinement of Deptford in Robertson Davies' trilogy (*Fifth Business* [1970], *The Manticore* [1972], *World of Wonders* [1975]) drove the characters out into the wide world of experience.

In much of this small-town fiction, the harshness of the land and the disintegration of traditional values that once bound the community to that land were often reflected in the people who had to inhabit it. The varying degrees of human and geographical sterility and desolation of Susan Kerslake's *Middlewatch* (1976), Terrence Heath's *The Last Hiding Place* (1982), or M.T. Kelly's *The Ruined Season* (1982) were more than matched by the economic and physical violence wrought by and upon the people of the logging community of David Adams Richards' Miramichi Valley in New Brunswick (*Lives of Short Duration* [1981] and *Blood Ties* [1976]). These are all examples of what Leslie Fiedler (16-17) once called, in an analogy with the Western genre, the Northern. Here the small town, dwarfed by a hostile environment, was the setting for the struggle of the often (but not necessarily) sensitive individual against a puritanical society, often symbolized or incarnated in some patriarchal figure of authority, whose weight of guilt was internalized by the would-be rebel.

The heirs of Grove, Stead, Buckler, and Ross were writers like Richards or like Marian Engel in *The Glassy Sea* (1978). In that novel, the pain of growing up plain, smart, and female in small-town Ontario revealed the consequences of rebellion, as well as of coming to terms with the repressive past. More and more, though, in novels like Atwood's *Bodily Harm* (1981) and Laurence's *The Diviners* (1974), alleviation of this guilt and pessimism seemed possible through a more mature acceptance of the pain of living and of having lived. In the work of Jack Hodgins and other West Coast writers, it has been argued, there was even more clearly a move away from the 'Puritan' to what has been called the 'Anglican' mode: 'the enjoyment of the creation as opposed to the Puritan alienation from nature . . . belief in the goodness of life combined with the recognition of human limitations, valuing of community as balancing private judgment and private myth' (Pritchard 45).

There was less cause for optimism in the urban novels of the period. In these, the same double pull could be seen between the documentary impulse and the drive toward symbolic universalization, that is, toward the presentation of the Eliotian Unreal City. Not surprisingly, perhaps, the city as the final place of social and psychological alienation was the most common image during the 1970s and early 1980s. Austin Clarke's moving trilogy about Barbadian immigrants in Toronto (*The Meeting Point* [1967], *Storm of Fortune* [1973], *The Bigger Light* [1975]) showed the city's multiculturalism and racial diversity in a less than flattering light, as, for instance, the excuse for hierarchies of power that even money could not move. Attacks on the mores and values of Canadian urban society could take the form of hallucinatory surreal fantasy, as in Juan Butler's *The Garbageman* (1972), or of documentary and didactic realism, as in the Cabbagetown and suburban novels of Hugh Garner (e.g., *Death in Don Mills* [1975], *The Intruders* [1976], *Murder Has Your Number* [1978]). The Vancouver streets of Helen Potrebenko's *Taxi!* (1975) and the Victoria subculture of britt hagarty's *Prisoner of Desire* (1979) were equally unappealing, but likely naturalistic, portrayals of one side of urban Canada.

The city was also usually seen as the cause, as well as the scene, of middle-class marital breakdown, of lives of quiet desperation, as in some of the carefully crafted, rather low-key novels of Richard B. Wright: *In the Middle of a Life* (1973), *Final Things* (1980), and *The Teacher's Daughter* (1982). In reading such tales of sociological horror and cosmic despair, one certainly could come to yearn for more novels like Adele Wiseman's wonderfully affirmative moral novel, *Crackpot* (1974), deeply rooted in the concrete world of the north end of Winnipeg, and yet reaching mythic dimensions in her exploiting, yet inverting, of even the most grotesque of ethnic and cultural stereotypes.

The hearty humour of this novel located it within a long

tradition in Canadian letters: since Leacock and Haliburton, satire and laughter have been standard ways for Canadians to come to terms with where and how they live. Rick Salutin (266) once implied that the trick in covering Canadian culture was to figure out what to do *besides* satirize. Mordecai Richler continued to 'have at' his own generation of urban middle-class Jewish professionals and intellectuals in *Joshua Then and Now* (1980), without leaving the WASP establishment unscathed, however. The novels of Morley Torgov (*A Good Place to Come from* [1974], *The Abramsky Variations* [1977], *The Outside Chance of Maximilian Glick* [1982]) and of Seymour Blicker (*The Last Collection* [1976]) continued this familiar North American vein of Jewish satire and comedy. In the comic novels of Max Braithwaite, Ontario cities and towns came under this same satiric scrutiny. In fact, much Canadian humorous writing was in the traditional moralistic or satiric mode which affirms 'the good and true' (Moss 200) in some way. And hardly a Canadian institution escaped ironic or satiric investigation: the RCMP (Ken Mitchell's *The Meadowlark Connection* [1975]), the literary and academic communities (Rachel Wyatt's *Foreign Bodies* [1982]), politics (Ian MacNeill's *The Battle for Saltbucket Beach* [1975] and Eric Koch's *The Leisure Riots* [1973]), tourism (Richard B. Wright's *Tourists* [1984]), or Canadian education and its effects on our culture (John Metcalf's *Going Down Slow* [1972] and *General Ludd* [1980]).

The humour ranged from the genially playful to the condescendingly withering. Often satiric fiction of this period took the structure of the modern picaresque: Ken Mitchell's *The Con Man* (1979), Richard Wright's *Farthing's Fortunes* (1976), and Anthony Brennan's *The Crazy House* (1975). However, it was not just urban novels that had the so-called sophistication to poke fun at themselves in the spirit of witty, but cogent, criticism. The fictive small town of Plum Bluff, Manitoba was the scene of Helen Levi's trilogy (*A Small Informal Dance* [1977], *Tangle Your Web and Dosey-Do* [1978], and *Honour Your Partner* [1979]) that offered a sharp and ironic portrait of middle-class innocence and decency. It was in a similar social milieu—though in the Ottawa Valley—that was born one Bartholomew Bandy, the foolish, feckless hero who goes to war and returns to adventures in Donald Jack's continuing series of *The Bandy Papers*.

Out of the Canadian *farm* experience, however, little such variety of tone seemed possible. Whether the farm was in Québec

(Jean-Guy Carrier's *Family* [1977]), northern Ontario (Gail Henley's *Where the Cherries End Up* [1978]), or Saskatchewan (Mary Ann Seitz's *Shelterbelt* [1979]), it was equally both a lure and a burden. It was the place where a family—often an immigrant family—put down its roots, and it was also the place from which the family could never escape. This ambivalence was as strong in the novels about Ukrainian new arrivals on the prairies as it was in those about multi-generational farms in WASP southern Ontario. In Matt Cohen's powerful *The Disinherited* (1974), the farm novel took on the dimensions of the family saga, of the conflict between generations, between the older one that was firmly rooted in the mythic and mundane reality of the soil and the younger one, willingly exiled from the land, but disinherited and rootless.

Of course, this kind of generational novel of family conflict could be, and was, set in cities as well: witness Robert Harlow's *Paul Nolan* (1983). T.D. MacLulich (194) has suggested that the frequency of this generational conflict novel in Canada may reflect a transferred exorcism of Canadian writers' own relationship to a utilitarian, materialistic, pragmatic society against which they must define themselves. Novels like David Williams' *Eye of the Father* (1985) or F.G. Paci's *The Italians* (1978), *Black Madonna* (1982), and *The Father* (1984) were, in this light, more than tales of specifically immigrant displacement and assimilation (though they were definitely that); they also became allegories of the artist's struggle with Canadian society at large.

What was perhaps most noteworthy about all of this 'regional' Canadian fiction was that it seemed to retain, for the most part, the well-known and accepted form of the traditional realist novel. Novelists themselves offered a number of theories to account for this constant in our fiction. George Bowering, for instance, has blamed 'good old puritanism' (5)—realist novels somehow seem more useful, for they reflect our values and culture. Matt Cohen, defining the realist novel rather basically (as one that is about 'reality' and 'in which not only does thought or action lead to subsequent connected thought or action, but does so in groups of words organized into logical sentences, paragraphs, chapters, etc.' [69]), explained this realist impulse in terms of the Canadian need to invent, not just reflect, reality. The realist conventions allow novelists, he argued, to fill a gap in their consciousness—the gap caused by the lack of a country. For

Cohen, Canada is a concept too large to hold in the mind, too diverse to unite in the imagination or in reality, and so the manageable and familiar conventions of the realist novel allow writers to invent a country which they *can* imagine. Perhaps. It is nevertheless difficult to avoid noticing that contemporaneous American, French, British, and Italian novels also continued to find the realist mode congenial.

In other words, whatever the local theory about the geographic size or the puritan mores of Canada, Canadian literature did not exist in a *literary* vacuum. It shared its formal and often thematic preoccupations with the literature of many other nations. Like the European and American novel, Canadian fiction was heir to both nineteenth-century realism and twentieth-century modernism. The constant staples of the novelistic tradition—of social analysis and psychological investigation—buttressed the Canadian novel too. Robert Kroetsch may have speculated that, because we lacked an Eliot or a Pound, we skipped modernism in Canada and went right from the Victorian to the Postmodern (Neuman and Wilson 111), but the *Bildungsroman* of the 1970s and 1980s was clearly the offspring of the modernist concern for psychological realism. Not that there was any obvious uniformity in the use of this convention. Some tales of growing up were quite radically experimental (David Young's *Incognito* [1982]). And, even among the many comic versions, there was a range from the light and sentimental irony of Ted Allan's *Love is a Long Shot* (1984) to the darker humour of W.O. Mitchell's *How I Spent My Summer Holidays* (1981) to the comic verbal exuberance of Armin Wiebe's subversion of English syntax and lexicon in the Mennonite dialects of his *The Salvation of Yasch Siemans* (1984).

Frequently, the story of the coming of age of the protagonist took place in a small town—the grim New Brunswick mill town of David Adams Richards' *The Coming of Winter* (1974), the Nova Scotian frontier community of Alden Nowlan's *Various Persons Named Kevin O'Brien: A Fictional Memoir* (1973), Stan Dragland's more comically treated Depot, Alberta in *Peckertracks: A Chronicle* (1978), or small-town Ontario in documentary poet Don Gutteridge's *Bus Ride* (1974) and *All in Good Time* (1981). In most cases, the limitations (geographical, emotional, and moral) of the town did not make growing up any easier. In many, the village took on the power of potential destruction. Whether the *Bildungsroman* was set in the country or the city, or both (as in Betty Wilson's tale of a Métis youth growing up in both locales in *André Tom Macgregor* [1976]), the experience of coming to maturity was almost always one that transcended the individual.

Often the quest for self involved a coming to terms with the past, both public and private, as in W.D. Valgardson's *Gentle Sinners* (1980) and T.F. Rigelhof's *The Education of J.J. Pass* (1983). Sometimes that past was a European one that was never really left behind: the Venice of Caterina Edwards' *The Lion's Mouth* (1982), the war-torn Poland of Ann Charney's *Dobryd* (1973) or Abraham Boyarsky's *Shreiber* (1983), or the omnipresent Ukraine in Maara Haas's *The Street Where I Live* (1976). Maria Ardizzi's *Made in Italy* (1982) was typical of many of these *Bildungsromane* written by those who emigrated to Canada, in that it was a tale of dislocation and isolation (linguistic, cultural, familial) and of the desperate desire to integrate and communicate. These were themes familiar to many stories of youthful development, but made more acute by the immigrant status of the protagonist.

Although many of the novels of growing up dealt with particularly male experience—Keith Maillard's *Alex Driving South* (1980), Barry Dickson's *Home Safely to Me* (1973), Dennis T. Patrick Sears' *The Lark in the Clear Air* (1974), or Peter Gault's *Golden Rod* (1983)—none explored more dramatically the dark side of maturing in an alien and sexually dangerous landscape than Clark Blaise's *Lunar Attractions* (1979). But one of the most interesting developments during the 1970s and early 1980s was that young women, as well as men, became the focus of the *Bildungsroman* form. Shirley Faessler's *Everything in the Window* (1979), Cecelia Frey's *Breakaway* (1974), Sylvia Fraser's *Pandora* (1972), Nessa Rapoport's *Preparing for Sabbath* (1982), Sondra Gotlieb's *True Confections or How My Family Arranged My Marriage* (1978), and, in a more Proustian vein, Oonah McFee's *Sandbars* (1977) were among the many novels that dealt with a woman's experience of coming of age. In the female variant of the *Bildungsroman*, in contrast to the traditional male form, familial ties were often rejected in the name of broader social and personal possibilities for women: the maternal, as associated in patriarchal culture with subservience and impotence, had to be redefined as either matriarchally powerful or as more positively feminine.[5]

The *Bildungsroman* was only one of the many forms taken by the fiction that followed the general questioning of gender and of sexual roles by a growing body of feminist criticism. Most, but certainly not all, of the novels about these issues were written by women. This is not at all to say that men did not deal sensitively and provocatively with feminist political and personal themes. We need only recall Ian McLachlan's *Helen in Exile* (1980) or the novels of David Helwig, especially *Jennifer* (1979), *It Is Always Summer* (1982) and *The Only Son* (1984), all novels concerning sexual wars and the power relations between men and women. Some male writers told, with varying degrees of credibility, the stories of women—from the inside: David Lewis Stein in *The Golden Age Hotel* (1984), Leon Rooke in *Fat Woman* (1980), Jack Ludwig in *A Woman of Her Age* (1973), and Howard O'Hagan in *The School-Marm Tree* (written in the 1950s, but published in 1977). The acute portrayal of the sensibility of a perfectly ordinary young woman in Kent Thompson's *Shacking Up* (1980), followed upon his equally incisive presentations of the male psyche in *The Tenants Were Corrie and Tennie* (1973) and *Across from the Floral Park* (1974).

Domestic dramas, whether by men or women, about the decline of modern marriage or about sexual politics in general, abounded in this period, some written by old hands at the game, like Brian Moore (*The Doctor's Wife* [1976], *The Mangan Inheritance* [1979], *The Temptation of Eileen Hughes* [1981], *Cold Heaven* [1983]), and others by newcomers like Wayne Tefs (*Figures on a Wharf* [1983]) and Sharon Butala (*Country of the Heart* [1984]). John Marlyn's *Putzi, I Love You, You Little Square* (1981) and George Jonas's *Final Decree* (1981) were novels written by men who gave the distinct impression that the women's liberation movement had had very few positive effects on human relations—at least from a European male perspective. However, more balanced and thoughtful fiction analysed the consequences of change: for instance, the results of switching family roles in George Szanto's *Not Working* (1982). Among the novels written by women on these sorts of subjects, the range of tone and approach was broad: at one end of the spectrum were the somewhat overtly anti-male novels[6] of Aritha Van Herk (*Judith* [1978] and *The Tent Peg* [1981]), and at the other, was a novel like Janette Turner Hospital's subdued study of the female condition in different cultures in *The Ivory Swing* (1982).

However, it was the *everyday* life of women, both with and without men, that was the staple of Canadian fiction written by women in this period. Family life, from both the female and male perspectives, was the occasion for considerable complex psychological analysis in *Small Ceremonies* (1976), *The Box Garden* (1977), and *Happenstance* (1980), all by Carol Shields; it was also the excuse for, at times, almost pathological solipsism in Joan Barfoot's *Abra* (1978) and *Dancing in the Dark* (1982). Other novels, like Betty Lambert's *Crossings* (1979), Elizabeth Brewster's *Junction* (1982), and Katherine Govier's *Random Descent* (1979), suggested that the search for present identity could be undertaken, for women as for men, only through coming to terms with the past. These different modes and perspectives should serve to dispel the cliché of some sort of monolithic entity called the 'feminist novel'. Fiction centred on professional women (Doris Anderson's *Two Women* [1978] and *Rough Layout* [1981]) differed in theme and tone from fiction about motherhood or old age—even when it was all written by the same writer: Constance Beresford-Howe's (respectively) *A Population of One* (1977), *The Marriage Bed* (1981), and *The Book of Eve* (1973). So-called feminist novels varied from the self-reflexive parable about a prehistorical creatrix, in Pegeen Brennan's *Zarkeen* (1982), to the satiric extravaganza of Rachel Wyatt's *The Rosedale Hoax* (1977) to the bizarre mixture of tall tale and history, of fantasy and biography, in Susan Swan's *The Biggest Modern Woman of the World* (1983).

In that novel, the reader is told: 'to be from the Canadas is to feel as women feel—cut off from the base of power' (274). The question of the relation of the individual female experience of powerlessness (so insightfully explored in all the fiction of Audrey Thomas) to a more generalized social and cultural experience was one that novels like Marian Engel's *Bear* (1976) and Jane Rule's *The Young in One Another's Arms* (1977) also investigated in some depth. In these novels, as in Atwood's *Surfacing* (1972), *Life Before Man* (1979), and *Bodily Harm* (1981), a broader rebellion emerged, not just against the patriarchal structures that controlled sexual politics, but against the paternalistic patterns of modern post-industrial capitalism. In Atwood's novels, this protest moved more and more into the public arena. Many of these women's novels also revealed an intense awareness of the relationship between bonding and bondage, that is, between a woman's need for connection with others and her equally strong need for freedom and independence. It was this theme that made novels like Audrey Thomas's

Intertidal Life (1984) and Margaret Clarke's *The Cutting Season* (1984) political novels in the broadest sense of the word.

Other novels, by both men and women, went beyond sexual ideology to use the male/female structure as a way of investigating, very self-consciously, the perhaps eternal question (recently declared to be the new question of postmodernism) of the relationship between art and life. But there was a most interesting difference in the way men and women used this metaphorical space. The writer figures in the women's fiction— in Audrey Thomas's *Latakia* (1979) or in Margaret Laurence's *The Diviners* (1974)—saw in the physical and passionate attraction of the sexes (and in its possible result) a model for the energy of creation, with a strong emphasis on maternal images of birth, of potential generation. However, in the men's novels—in Robert Kroetsch's *Alibi* (1983), Clark Blaise's *Lusts* (1983), and Rudy Wiebe's *My Lovely Enemy* (1983)—the relationship between sex and art was a more ambivalent one: while sexuality was still linked to the creative urge, there was also a strong awareness, less of the birth, than of the death impulse inherent in it.

Novels like this signalled Canadian fiction's arrival at another '-ism', at what we seem to have decided to call postmodernism. Some have seen this development as representing—finally—a loss of faith in the realist story (Bowering 8). Others explained that our national discontinuities made us ripe for the discontinuities of postmodernism (Kroetsch, in Neuman and Wilson 112). Still others sought to deny the change. Matt Cohen felt that in Canada there were only isolated postmodernist experiments by only a few writers: 'although these experiments have often been enthusiastically welcomed by critics eager to see the emergence of a "postmodern" Canadian literature, postmodernism in Canada is more alive as a critical theory than as a group of books' (69). However, *pace* Cohen, many books written in the 1970s and 1980s were indeed 'metafictional' or postmodernist. Indeed, this movement toward fiction about fiction was perhaps the single biggest development in Canadian fiction—long or short—during the seventies and eighties. Interestingly enough, the Canadian novel by no means lost faith in the realist story: what was striking about the fiction of this period was that the postmodernist challenges to convention all came from *within* the conventions of realism itself. Canadian fiction rarely took on that familiar American or French mode of increasing self-reflexivity or of increasing focus on literary materials (narrative or linguistic) in and for themselves, that is, outside of the context of some sort of realism or, at least, of a direct parody of its conventions. Such an unwillingness to jettison realism might well be analogous to what Laurie Ricou has called the nostalgia for the referential function of language in contemporaneous Canadian poetry. In fiction, we need only think of those Canadian novels about the artistic process, such as H.R. Percy's *Painted Ladies* (1983), Keith Harrison's *Dead Ends* (1981), Leo Simpson's *The Peacock Papers* (1973), Robert Harlow's *Scann* (1972), or even Guy Vanderhaeghe's *My Present Age* (1984) where, as in *Don Quijote*, people learned that they could not live in, or even as in, books.

On the other hand, many more determinedly experimental novels were written in Canada in those years. Elegant productions came from Coach House Press, such as Geraldine Rahmani's *Blue* (1981), where each of the three narrators was given a horizontal piece of the page, and Robert Sward's The *Jurassic Shales* (1975) with its distorted photographed heads of the Queen and equally distorted play with plot and character conventions. Other verbal and graphic effects were achieved in Ann Rosenberg's *Bee Book* (1981). The visual collage form that Cozette deCharmoy played with in *The True Life of Sweeney Todd* (1973) (from Oberon Press) was brought to a surreal extreme in the discontinuous form of collage and fragment of Audrey Thomas's *Blown Figures* (1974). Yet, even in Thomas's formal play, the experimentation was presented as a sort of mimetic analogue of the psychology of a distressed woman. The challenge to the linearity of print, the breakdown of convention on a formal level, was echoed in the difficulties that both character and reader faced in trying to understand. The linguistic play in her *Intertidal Life* (1984) was also not pure poststructuralist 'dissemination' of language: it was thematically motivated by the fact that Alice, the aptly named protagonist, was a writer. That she was also a mother provided the focus, not only of the plot, but also of the verbal associations that tied the novel together, as well as of the many echoes of other texts that gave such resonance to the work (echoes of Virginia Woolf, Margaret Atwood, George Bowering, Lawrence Durrell, D.H. Lawrence, Radclyffe Hall, and others). Among other novels to use fragmentary forms of composition, Sinclair Ross's *Sawbones Memorial* (1974), with its many unnumbered episodes, recalled the interior monologues of British and European modernist fiction, interwoven as they were with speeches and conversations. The overlappings of theme, character, and plot worked to pull together four generations of the fictive town of Upward. Helen Weinzweig's *Passing Ceremony* (1973) constantly altered the narrative perspective, providing the reader with a formal illustration of the failure of human relations that was the subject of the novel. Her *Basic Black with Pearls* (1980) took us into a mind and a fragmentary form that did not distinguish between realism and fantasy in the 'funhouse of appearance and illusion'. That many of these explorations of both psyche and form were of and by women might not be coincidental, for it was women writers who perhaps most obviously questioned the inheritance, both thematic and structural, of the novelistic patrimony.

Postmodernist (and modernist) possibilities of perspective also invited self-conscious play. Once again, realist conventions were contested from within the conventions themselves. Leon Rooke's *Shakespeare's Dog* (1983) was a comic realist novel, even if the perspective was that of a dog and the language that of Elizabethan England. In Ken Ledbetter's *Too Many Blackbirds* (1984), sixteen retellings of a story, a tale that was itself an unsolved mystery, asserted the impossibility of telling reality from fiction. The seven episodes of Ray Smith's experimental *Lord Nelson Tavern* (1974) altered point of view and narrative time in such a way that the readers' involvement in piecing together the relationships among the characters made manifest—in a postmodern way—the task readers have always had in the novel genre: the imaginative creation of a world of fiction.

In other words, many of these novels made explicit the conventionality of fiction; they were examples of 'metafiction', fiction about fiction-making. At times, as with Robert Allen's two-part novel *The Hawryliw Process* (1980 and 1981), the cleverness and inventiveness seemed to be victorious over any narrative power, but in general in Canada, this auto-referentiality was seldom achieved at the expense of narrative interest. In fact, very little of what American critics have called 'surfiction' (Federman) was written in Canada. The strength of the realist tradition could always be seen here. For example, Clark Blaise's *Lusts* (1983) was basically an epistolary novel, but his more postmodern version of that canonical (and realist) form actually *enacted* the changing shapes of the relationship of the letter writers. Kroetsch's *Alibi* (1983) was in some ways a very traditional journal novel, but it had a totally metafictional twist. In each of these novels, as in many others, it was the role of the reader—and his or her surrogate within the novel—that made these novels different from modernist ones (with their primary emphasis on the act of *writing*). In postmodernist fiction—long or short (Hancock 5)— it was the politics of how and why we read that came to the foreground. Reading became an act of co-creation. Given that so many Canadian novelists have been academics, it was not surprising that they should have been self-conscious about the material nature of their work and about the interpretive power of the reader: their students would have taught them about that! The fact that many of these novelists have also been poets (for example, Atwood, Kroetsch, Ondaatje, Bowering, and Musgrave) might well have contributed to opening up the novel to new possible forms, as well as teaching novelists to learn to trust their readers. Poets have never had the luxury of helpful paragraphs of explanatory prose.

Aside from the continuing strength of Canadian 'regionalism' and realism (though not without alterations), this kind of broader international trend in fiction had the greatest impact on the Canadian novel of the 1970s and 1980s. Perhaps the single largest of these was the internalized challenge to realism offered by Latin American fiction, a challenge that was often called magical realism (Flores). This kind of realism was less a rejection of the realist conventions than a contamination of them with fantasy and with the conventions of an oral story-telling tradition. This very mixture seemed to prove especially attractive to the Canadian novel, itself working within, but questioning and pushing the limits of realism. Among the many heirs of Gabriel García Márquez's *One Hundred Years of Solitude* in Canada were Kroetsch's *What the Crow Said* (1978), Susan Swan's *The Biggest Modern Woman of the World* (1983), Jack Hodgins' *The Invention of the World* (1977) and *The Resurrection of Joseph Bourne* (1979), and Michael Ondaatje's *Running in the Family* (1982). The fact that this last work was also a biography and autobiography, in a sense, raised the question of the limits of the *novel* genre. In fact, one of the results of postmodernism, as Laurie Ricou also points out in his chapter on the poetry of these years, was that textual self-reflexivity led to a general breakdown of the conventional boundaries between the arts, and, by extension, between genres. Borders between the novel and forms of what had been traditionally considered non-fictional genres were constantly being crossed: the metafiction of the 1970s and 1980s played with the boundaries between fiction and history, biography, and autobiography. In other words, there was not just a deliberate confusion between the novel and the short-story collection (in the work of Alice Munro and Ray Smith) or the novel and the long poem or poem sequence (Derk Wynand's *One Cook, Once Dreaming* [1980], Stephanie Nynych's . . . *and like i see it* [1972], Frank Davey's *Edward and Patricia* [1984]), but it appeared that fiction and non-fiction were interpenetrating in what were new and different forms from the usual fictionalized biography or historical novel. The difference from these traditional forms would appear to rest in the degree of metafictional self-consciousness within the work itself: these works were unabashedly fictional artifice—stories made up of words—but they also laid claim to a real, historically verifiable context. As in the documentary long poem of the same years, there was a strong pull toward the authoritativeness of fact. Sometimes these were Canadian historical facts: George Bowering's *Burning Water* (1980) told the tale of the writer writing *and* of the analogous process of discovery of the West Coast by George Vancouver, and in *A Short Sad Book* (1977), also by Bowering, figures of the modern Canadian literary scene mingled with Sir John A. Macdonald. Sometimes it was not really a Canadian historical context at all: in both Chris Scott's masterly *Antichthon* (1982) and Mark Frutkin's *The Growing Dawn* (1983), the metafictional focus was on the reading and writing about two more distant figures—respectively, Giordano Bruno and Marconi.

The writing of history had itself, of course, come under considerable scrutiny in the same decade, and its links to fictional narrative forms were among the main foci of attention. Historiography was redefined as a poetic construct. To write history was to narrate, to reconstruct by means of selection and interpretation (White lx). History began to be seen as being *made* by its *writer*, even if the events seemed to speak for themselves. Narrativization was seen as a form of human comprehension, a way to impose meaning and form on the chaos of historical event (Jameson). Given this new historical self-consciousness, it was not odd, perhaps, that when the Canadian novel chose to represent actual, historic personages—the Duke and Duchess of Windsor in Findley's *Famous Last Words* (1981) or Riel and Big Bear in Wiebe's *The Scorched-Wood People* (1977) and *The Temptations of Big Bear* (1973)—it should have done so equally self-consciously. Like history, the novel too had to use emplotting strategies of exclusion, emphasis, and subordination of the elements of the story, and it too had to deal with the chaos of already consitituted events. But it also had another set of conventions to confront: those of fiction. And so, in the 1970s and early 1980s, a paradoxical new form emerged, one that might be called 'historio*graphic* metafiction', with the stress on the processes of writing both fiction and history. These processes could be overtly thematized, as in Robert Harlow's *Scann* (1972), or they might be presented more allegorically, as in Graeme Gibson's *Perpetual Motion* (1982).

The reason for the attraction to historical modes might well have been, as Gibson claimed (E17), a late post-colonial need to reclaim the past. Such a theory might account for the large number of historical novels (as well as of historiographic metafictions) written in the dozen years since 1972. Or this attraction to historical modes might have reflected the lure of 'alterity' that each writer had to come to terms with (Scobie 277), even if only by actual personal appearances within the work itself: the narrator (Ondaatje) entering at the end of *Coming Through Slaughter* (1976). Or such novels might have intended to challenge—in a very conscious way—the formal borders of generic distinctions, to push realism as far as it could go—that is, into document, on the one end, and into metafictional mimesis of the process of writing and reading, on the other.

In the emerging postmodern fiction, the genres of history and biography overlapped considerably. In both an overt dialectic opposed the 'fact' of historically verifiable document to the structuring and interpreting acts of both writer and reader. Unlike the more or less traditional fictionalized biography (William Goede's *Quantrill* [1982], Roy MacGregor's *Shorelines* [1980] about Tom Thomson, Heather Robertson's *Willie: A Romance* [1983] about Mackenzie King), metafictions like Ondaatje's *Coming Through Slaughter* deliberately forced the reader to separate life and art, biography and fiction, at the same time as they structurally united them. Timothy Findley's *The Wars* (1977) was a variant of this form: a war novel (a familiar fictional genre) and, at the same time, a novel very much about the writing of history and biography, just as John Mills's *Skevington's Daughter* (1978) was about the writing of both biography and fiction. The relationship between metafiction and autobiography was perhaps a less problematic one, given that there has always been an accepted fictionalizing (or at least ordering process) built into the concept of the writing of the story of one's life. The self-reflexive *Bildungsroman* appeared in a number of forms, from the straightforward structure of Lorris Elliott's *Comin' for to Carry* (1982) to the more self-dismantling use of convention in Audrey Thomas's *Songs my Mother Taught Me* (1973). But these were not quite the same as a metafictional autobiography, a self-aware and self-reflexive fictionalizing of one's own life, or of the roots of the personal past. The most successful example of this mode in this period was certainly Michael Ondaatje's *Running in the Family* (1982), in which the author sought to write the history of the people of his familial past, to 'touch them into words'.

To overlap with history, biography, and autobiography, to challenge the boundaries of the novel genre, was one way for novels to work within the conventions of realism and still contest them. Another way was to take the major structures of the realist novel and work variations on them, play with them, parody them. The realist novel, for instance, pretended to present 'reality', usually authorized by either written or oral sources. In Canadian metafiction after 1970, an interesting split developed between the use and awareness of these two kinds of sources, specifically between the written chronicle and the oral tale. On the one hand, many novels dwelt almost obsessively on the written product of history as something fixed and fixing; on the other hand, novels also played with the overt fictionality and the transience (if immediacy) of the oral tradition. The chronicle, the mode of written history, was clearly an attractive structuring device for even the most self-reflexive of metafictions. But it was not just at the level of structure that this model had its impact. In this fiction, new 'trappings' of realism were made possible by modern technology. There was no need to rely only on historical documents of the old kind, for newspapers and, especially, photographs, films, tape-recordings, videos, and data banks also provided 'facts'. And novels duly used these devices as ways to suggest the verification and, by implication, verifiability of even their most fictive creations: witness Becker's tape-recording transcripts and scrapbook in Jack Hodgins' *The Inven-*

tion of the World (1977). However, these new trappings of realism were not presented in the usual realist fashion: their contexts often suggested something rather sinister, while at the same time paradoxically suggesting that the act of taping or photographing was the direct analogue of the novelist's act. The fixity of the photo (in Findley's *The Wars* [1977], Kroetsch's *Badlands* [1975], Munro's *Lives of Girls and Women* [1971], Ondaatje's *Coming Through Slaughter* [1976]), the illusory kinesis of the moving picture (in Atwood's *Surfacing* [1972]), the deceiving orality of the tape recording (*The Wars* and *The Invention of the World* again)—all these were compared to the fixing on paper that constituted the act of writing. All were acts of reducing open, imaginative immediacy to framed form. It took, argued these metafictions, the reverse, dynamizing process of the act of reading to resurrect the creative immediacy that once lived in the imagination of the writer.

The poststructuralist literary theory contemporaneous with such fiction suggested that writing had been historically undervalued by our society, that it had been degraded as the petrified, ossified form of oral speech. And Canadian novels were extremely self-conscious of the paradox of looking, within a written genre, for new, specifically oral narrative forms that might grant them both more immediacy and a broader social context. In Margaret Laurence's *The Diviners* (1974), the oral Scottish narratives and Métis songs were set against Morag's writing—and implicitly, against Laurence's own. In Wiebe's *The Temptations of Big Bear* (1973), the oral (immediate and transitory) power of Big Bear's speeches was opposed to the written (fixed and permanent) power of the white treaties and the trial evidence. But both novels could not escape one final irony: the only way to explore the oral/written dialectic was in print. Big Bear's dynamic oral presence lived on in static print, just as his historical existence lived on, in part at least, in a fiction.

Perhaps these two poles—the oral tale and the written chronicle—reflected as well the legacy of the theories of Marshall McLuhan's work, including *The Gutenberg Galaxy*. For McLuhan, oral cultures were collective, simultaneous, auditory, and oriented toward the present, while written cultures were individual, signed, linear, visual, and under the control of the past, of the causality and succession imposed by history (*Counterblast* 13-14). But McLuhan, like Wiebe, Hodgins, Laurence, and so many others, could only express these ideas, could only pass them on to us today, through the written medium of print. Even the metafictions most based on oral traditions of narrative only existed as written, individual, signed works—as, of course, did that paradigm of postmodern fiction, *One Hundred Years of Solitude*. In Canadian fiction, this paradox was often explored by polarizing the two extremes. One model tooks its form and modality specifically from oral gossip and communal, often mythic, memory; the other was modelled on the historical chronicle and the individual need to record in writing. The first, the oral mode of communal gossip, was tied to myth, legend, fairy stories, and the tall tale; the *written* one was linked, instead, to the cause-and-effect rationality and realism of historical narrative. In the latter were found most often those new technological trappings of literary realism—the tape-recording transcripts, the (descriptions of) photographs and films, or the more traditional historical archives. None of these resolutely written novels really seemed to manifest what Kroetsch saw as a terrible longing for validation by stasis (Neuman and Wilson 126). Rather, they were more likely open acknowledgements of the problematic nature of those conventions of realism that were usually taken for granted. In works using the other model, however, instead of this serious earnestness, there was the Rabelaisian scatology and obscenity of Kroetsch's *What the Crow Said* (1978), with its emphasis on animal and animal-like noises, on folk legend, and, in general, on the traditions of story-telling (story in the sense of a lie, as well as a narrative). Metafiction met oral history, with all the paradoxical implications which that might suggest.

Canadian postmodernism was not only characterized by metafictional self-consciousness about genre and the conventions of realism, however. The important role of parody in challenging accepted modes and themes *from within* them was another strategy that Canadian fiction shared with many other nations. Some novels were overtly ludic and parodic: John Mills's *The October Men* (1974) was an example of what has been called 'centripetal comedy' (MacKendrick 347) in parodic forms. Novels by women used parody in a much more ideological fashion; all 'intertextual' echoing of other works (parodic or otherwise) implicitly acted to contest the (male) Romantic belief in aesthetic uniqueness and originality. Parodic play, in particular, implied a kind of ironic distance and difference at the very heart of similarity, a distance that allowed a text to speak *to* its culture, from *within* that culture, but without being totally co-opted by it. Parody could be a weapon against marginalization, for it literally incorporated that upon which it ironically commented. It could be both inside and outside the dominant discourses whose critique it embodied. For example, Marian Engel's *Lunatic Villas* (1981) offered an ironic parody of the picaresque form, a form more usually used by men to write about men. Here the usual male rogue-figure—footloose and fancy-free—travelling 'on the road', was inverted to become the woman into whose house and life various rogues enter. As in Thomas's *Intertidal Life* (1984), male models, be they of explorers or rogues, did not adapt to the common female reality of children and social responsibilities. And many novels of the late 1970s and early 1980s investigated the available alternatives—both aesthetic and ideological.

Similarly, in an attempt to question the class-inspired highbrow/lowbrow hierarchies of an Arnoldian classification of art, contemporary metafiction also worked to democratize the 'serious' novel form: it assimilated not just history, biography, autobiography, poetry, and the short-story collection, but also, frequently through parody, it incorporated 'popular' or formula modes of fiction that were otherwise usually shunned. In these novels the structures of the 'popular' forms of fiction—the mystery story, the sports tale, the romance—were internalized and used as markers of metafiction: they overtly signalled that these works were fictive. Often this play was parodic, as in Atwood's use of the costume gothic in *Lady Oracle* (1976). There, when life (in fiction) began to imitate art, parody took on an important structural role and also offered a mode of voicing a social and cultural critique of the destinies of women: as characters, as authors, and as readers. Other forms usually considered as lowly and 'popular' that were used to metafictional ends were the spy story (Chris Scott's *To Catch a Spy* [1978] and *Hitler's Bomb* [1983]) and the sports tale, be it about horse-racing (Robert Harlow's *Making Arrangements* [1982] or baseball: both Paul Quarrington's *Home Game* (1983) and W.P. Kinsella's *Shoeless Joe* (1982) were delightful metafictional mixtures of fact and fantasy in which the reader joined the writer in becoming an active part of the process of making sense of the narrative. It was not that these novels were hard to read, but that the process of creating them was enacted in the texts themselves and was, in fact, the subject of both.

In her famous piece on 'Canadian Monsters', Margaret Atwood once claimed that the supernatural was not part of the mainstream of Canadian socio-realistic fiction (*Second Words* 230). Yet, fantasy was very well represented in the fiction of the 1970s and 1980s, both in its regular and in its metafictional variants. On topics as diverse as the Canadian identity (Stephen Franklin's *Knowledge Park* [1972]) and computerized two-dimensional worlds (Alexander Dewdney's *The Planiverse* [1984]), fantasy emerged as an important mode. Sometimes such fabulation was presented in more or less realist narrative forms (Ruth Nichols' *Song of the Pearl* [1976]); other times it appeared in a more experimental surrealist style (Frances Duncan's *Dragonhunt* [1981]), or set in an indeterminate time and space (Leon Rooke's *The Magician in Love* [1981]). Frequently these modes of fantasy also involved mythic dimensions, especially in their metafictional forms. Often, once again, the influence of that Latin American 'real maravilloso' (Carpentier) could be seen in the bizarre mixture of fact and mythic fantasy that is possible in a society that has enough 'peasant' faith to grant plausibility to the whole (Wilson). The hero of Leo Simpson's *Kowalski's Last Chance* (1980) had an innocent faith, of sorts, in leprechauns, and the people of Port Annie (in Jack Hodgins' *The Resurrection of Joseph Bourne*, subtitled *Or a Word or Two on those Port Annie Miracles* [1979]) accepted the 'Peruvian seabird' and the bizarre consequences of her arrival with an equanimity worthy of the inhabitants of García Márquez's Macondo. In Hodgins' novel, the fantasy—or imagination—of the characters and of the reader made communication possible (in both art and life). Frequently this metafictional concern for the power of the creative imagination took on psychological dimensions. In Brian Moore's *The Great Victorian Collection* (1975), a Montreal history professor found exactly that— a collection of Victorian memorabilia—outside his California motel. Was it real? a hallucination? a fantasy? The novel never fully resolved the mystery. In other fiction, we seemed to enter a fairy-tale or dream world with metafictional links to our own (through concentration on the acts of creating and interpreting), but in which the unconscious and the irrational seemed to take over, as in part of David Helwig's *The King's Evil* (1981). In Graham Petrie's *Seahorse* (1980), were we in the nightmarish world of the id? a Kafka-esque fantasy of deadly magic? The allegorical temptations of this novel, like those of the more satirically distopic *The Carbon Copy* (1973) by Anthony Brennan or those of the adventure-tale variant in Guy Gavriel Kay's *The Summer Tree* (1984), suggested further dimensions which metafictional fantasy could possess. In all of these self-reflective forms, despite their formal introversion, parodic play, and often totally unrealistic plots, the connection to the mimetic and realistic tradition was never quite totally severed. In a novel like Leo Simpson's *The Peacock Papers* (1973), no matter how overtly authorially manipulative, no matter how absurd the plot and its resolution, no matter how parodic (of Thomas Love Peacock's style, of the mock heroic genre), the satiric drive in the name of saving 'civilization' from the barbarians of technocratic efficiency maintained the mimetic link.

Fantasy could clearly be used as a vehicle for many kinds of messages. It could allow a novel to escape linear history and plunge into visionary, mythic dimensions, as in Geoffrey Ursell's *Perdue: or How the West Was Lost* (1984). It could also be used to confront moral issues in allegorical form. Perhaps the most daring such use of fantasy in the 1980s was Timothy Findley's *Not Wanted on the Voyage* (1984). The apocalyptic vision of Findley's earlier novels here took on comic yet moving and serious form in the retelling of the story of Noah's flood. This was a political and moral retelling, though, a story about evil and destruction, both biblical and future. In this novel, as in Jack Hodgins' *The Invention of the World* (1977), the power of imagination and legend, of fiction and myth, confronted the stubborn tenacity of fact and document.

To write self-reflexively and often parodically of fantasy and imagination, of games and of play, of history as process in progress (instead of as completed product)—all these were ways to break down the finality of narrative closure that was a legacy of the realist novel. They challenged that closure *from within*. None of these modes of writing denied the mimetic connection between art and life; they merely relocated its site of operation— from the products of fiction to the processes. The 1970s and early 1980s were, indeed, times of '-isms', times of theoretical suspicion and questioning, when new voices were demanding to be heard, and in fact, were heard. The formal consequences of novels like *Running in the Family, Intertidal Life, Famous Last Words, The Res-*

urrection of Joseph Bourne, and *Antichthon* for the development of narrative genres revealed best what Canadian fiction did to open up the borders, to challenge the boundaries, not just between genres, but between the two sides of what has been called the basic and most misleading assumption of much modern criticism: 'that fiction is an antonym of reality' (Iser 53).

Notes

1 This chapter has been prepared with the bibliographic assistance of Ken Durkacz and Heather Jones, the editorial help of Laurie Ricou, and was supported by a Leave Fellowship from the Social Sciences and Research Council of Canada.

2 For an example of this major concern, see the special issue of *Critical Inquiry* devoted to the question of the canon (10, 1 [September 1983]).

3 See Margaret Atwood's 1981 Address to Amnesty International, reprinted in *Second Words*, pp. 393-7.

4 I should like to thank here all those Canadian publishers who responded to my inquiries and whose remarks have contributed to my understanding of Canadian publishing. In particular, my gratitude goes to James Polk of the House of Anansi and Jack McClelland of McClelland and Stewart, but also to Robert Lecker of ECW, Glenn Clever and Frank Tierney of Borealis, Ann Reatherford of Porcupine's Quill, and John Harris of Repository Press.

5 See Lee Easton's MA dissertation on 'Patterns of (Af)filiation in the Modern Canadian *Bildungsroman*', McMaster University, 1985.

6 However, one should probably recall Atwood's warning: 'If a man depicts a male character unfavourably, it's The Human Condition; if a woman does it, she's being mean to men' (*Second Words*, p. 421).

Works Cited

Atwood, Margaret. *Survival*. Toronto: Anansi, 1972.

——. *Second Words: Selected Critical Prose*. Toronto: Anansi, 1982.

Bowering, George. 'Modernism Could Not Last Forever'. *Canadian Fiction Magazine* 32-3 (1979-80), pp. 4-9.

Carpentier, Alejo. 'De lo Real Maravillosamente Americano'. In *Tientos y Diferencias*. Mexico: Universidad Nacional Autonoma de Mexico, 1984. Pp. 115-35.

Cohen, Matt. 'Notes on Realism in Modern English-Canadian Fiction'. In W.H. New, ed. *Canadian Writers in 1984: 25th Anniversary Issue of Canadian Literature*. Vancouver: University of British Columbia Press, 1984. Pp. 65-71.

Cude, Wilfred. *A Due Sense of Difference: An Evaluative Approach to Canadian*

Literature. Lanham, MD: University Press of America, 1980.

Federman, Raymond. *Surfiction: Fiction Now . . . and Tomorrow.* Chicago: Swallow Press, 1975.

Fiedler, Leslie, *The Return of the Vanishing American.* New York: Stein and Day, 1968.

Flores, Angel, 'Magic Realism in Spanish American Fiction'. *Hispania* 38, 2 (1955), pp. 187-92.

Gibson, Graeme. 'Gothic Shocks from History: The Birth of a New Novel'. *The Globe and Mail* 4 June 1983, p. E17.

Goldie, Terry. *Fear and Temptation: Images of Indigenous Peoples in Australian, Canadian, and New Zealand Literatures.* Montreal: McGill-Queen's University Press, 1988.

Hancock, Geoff, ed. *Metavisions: An Anthology of Short Stories.* Dunvegan, Ont.: Quadrant, 1983.

Iser, Wolfgang. *The Act of Reading.* Baltimore: Johns Hopkins University Press, 1978.

Jameson, Fredric. *The Political Unconscious.* Ithaca, NY: Cornell University Press, 1978.

Kreisel, Henry. 'The Prairie, a State of Mind'. *Proceedings and Transactions of the Royal Society of Canada* 4th series, 6 (1968), pp. 171-80.

MacKendrick, Louis K. 'The Comic, the Centripetal Text, and the Canadian Novel'. *English Studies in Canada* 10, 3 (1984), pp. 343-56.

McLuhan, Marshall. *The Gutenberg Galaxy.* Toronto: University of Toronto Press, 1962.

——. *Counterblast.* London: Rapp and Whiting, 1970.

MacLulich, T.D. 'Our Place on the Map: The Canadian Tradition in Fiction'. *University of Toronto Quarterly* 52, 2 (1982-3), pp. 191-208.

Moss, John. *A Reader's Guide to the Canadian Novel.* Toronto: McClelland and Stewart, 1981.

Neuman, Shirley, and Robert R. Wilson. *Labyrinths of Voice: Conversations with Robert Kroetsch.* Edmonton: NeWest Press, 1982.

Pritchard, Allan. 'West of the Great Divide: Man and Nature in the Literature of British Columbia'. *Canadian Literature* 102 (Autumn 1984), pp. 36-53.

Ricou, Laurie. *Vertical Man/Horizontal World: Man and Landscape in Canadian Prairie Fiction.* Vancouver: University of British Columbia Press, 1973.

Salutin, Rick. *Marginal Notes.* Toronto: Lester & Orpen Dennys, 1984.

Scobie, Stephen. 'Amelia or: Who Do You Think You Are? Documentary and Identity in Canadian Literature'. In W.H. New, ed. *Canadian Writers in 1984: 25th Anniversary Issue of Canadian Literature.* Vancouver: University of British Columbia Press, 1984. Pp. 264-85.

Steele, Charles, ed. *Taking Stock: The Calgary Conference on the Canadian Novel.* Downsview, Ont.: ECW Press, 1982.

Swan, Susan. *The Biggest Modern Woman of the World*. Toronto: Lester &
    Orpen Dennys, 1983.
White, Hayden. *Metahistory: The Historical Imagination in Nineteenth-Century
    Europe*. Baltimore: Johns Hopkins University Press, 1973.
Wilson, Robert Rawdon. 'On the Boundary of the Magic and the Real:
    Notes on Inter-American Fiction'. *Compass* 6 (1979), pp. 37-53.

Bibliography

In the 1970s and 1980s, Canadian fiction criticism (and criticism
in general) reached a kind of maturity which allowed overt
dissension (e.g., B.W. Powe's *A Climate Charged: Essays on Canadian
Writers* [Oakville: Mosaic Press, 1984]), comparative analysis
(Ronald Sutherland's *The New Hero: Essays in Comparative Quebec/
Canadian Literature* [Toronto: Macmillan, 1977], E.D. Blodgett's
Configuration: Essays on the Canadian Literatures [Downsview, Ont.:
ECW Press, 1982], the special issue of *Essays in Canadian Writing*
on 'Canadian-American Literary Relations' [no. 22, 1981], for
example), and serious re-examination (Frank Davey's *Surviving
the Paraphrase: Eleven Essays on Canadian Literature* [Winnipeg:
Turnstone Press, 1983], Gaile McGregor's *The Wacousta Syndrome*
[Toronto: University of Toronto Press, 1985]). We even tried to
define literary Canada to the Americans: David Staines, ed., *The
Canadian Imagination: Dimensions of a Literary Culture* (Cambridge,
Mass.: Harvard University Press, 1977). Meanwhile, other nations
attempted to explain Canadian writing to themselves and to us.
To mention only a few: France's journal *Etudes Canadiennes*; Italy's
Giovanna Capone, *Canada, il villaggio della terra: letteratura canadese
di lingua inglese* (Bologna: Pàtron, 1978); and Germany's Walter
E. Riedel, *Das literarische Kanadabild: eine Studie zur Rezeption
kanadischer Literatur in deutscher Übersetzung* (Bonn: Bouvier, 1980).
    Novelists writing as critics were frequently very influential
in leading the way to new concerns for literary criticism: political
issues such as nationalism, feminism, and human rights (Margaret Atwood in *Survival: A Thematic Guide to Canadian Literature*
[Toronto: Anansi, 1972] and *Second Words: Selected Critical Prose*
[Toronto: Anansi, 1982]), and also contemporary postmodernist
and poststructuralist literary theory (especially Robert Kroetsch,
in his essays collected by Frank Davey and bp nichol in *Open
Letter* 5th series, no. 4 [1983] and in his interviews with Shirley
Neuman and Robert Wilson in *Labyrinths of Voice: Conversations*

with Robert Kroetsch [Edmonton: NeWest Press, 1982], but also George Bowering, in such provocative essays as 'Modernism Could Not Last Forever', *Canadian Fiction Magazine* 32-3 [1979-80], pp. 4-9).

In the wake of the 1978 Calgary Conference (Charles Steele, ed., *Taking Stock: The Calgary Conference on the Canadian Novel* [Downsview, Ont: ECW Press, 1982]), the questions of canonization and evaluation of Canadian fiction were raised and debated widely. Perhaps the best known exchange was that between Kroetsch ('Contemporary Standards in the Canadian Novel', *Essays in Canadian Writing*, 20 [Winter 1980-1], pp. 7-18) and Barry Cameron ('Criteria of Evaluation in the Canadian Novel: A Response to Robert Kroetsch' in the same issue, pp. 19-31). A contemporaneous exercise in the act of canon-formation was Wilfred Cude's *A Due Sense of Difference: An Evaluative Approach to Canadian Literature* (Lanham, Md: University Press of America, 1980). However, the new voices heard in the fiction implicitly demanded a reconsideration of what constituted the canon and how it was formed. This was especially true of so-called 'ethnic' writing, as the increasing number of volumes devoted to it revealed. Jars Balan edited *Identifications: Ethnicity and the Writer in Canada* (Edmonton: Canadian Institute of Ukrainian Studies, 1982); Joseph Pivato collected and contributed to a critical anthology entitled *Contrasts: Comparative Essays on Italian Canadian Writing* (Montreal: Guernica, 1985); and *Canadian Ethnic Studies* devoted a special issue to 'Ethnicity and Canadian Literature' (14, 1 [1982]). More regional studies, especially (but by no means exclusively) of the West, also followed the publication of Laurie Ricou's *Vertical Man/Horizontal World: Man and Landscape in Canadian Prairie Fiction* (Vancouver: University of British Columbia Press, 1973): for example, Dick Harrison's *Unnamed Country: The Struggle for a Canadian Prairie Fiction* (Edmonton: University of Alberta Press, 1977). Similarly, studies of the indigene began to appear: Leslie Monkman's *A Native Heritage: Images of the Indian in English-Canadian Literature* (Toronto: University of Toronto Press, 1981).

Scholarly articles and reviews of Canadian fiction continued to be published by journals such as *Canadian Literature, Essays in Canadian Writing, Books in Canada, Quill and Quire, Canadian Fiction Magazine, Journal of Canadian Fiction, Studies in Canadian Literature, Open Letter, Fiddlehead, Atlantis, World Literature Written in English, Journal of Commonwealth Literature*, the university and association journals, and too many smaller journals to mention. *University of Toronto Quarterly*'s annual *Letters in Canada* volume (summer issue) provided an annual overview of a selection of novels. *Canadian Literature* published two particularly valuable special issues: *Fiction in the Seventies* (no. 92 [Spring 1982]) and *Canadian Writers in 1984* (25th Anniversary Issue, Vancouver: University of British Columbia Press, 1984). In the latter, the writers themselves again discoursed on pet topics, as they did in various collections of interviews like Donald A. Cameron's *Conversations with Canadian Novelists* (Toronto: Macmillan, 1973), Alan Twigg's *For Openers: Conversations with 24 Canadian Writers* (Madiera Park, B.C.: Harbour, 1981), and Bruce Meyer's and Brian O'Riordan's *In Their Words: Interviews with Fourteen Canadian Writers* (Toronto: Anansi, 1984).

During this period, there were far too many introductory studies, detailed academic books, special issues of journals, and conference proceedings published on individual Canadian novelists to begin to list them here. Readers seeking chronological studies of writers' works should consult these or the *Canadian Encyclopedia* (Edmonton: Hurtig, 1985) and the three forthcoming *Dictionary of Literary Biography* volumes on Canadian writers. For detailed bibliographies, they should consult Helen Hoy's *Modern English-Canadian Prose: A Guide to Information Sources* (Detroit: Gale Research, 1983) or the earlier works by Margery Fee and Ruth Cawker, *Canadian Fiction: An Annotated Bibliography* (Toronto: Peter Martin, 1976) and by Michael Gnarowski, *A Concise Bibliography of English-Canadian Literature*, revised edition (Toronto: McClelland and Stewart, 1978). ECW Press also initiated a series of very useful annotated bibliographies of 'Canada's Major Authors'.

The vast number of books that offered general overviews or collections of essays or colloquium papers also precluded their being listed here. Clearly Canadian Literature came to be a recognized academic field of study during the 1970s and early 1980s. The publication of William Toye's edition of *The Oxford Companion to Canadian Literature* (Toronto: Oxford University Press, 1983) marked some sort of consolidation of reference sources in this field, a process which had been started by Frank Davey's useful *From Here to There: A Guide to English-Canadian Literature Since 1960* (Erin, Ont.: Press Porcépic, 1974). Several new series of studies also appeared: ECW's multi-volumed *Canadian Writers and their Works*, and four volumes of *Profiles in Canadian*

Literature, edited by Jeffrey Heath (Toronto: Dundurn, 1980-). Most recently, we have seen the inauguration of *Swift Current,* an annual Canadian literary database accessible by telephone from a CP/M or MSDOS personal computer.

Clearly Canadian novelists continued to be heard as major critical voices on their own and on others' works (in addition, see Douglas Daymond and Leslie Monkman, eds, *Canadian Novelists and the Novel* [Ottawa: Borealis, 1981]). And despite the attacks on thematic criticism (besides Davey's *Surviving the Paraphrase,* an especially provocative introduction to an issue of *Studies in Canadian Literature* (2 [Summer 1977]) was entitled a 'Mandatory Subversive Manifesto: Canadian Criticism vs. Literary Criticism'), thematic essays and books continued to appear. The prolific John Moss's *Sex and Violence in the Canadian Novel: The Ancestral Present* (Toronto: McClelland and Stewart, 1977) was typical. Critics of fiction did start to employ other modes of analysis, however—formalist, generic, reader-oriented, feminist, and poststructuralist. While there have been attempts to provide a broader sociological context for Canadian literature (e.g., Paul Cappon, ed., *In Our House: Social Perspectives on Canadian Literature* [Toronto: McClelland and Stewart, 1978]), two of the most promising new directions for literary theory at the end of this period were toward defining a feminist poetic and toward distinguishing the Canadian variant within the international frame of reference known as postmodernism.

Index